REVISED EDITION

The Fine Wines
of
California

Robert S. Blumberg
and Hurst Hannum

Doubleday & Company, Inc.
Garden City, New York

ISBN: 0-385-02300-X
Library of Congress Catalog Card Number: 73–81427
Printed in the United States of America
Revised edition

*This work is dedicated to Enjoyment and,
since without it true Enjoyment is impossible,
to Peace.*

ACKNOWLEDGMENTS
TO THE SECOND EDITION

We must again thank the many vintners without whose assistance the task of keeping up with the changing California wine industry would have been much more difficult. In large part because of their cooperation, we hope that this edition will be even more comprehensive and certainly more current than the previous one. While we cannot acknowledge everyone who was kind enough to help us, we would like to thank those whose friendliness and openness went beyond the call of duty or public relations, among whom are Joseph S. Concannon, Jr., Paul Draper, Mike Elwood, Jim Lucas, Joe Maganini, Bruce Nyers, Mike Richmond, Mike Robbins, Sam Sebastiani, Jr., Dan Shoemaker, Robert Travers, and Bud van Loben Sels.

Special thanks should be extended to Hans. J. Greenberg; to Marion Koerper, who again weathered all our crises in superb form; to Mrs. Estelle Goldstein, for preparing the manuscript and struggling with Bob's handwriting; and to Jim Olsen, for his excellent palate, endless cigars, and friendship.

And once again our thanks to our friends who participated in our tastings, both good and bad.

ACKNOWLEDGMENTS
TO THE FIRST EDITION

Many people have given us invaluable aid and information in the course of preparing this book, and we would like to take this opportunity to thank at least some of them.

First, of course, our task would have been much more difficult without the cooperation and wines provided by many of the wineries themselves. For the extra time and effort which they expended in our behalf, we would particularly like to thank Mr. James Friedman of Paul Masson, Mr. Daniel Mirassou, and Mr. Joseph S. Concannon, Jr.

Our special thanks go out to Miss Marion Koerper and Miss Elizabeth Gross for the help and inspiration they have offered us since the commencement of this work, to Dr. Seth L. Wolitz for his timely suggestions and the unique tasting experiences he provided for us, to Mrs. Estelle Goldstein for an excellent job of preparing and typing the manuscript, and to Mr. Stephen Sussman for researching the legal aspects of wine production and labeling in California.

And, although space does not permit us to name each one individually, our deep-felt thanks to our many friends who took part in our tasting programs and thus helped us gain insight into the reaction of the average wine drinker to many of the wines described in this book. Finally, to all the others who have offered advice and encouragement along the way—tour guides, retail store owners, wine aficionados—we would like to express our appreciation.

Contents

xiv   *Contents*

PART ONE

Some General Topics

Why Another Wine Book?

Selecting a bottle of wine from the shelves of a well-stocked gourmet shop or liquor store can indeed be a puzzling and frustrating experience for the novice buyer, and too often his selection turns out to be disappointing. There are two ways to make this task easier and more rewarding. The first is to taste as many wines as possible and thus to become familiar with all wineries and wine types. The second, a bit less time consuming and certainly less expensive, is to read this book.

We were originally stimulated to write this book by the lack of any other existing work dedicated to a consumer-oriented description and analysis of California wines. There certainly has been a wealth of books available on wine making, wine country touring, and wine romance and history, but until recently there has been little dedicated to the wines themselves.

Today there are several wine magazines and newsletters that have descriptions and rankings of wines, although frequently these are tempered by the fact that some of the publications are dependent on advertising revenue from wineries. Others have adopted a committee approach to the judging of wine. This can produce interesting results, although quite often the simple, palatable wines do very well, while the most interesting and complex ones place somewhere in the middle (because of both high and low votes) in a position that does not adequately reflect their individuality. Still the growing number of people talking about and actually judging California wines is a welcome sign, and we hope this book will serve to further widen the discussion and interest in California wines.

We first began delving into California wines as a hobby inspired by a year spent in Bordeaux, the wine capital of Europe. When we returned we launched our own investigation into American wines. Since neither of us could afford to go out and simply start buying random samples, we headed off for the wineries themselves and the tasting that is an integral part of their public relations. We were, to say the least, surprised.

We soon discovered that the quality of many wines (speaking in a general, not a technical, sense) was subject to considerable variation despite the apparent equality reflected in their similar retail price tags. After several comparative tastings, it became evident that we hadn't just stumbled on a few exceptions; the price of a fifth of California table wine bore little if any relationship to what was inside! In recent years prices have risen, but the general irrelevance of price to quality remains.

How then should you select a bottle of California wine? Even winery reputation isn't a wholly adequate guide, for most of the better-known wineries make so many different wines that some come out distinctly better than others.

Since the ridiculous pronouncements that often adorn a bottle's back label or the winery's mailing circular offer no real help to the average consumer, we have tried to cut through the thicket of advertising and promotion to present meaningful descriptions of the many wines and wine types. Our primary purpose remains to provide you, the consumer, with a way of differentiating among the many modestly to exorbitantly priced wines available today and to spare you some of the not always pleasant surprises that we have encountered in our own tasting experiences.

Of course, whether we "like" one wine more than another may result from simple differences in taste and not be because one wine is "better" than the other. But it *is* possible to judge color, varietal character, acid balance, and other such attributes against a fairly objective standard, and in this sense compare the taste quality of two different wines.

While wine has a long way to go to overtake beer in national sales, the rise in wine consumption and production in recent years has been nothing short of spectacular. In 1971 the adult consumption of wine was up 12 percent to 2.4 gallons per person, and Americans consumed over 300 million gallons of wines of all kinds. Nearly three fourths of this came from California vineyards, under scores of different labels. No one can hope to keep track of the hundreds of wineries and wine types available, particularly in today's geysering industry, so we have been forced by several factors to limit the wines we discuss here.

First, we deal only with table wines—unfortified, natural wines of 10 to 14 percent alcohol. This excludes all of the celebrated California sherries, ports, and brandies, as well as the new flavored "pop" wines; their mysteries will have to be unraveled at some other time.

Secondly, we have restricted ourselves primarily to those wines we have denominated "premium wines," those wines that are normally bottled in corked, fifth-size bottles rather than in half-gallon or gallon jugs. This limitation is *not,* however, intended to imply that the less expensive wines, produced by such wineries as Gallo, Italian Swiss Colony, Guild, and Franzia, are beneath consideration. On the contrary, these wines constitute by far the lion's share of California wine, and they are largely responsible for the growing interest in wine in America today. Most of them are sound, perfectly marketable wines of a quality commensurate with their price; a few can compare very favorably with some of their "premium" brethren. We have tried to examine the differences among the major brands in Part Four. But California's jug wines are not, and are not intended to be, highly interesting or complex wines from a tasting standpoint and have neither the individuality nor the finesse of most premium wines.

Finally, we realize that where descriptions as detailed as ours are presented, space and time limitations render it impossible to cover in depth every winery in California that produces premium wines. We have tried to include all the major producers, those whose products can be found throughout California as well as in many other areas of the United States. In addition, we have included many smaller wineries of more limited distribution whose wines have provoked interest or controversy in wine circles. No winery has been intentionally excluded; those we have missed are not here either because time prevented us from giving them a fair and complete evaluation or simply because we didn't know about them. And while this revised edition includes many new wineries, their numbers are rising faster than the national debt. Since this writing, several more will undoubtedly have surfaced, so you'll have to get out and do some discovering for yourself!

With this edition we have added a fairly detailed chapter on how wine is made, although it is certainly true that appreciating a wine does not require expertise in wine making. Yet much of a wine's character comes from the way in which it is fermented and aged, and some technical knowledge should help those consumers who want to probe deeper into the mysteries of wine. Those of you who find your scientific appetite whetted are referred to several excellent technical works listed at the end of this book.

We have also scattered brief paragraphs here and there dealing with visits to the wineries themselves. While this is not the primary purpose of the book, we do want to recognize those wineries that treat their visitors with courtesy and whose guides are well informed beyond their memorized speeches.

We cannot recommend too strongly a personal visit to the California wine country, particularly the Napa Valley. There are many wineries in a more or less central location, and most welcome tourists (with varying degrees of commercialism).

The valley itself is beautiful, with thousands of acres spreading out on both sides of California Route 29. Even without the added enticement of the tasting that accompanies every tour, the cellars, vats, and vines alone are well worth the one-and-a-half-hour drive from the San Francisco Bay Area. One warning, however: the wineries are very crowded on weekends, especially during the summer. Traffic is often bumper to bumper, and the tasting rooms may be several people deep. You'll be much more comfortable on a weekday or during a season other than summer, and the earlier in the day, the better. Perhaps the ideal time would be late some weekday morning during the harvest season in late September or October. At this time the presses and crushers are working to capacity, and the picture is much more exciting than merely hearing a description of how everything is done.

Of course, there are several wineries outside the Napa Valley with excellent tours, but Napa offers the largest concentration of wineries in the state.

We have been as honest as possible in our discussions of individual wines and wineries. We have not hesitated to be critical, though we hope that we have also offered praise where it is deserved. But please remember that this book is intended only as a guide to California wines, not as a definitive ranking. If you agree with our tastes—if your prejudices and preferences match ours—so much the better. Our classes in wine appreciation have shown us that there is often more agreement on "good" and "bad" wines than some care to admit, but our real purpose here is to encourage experimentation and to introduce you to some of the many exciting wines available from California's wineries. It is our hope that this book will help in guiding that experimentation through some of the intricacies and culs-de-sac that do, unfortunately, await the unwary. If we can promote greater comprehension, conversation, and even controversy on the subject of wine and California, we feel certain that the effect on both the consumer and the wine industry will be positive.

A Brief History of Wine Making in California

The first grapevines in California were introduced to San Diego in 1769 by Spanish missionaries. As the fathers pushed their missions northward, the vineyards followed, and within a few decades wine was being made at most of the Franciscan missions. The grape which was almost universally planted, appropriately named the Mission, produced a rather unsatisfactory wine, and by the time of the Gold Rush in 1849 many of the original vines had greatly deteriorated. But while the Mission did not produce a great (or even a good) wine, its introduction did demonstrate the practicality of viticulture in California.

Along with the Gold Rush came Colonel Agoston Haraszthy, a Hungarian count (he became a self-proclaimed colonel after his arrival in the United States) who was in large part responsible for the introduction of quality European grapes to California. The life of Colonel Haraszthy, one of early California's most colorful and forceful characters, would in itself be a fascinating subject for a book, but here we will limit ourselves to his wine-making dreams and schemes. Convinced that California had the potential to surpass the wine-producing regions of Europe, in 1861 he embarked on a tour of European *vignobles,* returning some months later with two hundred thousand vines and cuttings culled from the most celebrated vineyards in Europe. Though the theory is unsupported by any solid evidence, some feel that the mysterious Zinfandel grape, now indigenous to California, first arrived here in the Colonel's mass importation. While his own winery in the Sonoma Valley did not rise to great heights, his experimental plantings throughout the state appreciably improved the varietal complement of California vineyards and marked the beginning of a new expansion of the California wine industry.

Unfortunately, Haraszthy's diligence was followed by entrepreneurs who leaped into California wine making more interested in profits than in honest wine-making techniques. The gross abuses often perpetrated on the consumer finally resulted in the passage of the first California Pure Wine Law in 1880, a measure strongly supported by the better vintners. Soon the worst types of fraud disappeared, and California wines began to overcome the bad reputation they had acquired.

California's troubles were not yet over, however, for the dreaded phylloxera (a plant louse that destroys vine roots) began attacking the European vines (*Vitis vinifera*) now planted in California vineyards. European vineyards were also in the process of being decimated by this pest, although there the havoc was even greater than in America. Then it was discovered that the roots of American vines native to the East (*Vitis labrusca*) were resistant to the American-bred phylloxera. Although hardly an area was left untouched, and many vineyards were completely destroyed, the development of phylloxera-resistant roots finally enabled California growers to save their vines. Perhaps in an unconscious repayment for Colonel Haraszthy's importations, American rootstocks were shipped to Europe by the hundreds of thousands, and today nearly all European wine vines (as well as Californian) are grafted onto phylloxera-resistant roots, which originated in the United States. So the next time a French wine connoisseur begins overpraising his own vineyards, remind him that were it not for American rootstocks perhaps all he could boast of today would be an extensive insect collection!

Despite two wine depressions, in 1876 and 1886, caused by overplanting and the sale of poor-quality wine, by 1900 California was producing some excellent and well-known wines. Several very large wineries were founded in this period, including the Italian Swiss Colony at Asti. A conscious effort was also made to match vine types with the climate and soil best suited to them.

Then came Prohibition. As might be expected, the Eighteenth Amendment was a disaster for California wineries. Only a very few were able to remain in business by producing medicinal and sacramental wine; other companies continued to grow grapes for home use but were forced to shut their doors to wine making on a commercial scale.

Of course, the industry was hurt by the years of idleness and the mass exodus of trained personnel into other professions, but an even greater impact resulted from the demand for wine grapes that arose among amateur home wine makers in the East. Even during Prohibition home wine making was legal, and thousands of thirsty Americans turned to this practice. It did not take long to discover that the thin-skinned varieties which produced the best wine in California were not suited to the long rail voyage to the East Coast. Even when they were available, the rather plain, small Cabernets and Pinot Noirs were usually passed over by the amateur wine maker in favor of the larger, prettier grapes. To meet the rising demand (and prices) for wine grapes, the premium grapes of many of California's vineyards were uprooted and replaced with popular thick-skinned varieties which would ship well—but which could produce at best mediocre wine. The two grapes which most frequently appeared on Eastern markets were the Alicante-Bouschet and the Carignane, both of which would be better eaten than drunk.

After thirteen years of unused cooperage, acres replanted in common grapes, and the absence of skilled wine makers and a knowledgeable clientele, repeal in 1933 found the California wine industry in complete disarray. There was of course a great flurry of wine making, but the results were far from spectacular. Quality was low, and the wines of the 1930s certainly did not live up to the reputation enjoyed by those of the decade before Prohibition.

During these dark days the great majority of California wineries banded together in an attempt to improve industry-wide quality standards and founded the Wine Institute, a nonprofit organization dedicated to the advancement of California wine. The Institute has been instrumental in reducing import restrictions placed on California wines by other states, has done much to improve technical standards of the industry, and acts as the wine industry's lobbyist in Sacramento and Washington. Today the Wine Institute is very active in public relations, with a substantial budget devoted to promoting California wine.

The University of California at Davis has also made great contributions in the fields of enological and viticultural research, not only to California but to all wine-making areas of the world. In recent years it has devoted considerable energy to developing new varieties of grapes that will give increased production while not sacrificing too much of the quality of low-yielding premium grape varieties.

World War II brought increasing financial success to California wineries, but this ended abruptly with the wine depression of 1947, which resulted in a marked drop in the price of California wine. Although many excellent wines were produced in the postwar years, and consumption gradually increased, California wineries still could lay no claim to real prosperity.

The major event in the wine industry during the postwar period was the consolidation of wine making in the hands of fewer and larger wineries. M. A. Amerine and Vernon Singleton, professors of enology at the University of California at Davis and recognized authorities on wine, estimate that by 1965 five or six companies controlled from 65 to 75 percent of the total production of California wine. And today two companies, E. and J. Gallo and United Vintners (owned by Heublein), produce well over one half of all wine made in California. Gallo, in fact, produces so much wine that it has found it more economical to make, rather than buy, its own bottles. These large wineries enjoy certain economic advantages over their smaller counterparts and are well suited to produce great quantities of sound, inexpensive, ordinary wine. They are very commercially oriented and are in no small part responsible for the growing consumer interest in California wines that has become evident in the past decade.

As wine in the past few years has become more and more attractive as a business venture, many large corporations have diversified and entered the California wine scene. Many small independent wineries (and some large ones) receive purchase offers every week, and the list of corporate interests in California reads like a page from Dun & Bradstreet: Heublein, Inc. (Italian Swiss Colony, Petri, Inglenook, Beaulieu); National Distillers and Chemical Corporation (Almadén); Young Brothers Markets (Buena Vista); Seagram's, Inc. (Paul Masson); Nestlé (Beringer Bros.); and Sterling International (Sterling Vineyards). It is impossible to generalize about the effects of this increasing corporate involvement in what in the past has been a primarily family-run and -owned industry; certainly some corporate acquisitions have meant new equipment and inspiration for aging wineries, while others are financial investments where consideration for improving wine quality does not always match the dedication to increasing wine sales. In any case, corporate ownership of many well-known California wineries is a fact, and the only test of the merits or disadvantages of the situation must rest in the wines themselves.

The corporate format has also allowed consumer participation in a booming business beyond just enjoying the finished product. Several wineries, including Windsor Vineyards, Franzia Brothers, and Almadén, are now wholly or partially held by individual stockholders and their shares are traded on the open market.

Yet along with this growing consolidation and big-business atmosphere has come an amazing proliferation of smaller wineries: at least thirty-five have appeared in the last few years. Most of these, as well as many existing small wineries, have continued to concentrate on the production of premium wines, hoping that limited production and personal attention will result in wines that will surpass those of their more widely distributed and advertised competitors.

At this moment California wines are truly in a golden age, as sales continue to soar, new wineries spring up, vineyard acreage is increasing dramatically, and nearly every winery can sell everything it produces. This wine boom is due to many factors, but the most important must be the efforts of the wineries themselves. The industry giants have made California wine available to all segments of the American public, while many of the smaller wineries have contributed much to the growing reputation of California wine at both the national and the international level. Together, they have ushered in a new renaissance for the wines of California.

From Vine to Wine

Wine is the product of the fermentation of fruit sugars by yeast into ethyl alcohol and carbon dioxide. Wine can be made from many fruit varieties, but the grape has the distinction of being virtually the only fruit that contains enough natural sugar and nutritional elements to support a yeast fermentation to a high enough alcohol content to ensure a stable product. Wines made from other fruits must have sugar and supplemental yeast foods added prior to fermentation, or else their wine will be of such low alcohol as to risk easy spoilage.

Many different varieties of grapes are cultivated or grow wild throughout the world, but centuries of wine-making experience have proved that the finest wines are made from the vines known as *Vitis vinifera*. From its origin, probably somewhere in the Middle East, this family of vines has been transplanted to all the great vineyards of Europe, Africa, Australia, and the New World, including California. The hardy native American vine, *Vitis labrusca*, which includes such well-known varieties as Concord, Delaware, and Catawba, is also extensively used in wine making in the Midwest and Eastern United States. In these areas the bitter winter cold and high summer humidity make cultivation of *Vitis vinifera* a difficult enterprise, while the native vines have adapted well to these hazards of climate. It is generally recognized by wine experts, though, that wines made from *labrusca* have a particularly strong flavor referred to as "foxy" and do not achieve the complexity and finesse of *vinifera* wines.

An adequate amount of sunshine during the growing season is necessary for the vine to adequately ripen its fruit. The young grape berry is very high in acid and low in sugar. Like any fruit, when picked green the grape is sour and mouth-curdling, but as it ripens and the sugar content increases it becomes sweet and luscious. The acid content decreases, primarily due to a volume dilution as the fruit increases in size, but there is also a certain amount of natural respiration and chemical change in the maturing berry that leads to a loss of acid. Perfectly ripe grapes must contain a natural sugar content sufficient to yield a wine of approximately 10 to 14 percent alcohol, and they also need to retain enough acidity to produce a wine with good fruitiness. Thus the cultivation of the vine for wine making is limited to those temperate areas of the world where the growing season is warm enough to ripen the grapes adequately, but yet not so hot as to cause the fruit to lose too much of its natural acidity.

In California the yearly cycle of the vine begins in mid-spring, when the dormancy of winter is interrupted by the appearance of the first green shoots. Flowering occurs in May to mid-June, with the cooler areas of Europe usually being several weeks behind California. During this time the vintner is watchful for frosts and worried by the prospect of hailstorms, for these two powers of nature can damage new growth and reduce the quantity of the coming harvest. If frosts are prolonged or sufficiently cold the vines can even be killed. New overhead sprinkler systems are popular in California for frost protection and are proving much more efficient than the old method of placing burning pots in the field. These sprinklers work by spraying a layer of water on the vines which freezes at a temperature that is not low enough to harm the plant, yet protects the delicate areas of the vine from getting any colder should the air temperature continue to drop.

Rain showers during the time that the vines are actually in flower are also damaging, for they will prevent pollination and setting of the fruit, and thus again greatly reduce the quantity of the harvest.

The vines continue to grow and the grapes to mature during the summer, and by August color begins to appear in the berries. A prolonged spell of very hot weather during this time can burn the vines and shrivel the berries, as well as reduce the fruit acids present in the grapes. This is exactly what happened with the 1972 vintage in many parts of northern California.

Harvest time usually begins in early September for the more precocious varieties, such as Chardonnay, Pinot Noir, and White Riesling, and continues through October for such late ripeners as the Cabernet Sauvignon. Good weather during harvest is important, for rain swells the berries with water and dilutes the sugar content. Too much moisture also encourages bunch rot to grow on those varieties with tightly packed clusters.

In a few selected areas of the world the vintage is often delayed several weeks to allow the *Botrytis cinerea* mold to work on the grapes. Unlike other plant molds which can ruin fruit, *Botrytis* imparts special flavors and makes the production of intensely sweet and luscious wines possible. For this reason it has been dubbed *"la pourriture noble,"* or the noble rot. Given the proper microclimate, individual grape berries become infected with this mold in late fall during periods of high humidity. The mold loosens the skins on the grapes, so that when the weather turns warmer considerable water evaporation occurs through the loose skin and the natural sweetness and flavor of the grape becomes more concentrated. The individual berries take on the shriveled appearance of raisins, but do not have the caramelized flavor of a raisin. When harvested, an intense, golden, sweet wine is made literally drop by drop from the shriveled berries. This is the secret of the famous Sauternes of France, the Trockenbeerenauslese of Germany, and the Tokays of Hungary. Although *Botrytis* is rare in California, in recent years a very few wines have been made from grapes partially infected by *Botrytis*. However, none have yet reached the complex depths of the great sweet wines of Europe.

Once the grapes are picked they are transported to the winery where they are placed in a machine that crushes the grapes and removes them from the stems. Picked fruit tends to brown, or oxidize, rather easily, and it is important to crush the grapes as soon as possible to preserve the freshness of the fruit. At this stage sulfur dioxide is often added to prevent oxidation. Some California wineries are experiencing success with mechanical harvesters that pick the grapes and crush them into tank trucks, under the protection of inert nitrogen gas, thus preventing virtually any oxidation. This is especially important for those wineries whose vineyards are many miles away from their crushing and fermenting facilities.

Until this stage, whites and reds have been treated identically, but now the different wines proceed by separate routes. White grapes are immediately pressed after crushing, thus removing the skin and pulp and leaving only the juice to ferment. Care must be taken not to use too great a pressure in the production of quality wines, even at the sacrifice of some quantity. Too strong a press produces a coarse wine with undesirable bitterness from crushed pips.

It is possible to ferment wine by using only those yeast cells naturally present on the skin of grapes. However, these are not always the hardiest varieties, and some wild yeasts can even impart off-flavors to the wine. Most California wineries rely on the sulfur dioxide added at the time of the crush to inhibit the natural yeasts, and they then add specially cultivated strains of wine yeast to ensure a complete, even fermentation.

Some California wineries are now using centrifuges prior to

fermentation to further clean the wines and remove as many small pieces of skins and pulp as possible. This is done under a carbon dioxide blanket to avoid aerating the wines, the thought being that white wines fermented from the purest juice will come out the freshest and fruitiest. The centrifuge may be used again after fermentation to remove yeast deposits.

Fermentation of white wines is best carried out under relatively cool temperatures for a long period of time, usually four to six weeks. Too warm a temperature will produce off-flavors and disturb the delicacy of a white wine. Fermentation vessels may range from wooden casks to concrete vats to stainless steel tanks. Despite their unromantic appearance, the latter have the advantage of being easy to clean, and the latest models are equipped with temperature-controlled cooling jackets, through which solutions can be passed to ensure a slow cool fermentation. Some vintners, however, feel that big white wines such as the Chardonnay benefit from fermentation in small oak barrels, allowing intimate contact of wine with wood, and in such small lots the fermentation does not usually generate enough heat to cause problems.

After fermentation the white wine is racked, or drawn, off the dead yeast sediment, called the lees, and transferred to a storage or aging container. This may be a stainless steel or glass-lined tank, a large wooden cask, or a small oak barrel, depending on whether the wine maker wishes his wine to extract flavor from wood. The wines are then aged to suit the tastes of the vintner, further clarified through racking or filtration, and bottled.

Dry white wines are made by simply allowing fermentation to proceed until virtually all the available sugar has been converted to alcohol. Sweet white wines may be made by several different methods. The first, and most obvious, would be the addition of sugar to the wine. In California direct sugaring is illegal, although vintners are allowed to add unfermented grape juice or grape-juice concentrate to the wine to sweeten it. This is widely practiced, especially for the less expensive sweet wines. It is also possible to produce a sweet wine by starting with grapes that are so high in sugar that an alcohol level sufficient to halt fermentation by killing the yeast will be reached before all the sugar has been fermented. In practice this is very rare, except for those grapes which have been affected by *Botrytis*. In fact, botrytized grapes are so intensely sweet that fermentation can sometimes barely proceed at all, and the resulting wines often end up with a low alcohol content and rely on their high sugar concentration for protection from spoilage, much the same way that jams and jellies are preserved by their high sugar content.

A common method for the production of premium sweet wines is to artificially stop fermentation before it is complete, thus leaving a small amount of residual sugar. This may be accomplished either by adding sufficient sulfur to kill the yeast or by sterile filtration methods that will remove all viable organisms from the wine. A combination of the two is often used, for the filtration process lessens the need for sulfur and decreases the likelihood of an objectionable aroma persisting in the wine.

In contrast to white wines, the skins and pulps are left in the fermenting tank in the production of red wines. The coloring matter of grapes is present in the skins rather than the juice, and the warmth and chemical processes of fermentation release this pigment and color the wine. Some heat is necessary to extract color from the grapes, and red wines are fermented warmer than whites, usually in the 65- to 75-degree range. Should the temperature rise much above this, cooling measures are necessary since too warm a fermentation will produce unpleasant odors and flavors.

In addition to the coloring pigments, an organic acid called tannin is also extracted from the skins during the fermentation of red wines. Tannin gives wine astringency and serves as an antioxidant during a wine's aging. The longer a wine is fermented in contact with the skins, the more color and tannin will be extracted, and the fuller and rougher the wine will be when young. Traditionally the great wines of Bordeaux and Burgundy were left in contact with the skins until the fermentation was completed. The result was a wine that required years of bottle aging to smooth out and reach its peak of drinkability. The trend today, both in Europe and California, is to produce wines that are lighter in style and ready to drink at a younger age, and one way of accomplishing this is by leaving the wine on the skins for a shorter period of time. Of course, there are still selected vintners in Europe and California who continue to follow the traditional method.

Carbon dioxide produced during fermentation pushes the skins to the top of the tank, forming a crust. To increase color extraction and prevent too great a buildup of heat, the wine must be circulated over the layer of skins several times a day. This may be accomplished by pumping the wine over the skins or by using a newly developed rotating fermentation tank in which the juice and skins are continually mixed.

When color and tannin extraction has reached the desired level, the wine maker pumps the juice out of the tank and removes the remaining pulp to a press. A little press wine is often added to wine produced from the free-run juice to give more body, though as with whites too great a pressure will produce wine of lesser quality.

Rosé wines are produced by leaving the juice in contact with the skins only long enough to pick up the desired pink color. If the grapes are highly colored, a few hours is often all that is necessary. Rosé wines can, of course, also be made by mixing a red with a white wine, but these are of inferior quality.

Red wines benefit from aging in wood, although wine makers do have differences of opinion as to the amount of wood flavors they wish to be present. Some feel that too much wood interferes with the natural fruitiness of a wine, while the classic French technique, widely followed in California, is to leave the wine in small oak barrels for one to two years. Other

California wine makers often favor longer periods of aging in large wooden casks, where the surface-to-volume ratio of wine to wood is less and many more years are required for the wine to pick up flavor qualities from the wood. A combination of the two methods, with some time in large tanks and a year in small oak barrels, is also commonly encountered in California.

Oak imparts considerable flavor to wine, while redwood is a more neutral wood. There is considerable variation in the qualities of oaks found throughout the world. Oak from the Limousin forest of France has traditionally been used for the aging of Burgundies, and it imparts a pronounced oily-sweet flavor and scent to the wine. Nevers oak is used in Bordeaux and is noted for contributing a more austere flavor. Both of these oaks have their own proponents and both are widely used in California, especially for aging Cabernet Sauvignon and Pinot Noir. Some vintners are also employing Yugoslavian oak and a considerable amount of oak from Eastern United States forests, in the form of both new and recured whiskey barrels. White oak from Germany is also imported; it is a rather neutral wood and is most commonly used for aging white wines. There is probably no one type of wood that is best for all wines, and the wide variety of aging containers now being used in California ensures the consumer a wide spectrum of flavors and styles from which to choose.

Malic acid is one of the important natural constituents of wine, and while red wine is aging it is common for it to undergo a second fermentation process known as the malolactic fermentation. This involves the conversion of malic acid to lactic acid, with the release of carbon dioxide. Lactic acid is a weaker acid than malic acid, so this fermentation is especially beneficial in those wines which are very high in natural acidity. In California this is not often the case, but the malolactic fermentation is still encouraged because it introduces some complex flavors to the wine and because the resultant product is more stable. Timing is very important with the malolactic fermentation; if it takes place in the bottle the carbon dioxide is trapped and the result is a fizzy red wine. Since California white wines are often deficient in acid, it is extremely rare that a California vintner wishes to induce a malolactic fermentation in his whites.

Red wines throw a heavy sediment while aging, and the wine maker must choose one of several methods of clarification to prepare them for market. The most natural method is to pump the clear wine off the sediment and into another container while the original is cleaned. This must be done several times a year, and is favored by some wine makers as their only means of clarification since it does not remove desirable flavor elements. Wines may also be clarified through fining, which involves the introduction of a material such as egg white, gelatin, or bentonite which will slowly settle in the tank, carrying with it undissolved solids. This is a very common practice throughout the world since, although some traditionalists would disagree, it does not seem to remove too much flavor from the wine. Even wine that has been fined will often throw some sediment after years of aging in the bottle.

Filtration is a very efficient method of clarification, although it is generally agreed that overfiltration can rob a premium wine of desired elements. Most California vintners do use some form of filtration since they are selling wine to a public that is not accustomed to seeing sediment in a bottle of wine.

Once the wine maker feels that his product has obtained the proper marriage of wine with wood, the individual barrels and casks will be blended into a holding tank to ensure uniformity of a particular vintage. Once bottled, wines should be laid to rest for at least a couple of months to overcome the shock of bottling, and then released to the public. Of course, the finest red wines require considerable additional bottle aging before they are at their best.

A Few Definitions

The amateur wine enthusiast will quickly pick up a wide variety of terms used to describe wines when he visits wineries or attends tasting parties. An understanding of the following terms will hopefully increase your appreciation of the world of wine and promote you to stage two on the way to aficionado.

Acidity

The fruitiness and tartness of a wine comes from its acidity. There are many different acids present in wine: tartaric, malic, lactic, acetic, and succinic are but a few examples. A correct acid balance is one of the most important aspects to look for in wine tasting, especially in white wines. Acidity is classified as either low, medium, or high; a wine particularly lacking in acid is termed "flat," and one whose high acidity ("sharpness") is due to unripe grapes is usually designated as "green." The important thing to remember is that acidity contributes fruitiness and helps to bring out an eye-appealing color in wine as well as complementing the body.

Aroma

Two terms, "aroma" and "bouquet," appear to be synonymous and are often interchanged by both the wine-drinking public and the wineries themselves. There is, however, an important distinction. The aroma of a wine is that part of the sensory impression that comes from the grape variety used in producing the wine. To be able to sniff a glass of wine and to determine what grape types were used in preparing the wine is a goal of both the serious connoisseur and the cocktail-party show-off. It is something that can be acquired with practice, especially for those grape varieties with very characteristic aromas. In California this ability has further reward, since state law requires that a varietal wine need be made from only 51 percent of the named grape. Detection of aromas from grapes other than the one named on the wine's label can be informative both from a quality standpoint and for comparing the products and wine-making practices of different wineries.

There are also several grape varieties that are capable of producing fine wines but do not have a distinctive aroma of their own. Such wines are usually characterized as having simply a vinous, or winelike, aroma.

Astringency

Tannin is an organic compound that is present in the skin and stems of the grape. It is one of the most distinguishing characteristics of red wine, as red wine is produced by fermenting together the juice, skins, and sometimes even the stems. White wine, on the other hand, is virtually devoid of tannin, since only the juice itself is fermented. One exception to this is whites that have been aged in new, small oak barrels, for they may extract a slight amount of tannin from the wood. Tannin can be easily recognized by the mouth-puckering, astringent sensation it produces. If you've ever taken a sip of a red wine and then felt as if your tongue were doing a double somersault, you know what tannin is.

A red wine's color comes from pigments in the skin of the grape which are released during the heat of fermentation.

When the skins are kept with the fermenting juice for a relatively long time in order to obtain a deep, richly colored wine, there is likely to be a correspondingly high tannin content. In a young wine high tannin can lead to a rough, perhaps even bitter-tasting wine. But fortunately tannin is one of those chemical elements that are smoothed out by aging; in fact, a high tannin content is a sign that a wine will age well, and knowledgeable wine lovers look for this when selecting young wines to put away or "lay down" for a few years until they are more mature. Tannin is also important since it serves as an antioxidant. Its presence is an extra guarantee that the wine will not spoil during its years of slow maturation in the bottle.

Body

"Body" is another important term in the vocabulary of wine, but unfortunately the word is subject to various interpretations by different authors. In this book we define body as the consistency of the wine; almost the "weight" of the wine on the tongue. For example, water would be classified as a very light-bodied fluid, while milk, a thicker, heavier-tasting liquid, has greater body. Body in a wine results from interaction on the taste buds of a wine's alcoholic content, flavor constituents, and the presence or absence of tannin.

Bouquet

The bouquet of a wine is that part of the odor that can be attributed to the aging of the wine as well as to the creation of various chemical constituents during fermentation. Sensory evaluation of a wine's bouquet is something more easily experienced than described. Because of the great complexity and extremely small quantities of odor constituents present, it has, up to this time, been nearly impossible to identify all of them even through chemical analysis.

Bouquet is enhanced primarily through aging, which introduces a soft, subtle complex of odors. The interested wine drinker would do well to obtain two bottles of a fine wine, one young and one well aged, and to compare the effects that aging can have on the odors released. Appreciation of the ever-changing bouquet of a wine as it slowly matures in the bottle is one of the benefits obtained from putting away a supply of wine in your own personal cellar.

Color

This word, of course, needs no definition, but careful attention to color can tell you much about the wine. Young red wines tend to have a pronounced purple tint to them. As they gain a few years of age this disappears and the color becomes a purer red. With age red wines take on a slight orange cast around the edges, and when very old a color approaching the orange-brown of tea may be reached.

The intensity of color in a white wine varies from virtually waterlike through shades of yellow and on to rich gold, and depends on the grape variety as well as vinification techniques. Young white wines sometimes have a refreshing green tint to their color, while whites that are heading over the hill acquire a brownish color due to oxidation. Sweet whites usually have a deep yellow or golden color.

Cuvée

A blend of wines, generally of different vintages, which are then bottled as one lot. Originally a Champagne term denoting the particular blend made up by each Champagne house before beginning the secondary fermentation, it is now also used for still wines as a means of identifying a given batch of wine.

Dry vs. Sweet

A dry wine is simply a wine that is not sweet, but this term is often mistakenly used as an index of a wine's quality. It is not uncommon for one to hear two table wines, both without noticeable sweetness, compared in conversation with a comment like, "Oh, this wine is much better; it's a drier wine."

The ability to detect sweetness varies considerably from individual to individual. The average threshold, that concentration at which some sweetness becomes noticeable, is between 1 and 2 percent sugar by volume. Table wines that are slightly above this limit in sugar concentration are referred to as medium dry or medium sweet, while those which are several percentages higher in sugar and have a quite noticeable sweet taste are classified as sweet. This system applies only to still table wines, however. With Champagne, for example, the term "brut" is used to describe a Champagne without noticeable sugar, while "extra dry" actually denotes a detectable sweetness.

Generic

A generic wine carries the name of a European wine-producing region, such as Burgundy, Sauternes, or Chablis. They may be made from any grape variety, and in California are generally less expensive and less distinctive wines than those labeled with the grape variety.

Must

A word often heard around wineries at harvest time, must is simply the mixture of grape juice, skin, and pulp undergoing fermentation.

Nose

A term used to refer to the smell of a wine, be it the aroma, bouquet, or both.

Pétillance

The presence of a slight sparkle in a wine is termed *pétillance*. The bubbles are from small amounts of carbon dioxide, although the pressure level of the gas is such that a *pétillant* wine is in the still, rather than the sparkling, category. Many vintners feel that a sparkle imparts freshness and thus purposely create a slight tingle in some of their whites and rosés.

Proprietary

Proprietary wines are similar to generics in that any grape variety may be used in their production. However, they are names coined especially by the producing winery (Paul Masson's Rubion or Baroque and Christian Brothers Château La Salle, for example), rather than being mere copies of European regions.

Varietal

A varietal wine is one whose label carries the name of the principal grape variety from which it was made, like Cabernet Sauvignon or Chenin Blanc. While many vintners do use a greater percentage, the legal requirement is only that 51 percent of the wine actually come from the named variety of grape.

The Characteristics of California Wines

For centuries men have written volumes describing the characteristics of European wines. The imagination and verbal creativity of wine lovers has been captured by the nuances of aroma and flavor that the sun and soil of a particular region have imparted to the grape varieties planted there.

Writers on California wines have often attempted to follow the same path as their European companions by offering descriptions of California Chardonnays, Cabernet Sauvignons, Pinot Noirs, and other fine wines. But while the many wine-growing regions of Europe are fairly small and it may indeed be possible to capture the general characteristics of a Bordeaux or a Burgundy in print, California is a large state with many different soil and climatic conditions, and any description of a California Chardonnay, for example, may in fact be true for only a very few of the many wines produced from this variety.

To further complicate the problem, California's vintners each have their own ideas as to fermenting, aging, and blending practices.

Indeed, the very fact that a California varietal need be made from only 51 percent of the grape variety named on the label means that many wines of different character will be produced. Some vintners insist on producing 100 percent varietal wines, others may blend judiciously, and still others choose to throw in whatever inexpensive grapes are around. The result is often three very different wines that may legally bear the same label.

California's bountiful sunshine makes it possible to grow virtually every wine grape known to man. This means that you have a multitude of California wines to select from, and it is our hope that a general knowledge of the different wine types will not only aid you in making your selections but will also encourage you to try those wines that sound most appealing. Thus we are offering in the next few pages general descriptions of the most popular varietal wines produced in California. But please remember that variations within the several wine types are very common, and our descriptions should not be construed as anything more than a simplified introduction. A more specific wine-by-wine analysis is found in Part Two to take care of the variations and discrepancies that do exist from year to year and from winery to winery.

THE WHITES

Chardonnay

The Chardonnay, or Pinot Chardonnay, as it is sometimes called, is one of the most famous white wine grapes of the world. Its homeland is the Burgundy district of France, where it produces such well-known wines as Chablis, Meursault, Montrachet, and Pouilly Fuissé. It is also one of the principal grapes used in the production of French Champagnes.

The best Chardonnays will always be expensive, both in France and in California, for the vine is a very temperamental one to grow and is a low yielder. Production of only one or two tons per acre is not unusual, compared to the six to eight tons of some other white varieties. But a great Chardonnay can be a truly magnificent wine.

At its best the Chardonnay is a full-bodied dry wine whose color ranges from greenish-tinged straw yellow to pale gold. It should have a complex aroma that lends itself to many descriptions. The wines of Chablis are said to have a fresh, flinty aroma, while those of the more southern areas of Burgundy often have a rich aroma of ripe fruit such as peaches or figs. Some California Chardonnays share this aroma of ripe fruit, while others have a delightful nose of fresh green apples. The Chardonnay can be a powerful wine which will withstand months of aging in small oak barrels, and the complexity of flavors added by the oak blends well with the natural fruitiness of the wine. For this reason most French Chardonnays spend considerable time in wood, and the use of small oak cooperage for California Chardonnays is expanding. Barrel aging imparts spiciness and a small amount of tannin to the wine, and these flavor elements make Chardonnay a fine accompaniment to full-flavored poultry and wild game dishes such as pheasant. Some of the lighter, crisper Chardonnays, such as the French Chablis and many from California, go quite well with seafood.

Several years ago it was not often that a California Chardonnay measured up to the greatness of its name. Recently, however, we have been increasingly impressed by the quality and strength of many California Chardonnays. This is particularly true for some of the very small wineries that can lavish extra time and energy on the wine, but many of the medium to larger wineries are also producing flavorful Chardonnays that are a considerable improvement over those of several years ago. Though still different in style from their French counterparts, being on the whole lighter and without the intense richness and oakiness of a White Burgundy, California Chardonnays have been scoring quite well in our comparative tastings with many a French wine.

This praise cannot, however, be taken as sweeping approval of all California Chardonnays. There are still many overpriced Chardonnays that are disappointingly lacking in varietal character. Those vintners who choose to blend a substantial proportion of less expensive, ordinary wine grapes with their Chardonnay do little more than dilute the character of the wine and increase their profits. And less than perfect grapes may produce a relatively ordinary wine that nevertheless will retain its premium price tag. While Chardonnay will almost always be a good wine, some care must still be exercised in your selection.

Chenin Blanc

The homeland of the Chenin Blanc is the beautiful Loire Valley of France, where, in vineyards around the city of Tours, it produces the famous wines of Vouvray. In California this grape does very well and usually leads to a soft, mellow, fruity wine of light- to medium-yellow color. Many Chenin Blancs are medium sweet with 1.5 to 3 percent sugar content. Those who prefer slightly sweet wines may enjoy these wines with dinner, while others will probably enjoy them more with dessert or after dinner for gentle sipping along with the conversation.

In France this grape is called *Pineau blanc de la Loire,* and several California wineries are now using this name or a shortened version of it on their labels. The French name has also led to some labeling confusion, for Pineau Blanc has been loosely translated as *White Pinot,* and for many years it has been the practice of many wineries to label their dry Chenin Blancs as White Pinots. This is one of the grosser errors in California labeling practices, for the Chenin Blanc is not at all a member of the Pinot family. It would be much clearer if all wineries would adopt the policy of labeling their dry wines from this grape Dry Chenin Blanc. In any case, whether labeled Dry Chenin Blanc or White Pinot, the wine inside is usually a dry wine with the pleasant fruitiness of the grape, though often without the richness of the medium-sweet Chenin Blancs.

Fumé Blanc—see Sauvignon Blanc

Gewürztraminer—see Traminer

Green Hungarian

This is a wine with an intriguing name that is made from another of the "mystery grapes" of California. The exact origin of the Green Hungarian grape and its mode of entry into the United States are not well recorded. One story has it that this variety's original home was somewhere in Germany and that it was transported to Hungary by a migrating group of Germanic people. They in turn attached the prefix "green" to the grape's name to distinguish it from native Hungarian varieties of different color.

Whatever this vine's true history may be, it is used by several California wineries, both large and small, to produce a white table wine with a fruity aroma and a fairly good acid content. Most Green Hungarians are dry, though a few retain a little sweetness. Probably as much mediocre wine is made from the Green Hungarian as is good wine, though at its best it can be a light, crisp wine that is very pleasant and easy to drink.

Besides the Green Hungarian that is bottled as a varietal table wine, several premium wineries use this variety as a blending grape in the production of California Chablis and Rhine Wine.

Grey Riesling

Not a true member of the Riesling family, this is actually the *Chaucé gris* grape of France. It does produce a wine similar in style to many California Rieslings, and this, coupled with the grey tinge present in the skin of the grape, led California vintners to christen the grape Grey Riesling. It sometimes produces a wine with an intriguing, spicelike flavor, and is generally dry, pleasant, and relatively low in acidity. While it can produce a good wine, it rarely reaches the heights of the best true Rieslings.

Muscat Varieties

The *Moscato di Canelli* from Italy and the *Muscat de Frontignan* and *Muscadelle de Bordelais* from France are employed by a few California wineries to produce medium to fairly sweet wines with a flowery, perfumed character. The *Malvasia Bianca,* another member of the family, is particularly characterized by a distinct orange-blossom aroma and is one of the most popular of the Muscat table wine varieties in California.

The sweetness usually present in these wines calls for them to be served with dessert or well chilled on a warm summer afternoon. If you have a friend who claims not to like wine, this may be the type to open, for the perfumed aroma and soft, slightly sweet flavor often particularly appeal to nonwine drinkers.

Pinot Blanc

This grape is a relative of the Chardonnay and generally produces a medium-bodied wine with good acid content. At its best the Pinot Blanc indeed resembles Chardonnay, though usually it is a little lighter in body and character. Some small wineries age their Pinot Blancs in small oak cooperage and produce a full, distinctive, spicy wine which may be the equal of some Chardonnays. Pinot Blancs from larger wineries usually do not see as much wood and are less complex, though they often are still quite fruity. The better California Chablis contain Pinot Blanc in their blend, and this grape is also used in many California Champagnes.

Riesling Varieties

In the cool northern European climates of Germany, the French province of Alsace, and in selected regions of Austria and Czechoslovakia, some delightful light-bodied, flowery white wines are produced. The principal grapes planted in these areas are in the Riesling and Traminer families, and because of their success in Europe they have been widely transplanted around the world, including California.

These grapes ripen earlier than most other varieties, and thus are among the few vines which may be planted in areas where late-spring snowfalls and early-fall frosts result in a fairly short growing season. In cool climates, the wines tend to be rather low in alcohol and high in natural fruit acidity, although in selected riverside vineyards in Germany they can also be very sweet and luscious through the miracle of the noble mold, *Botrytis cinerea.*

The most famous vine of this family is the *White Riesling,* or, as it is often called in California, the *Johannisberg Riesling.* In Germany this grape is so respected that it alone may be labeled "Riesling," and from selected Riesling vineyards in the Rheingau and Mosel regions of Germany come some of the most famous white wines in the world.

California also produces some very fine Rieslings, though often in a different style. Since there is more than enough sunshine during the growing season to mature a Riesling in California, they are often among the first grapes to be harvested. But while our more generous sunshine increases the sugar content of the grapes, ensuring more body and alcohol, this may be at the expense of natural acidity. Thus the classic dry California White Riesling tends to be fairly full-bodied, but it may have a slightly rough finish and lack the crispness and good acid balance of the best German wines.

Recently some California vintners, particularly those whose vines grow on cooler hillsides, have been finishing their

Rieslings with a little residual sweetness, and this seems to balance the wines and to add considerable finesse and fruit. At their best these wines have a pale-yellow color, perfumed floral nose, and a fresh flavor that goes well with lunch or a light supper, as an aperitif, or well chilled served alone on a warm afternoon or evening.

The *Sylvaner* grape is a second member of the Riesling family that produces premium wines, though ones with less flavor and distinction than the White Riesling. They are usually dry with a rather flowery nose, fairly light-bodied in Alsace and Germany and light to medium-bodied in California. They are generally quite drinkable and have the advantage of being less expensive than the White Riesling. In California the Sylvaner is also known as the *Franken Riesling,* since the vine is extensively planted in the German province of Franconia.

In contrast to those in Germany, wines labeled simply *Riesling* in California may be, and usually are, produced primarily from the Sylvaner grape.

Sauvignon Blanc and Semillon

These grapes come to us primarily from the Bordeaux region in France, where they yield the rich, sweet, perfumed Sauternes and the dry Graves. In Sauternes, the vines are predominantly Semillon, with between one third and one fifth Sauvignon Blanc. In Graves, this ratio is reversed.

The Sauvignon Blanc is a princely grape that produces a very fine medium-bodied white wine. It possesses an earthy, almost woody flavor that the French call *goût de terroir* (earthy taste). The grape is also grown along part of the upper Loire River in France, where it is known as the *Blanc Fumé* and produces a very dry wine with a distinctive grassy flavor. In California this appellation has been changed to *Fumé Blanc* and adopted by a few vintners to describe very dry, crisp wines produced by them from the Sauvignon Blanc grape.

The Semillon is generally more aromatic than the Sauvignon Blanc; it has a very lush, almost perfumed fragrance and lends softness and roundness to blends of the two varieties.

In California, these two grapes are used to produce a wide assortment of wines, both dry and sweet, and they are so often blended together that it is difficult to consider them separately. When sold as dry wines, they are usually labeled Dry Sauvignon Blanc, Fumé Blanc, Dry Semillon, or Dry Sauterne. The first three are often the more interesting and are generally extremely dry wines. Their earthy flavor is quite distinctive, much praised by some, and rather unpopular with others.

Sweet Semillon, Sweet Sauvignon Blanc, Haut Sauterne, and Sweet Sauterne are among the names given to the medium-sweet to sweet wines made from both Semillon and Sauvignon Blanc. When served well chilled these wines may be pleasant with good fruitiness, though all too often their sweetness masks other distinguishing characteristics and detracts from the quality of the wine. Those who enjoy a sweet wine should also investigate the "Château" wines put out by several of the wineries, such as Château Beaulieu or Château Semillon by Wente Bros.

The very best of these semisweet and sweet wines are the closest California approximation of a true French Sauternes. They can be quite good, but even though the names may be the same, please do not expect them to be exactly the same in complexity, flavor, and aroma as their French counterpart. The soil, climate, and growing conditions are far too different to expect a perfect duplication, and the *Botrytis cinerea* mold that is essential to the production of French Sauternes is relatively rare in California. For a few years the old Cresta Blanca Winery in Livermore produced a Premier Semillon from grapes that were inoculated with the noble mold in the winery after they had been harvested. The resultant wine was fairly rich and sweet and the closest California has yet come to the true Sauternes style. But a similar attempt today to produce a wine from Botrytised grapes would involve production costs that would probably place the wine's price tag out of reach of all but the wealthiest of wine fanciers.

Traminer and Gewürztraminer

The Traminer and Gewürztraminer are grapes that produce wine of a style similar to the Rieslings, but with their own distinctive character. *Gewürz* in German means spicy, and this is a good description of the wines' perfumed-spicy aroma and flavor. A perfect Gewürztraminer can be a delightful drinking experience. It is a versatile wine, blending particularly well with poultry and shellfish, and in Alsace it is used to accompany the regional specialty of sauerkraut garnished with sausages and smoked meats. A distinctive earthy aftertaste is often found in Gewürztraminers, particularly those from Alsace. When this is excessive the wines have a bitter finish that is not too pleasing. Some California Gewürztraminers are a little deficient in acid, but the Gewürztraminer is potentially one of California's most successful white varieties. Most vintners finish their Gewürztraminers dry, although a few choose to retain some residual sweetness.

The Traminer is similar to the Gewürztraminer, producing fruity wines that are just a little less distinguished. In fact, the Gewürztraminer originated as a clone selected from those Traminer vines which seem to produce the spiciest and most flavorful wines. In California some wines that are labeled Traminer are actually produced from a third grape, the *Red Veltliner*. This grape does have white juice, but receives its name from a red blush present on the skin. In addition to California, it is also grown in Austria and Czechoslovakia and produces a light, tart wine.

White Pinot—see Chenin Blanc

Other White Grape Varieties

Sauvignon Vert and *French Colombard* are two wines that are occasionally varietally labeled, although these grapes are more often used for blending. The Sauvignon Vert is not related to the more famous Sauvignon Blanc, and by itself produces a wine fairly low in acid. Large plantings of it were inaugurated soon after Prohibition because it is a high-yielding vine, and it is primarily the smaller wineries established years ago that still have a high proportion of Sauvignon Vert in their vineyards. The French Colombard has a natural high acidity and is a useful grape for blending with other grapes lower in acid. Its use is particularly prominent in many California Champagnes. The few wineries that have chosen to varietally label the wine have done a creditable job with a grape that is not generally considered among the premium varietals.

The *Folle Blanche* is another white variety with rather high acidity. It is varietally bottled only by Louis Martini, who produces a good, crisp wine, while other California wineries use it primarily for blending purposes. The Folle Blanche was until recently the principal grape of the Cognac district of France, where its tart white wine was distilled into one of the world's finest brandies. The *Ugni Blanc* is now the most important grape of the Cognac region, and it, too, is grown in California largely for blending purposes, though Wente Bros. has succeeded in making a fine white wine from a combination of this grape and the Chenin Blanc. Ugni Blanc is known in other areas of France as the *St. Emilion* grape, and in the Tuscany region of Italy it is called the *Trebbiano* and is used in the production of white Chiantis.

CALIFORNIA VIN ROSÉ

A wide assortment of rosé wines, ranging from quite dry to medium sweet, is available today from California wineries. Fortunately, there is usually ample indication of a particular wine's degree of sweetness on the front or back label of the bottle. While many connoisseurs tend to look down their noses at rosés and consider them merely a kind of pink bastard between red and white, rosés are probably the best-known wines among the general public. This is due to the esthetic appeal of their color and also to the fact that they may be drunk with virtually any type of food and are easily palatable to those people who do not often drink wine. Whatever the experts say, here is a fine example of where personal preference should prevail.

Grenache, Gamay, and *Zinfandel* are the most common grapes used in producing a rosé wine; some *Grignolino, Petite Sirah,* and *Cabernet Sauvignon* are also used.

A rosé made entirely or predominantly from *Gamay* or *Zinfandel* grapes is usually of the drier type. The aroma and fruitiness of the grape are usually maintained, but other characteristics of body, tannin, and of course color are lost due to the difference in wine-making technique. Rosé wines are made from dark grapes by leaving the skins in the fermenting tanks for only a few hours until the desired amount of color has been obtained. (For red wines, the skins stay in the tanks throughout fermentation.)

The *Grenache* is a lighter-colored grape variety that lends itself well to the making of rosé wines both in France and in California. The Grenache grape can be grown both in the cooler, premium-grape-growing areas of California and in the warmer Central Valley; for this reason, its sweetness can vary a good deal. Several of the wineries of the Napa Valley bring their Grenache grapes in from the Central Valley and thus have the option of producing dry or medium-dry rosés. Since the Grenache does seem to adapt well to different climates, a great deal of it is grown throughout the state. The result, as for the Zinfandel, is wine that varies in quality from very ordinary to very good.

Whether dry or sweet, a Grenache rosé should possess the delightfully characteristic Grenache aroma, which can perhaps best be described as a perfumed, flowery fragrance. It is one of the most easily distinguished grape aromas, and a novice interested in learning to identify the characteristic aromas of various wines might best begin with a good Grenache rosé. The color of a Grenache wine is generally a pink-orange, instead of the bold pink of most other rosés.

Some rosés produced from *Cabernet Sauvignon* grapes do preserve the character of the grape, though of course this is necessarily less intense than that found in the red wine made from Cabernet grapes. Most Cabernet rosés are dry and fruity, and some have a touch of astringency. Except in a light year, however, it does seem a bit of a shame to use the potential greatness of the Cabernet Sauvignon to produce a rosé when so many other varieties are available.

THE REDS

Barbera

This grape comes to us from the Piedmont region of northern Italy, where it produces some of Italy's finest red wines. It has adapted well to California sun and soil, and at its best can yield a wine of considerable character, dark color, berry-like aroma, and pleasing fruitiness. Young Barberas tend to be rather tart wines, due to the abundant natural acidity of the grape, but with a few years of bottle age, they often mature well and acquire softness and better balance. They are a fine accompaniment to many meat dishes, and their fruitiness and acidity blends especially well with highly seasoned cuisines.

Many of the small California wineries run by families of Italian parentage age their Barberas for five to eight years in large wooden casks. This lessens the acid content of the wine and makes it more palatable when finally bottled. This style of Barbera usually has the orange to onionskin hue of a well-aged wine and can be quite pleasant, though ultimately it may not be as full and flavorful as the bottle-aged variety.

Cabernet—see Ruby Cabernet

Cabernet Sauvignon

This grape is indeed capable of producing some of the finest dry red wine in the world. The fame of the great châteaux of Bordeaux is due primarily to the Cabernet Sauvignon, and, fortunately for us, it is one of the European varieties that has proven best suited to California's soil and climate. At its best, the Cabernet Sauvignon produces a deep-colored, medium- to full-bodied wine that can be immensely pleasing to both nose and palate. The aroma is often particularly complex, with overtones of mint, sage, or black currants. The wine is characteristically high in tannin and is one of the varieties that benefit most from aging. For this reason, several of California's fine wineries keep either all or part of their harvest for extra months of aging in cask or bottle before releasing it for sale. Unfortunately, adequate aging before the wine reaches the public is the exception rather than the rule, and a considerable amount of Cabernet Sauvignon reaches the market before it is really ready to drink. A young Cabernet can be a very sharp, rough wine, and is likely to disappoint a beginning wine drinker who has heard tales of its greatness. This is one wine usually worth the extra money necessary to obtain an older vintage. Of course, the best idea is to purchase good Cabernet when young and store it in your own home for several years.

Like all fine wine grapes, the Cabernet Sauvignon needs ample sunshine to fully mature and produce a great wine. A Cabernet produced from a cool year is likely to be rather thin in body and high in acid. This is particularly true of Bordeaux, where weather conditions can be marginal in some years, but it also applies to California, where there can be considerable variation in the general quality of Cabernet from one vintage to another. For example, 1968 and 1970 generally produced much fuller wines in the Napa Valley than 1967 or 1969.

The demand for Cabernet Sauvignon today is so great that many wineries are intentionally producing a wine that will be quicker-maturing, thus assuring a larger ready supply for the public. To accomplish this it is necessary to keep the tannin content of the wines relatively low by removing the skins from the fermenting tank earlier than they perhaps otherwise would have been. While this will give a smoother, less tannic wine, it will also result in a lighter-colored wine that may not mature to the greatness of which a Cabernet Sauvignon is capable. These young, more delicate Cabernets are often quite agreeable, but for a merely agreeable wine there are dozens of inexpensive red wines available. One does not plant a redwood tree merely for a little shade; neither should one attempt to make a *vin ordinaire* out of a Cabernet Sauvignon.

A wine made entirely from Cabernet Sauvignon grapes should be a powerful wine with strong flavor and a requirement of considerable aging. They can be magnificent, but they also run the risk of being too overpowering. For this reason virtually all Bordeaux and many California Cabernet Sauvignons are actually blended with several other grape varieties, and the selection of blending grapes is an extremely important determinant of style and character. In Bordeaux *Merlot, Malbec, Cabernet Franc, Bouschet,* and *Petit Verdot* are the principal blending varieties. Merlot adds softness and fruit to the wine, Malbec contributes strength and alcohol, while the other three modify the strength of the Cabernet Sauvignon without overly sacrificing flavor or character. All of these varieties, particularly Merlot and Cabernet Franc, tend to be earlier-maturing than the Cabernet Sauvignon and thus also reduce the time needed for the wine to mature. Most importantly, these grapes are very closely related to the Cabernet Sauvignon and therefore blend extremely well with it. Indeed, some Bordeaux wines from the districts of St. Emilion and Pomerol may have no Cabernet Sauvignon in them at all, being composed primarily of Bouschet and Merlot, and yet in a blind tasting they may be virtually indistinguishable in varietal character from a wine made primarily from Cabernet Sauvignon.

In California a number of the finer wineries do produce a 100 percent varietal Cabernet Sauvignon; some of these may be great wines that, if given the opportunity, can equal or exceed the aging potential of many of Bordeaux's finest. Small amounts of Merlot and Cabernet Franc are also grown for blending purposes in California, and to date have been used quite successfully. The Merlot in particular has shown excellent promise, and its acreage will surely increase in the next few years. Many California wineries still rely on other grape varieties, such as Zinfandel, Carignane, and Ruby Cabernet, for blending. Their results are often less successful, for these varieties tend to overly dilute the Cabernet Sauvignon character of the wine.

Gamay (Beaujolais)

Two different Gamay grapes are grown in California: one is called the Napa Valley Gamay and the other the Gamay Beaujolais. For years it was thought that the latter was the same grape grown in the Beaujolais region of France, the one responsible for the light, gay, early-maturing wines of that celebrated district. The exact origin of the Napa Valley Gamay was unknown and it was felt to be a grape unique to California. Recent research at the University of California at Davis, capable of tracing the ancestry of a grape by analyzing the pigments in the skin, has suggested that the reverse may be true—that the Napa Gamay is the true Beaujolais grape and that the California Gamay Beaujolais is actually a clone or a variant of the Pinot Noir. As a result of all this confusion, California law now permits the former Gamay Beaujolais grape to be labeled as Pinot Noir, which we find rather curious, since for years the Gamay Beaujolais was described on labels and in tasting rooms as a light, fruity wine, while the Pinot Noir was a full, robust one. In addition, the Napa Valley Gamay may now be labeled as Gamay Beaujolais. Isn't it good that all the confusion has been eliminated!

Whatever the ultimate decision may be regarding the true origin of these grapes, both California Gamays are usually fruity, fairly light-bodied, and low in tannin. The relative smoothness and amount of acidity vary somewhat from winery to winery, but, on the whole, a California Gamay Beaujolais can be counted upon to be a light, pleasant, and very fruity wine, often an ideal accompaniment for a luncheon or picnic. The Napa Valley Gamay is often a bit fuller and possesses deeper flavor, though at the expense of losing some fruit. Both of these wines can usually be drunk quite young and still be appreciated, and many Gamays are at their best for only a year or two after harvest. A very few are purposely made to age for at least a few years, but they are certainly exceptions. While the Gamay may lack the character and robust quality of a good Cabernet Sauvignon, it is a wine well worth investigating for its own merits and its often attractive price tag.

Petite Sirah

Varietal wine made from this grape is enjoying increasing popularity in California, though for years only a few wineries bottled a Petite Sirah, while most of their neighbors used this grape for blending into California Burgundies. Now at least ten wineries produce a Petite Sirah, and this number grows each year.

The true Petite Sirah has its homeland in the Rhone Valley of France. It is the legendary grape responsible for the rich, long-lived wines of Hermitage and Côte Rôtie, and it is an important grape in the blend that comprises Châteauneuf-du-Pape. Capable of producing a wine with inky-black color, a delightful peppery-spicy nose, and full, complex flavors, it is a varietal that well deserves to be considered one of the world's great wine grapes.

The Petite Sirah's slow start in California may have been due to the fact that some of the plantings originally called Petite Sirah were actually a different variety, the *Durif,* which is a rather ordinary grape best used for blending. As the true Petite Sirah becomes more appreciated and its potential realized, interest in this grape variety will certainly continue to grow.

We have tasted rich, full-bodied California Petite Sirahs that are high in tannin and will last for years as well as lighter, fruitier ones that are pleasant to drink when relatively young. The differences are probably due to climate variation throughout the state as well as to different wine-making techniques. In either case, this is a wine that provides an intriguing change from the more common red varieties and it is well worth trying to see if it fits in with your own taste preferences.

Pinot Noir

A thousand years of time have united the small black Pinot Noir grape and the hillsides of the French Burgundy country much as a well-formed glove clings to a hand. The result, in a good year, is a soft, full-bodied, velvety wine that gives the Château Latours and Lafites of Bordeaux a run for their money as the best red wine of France.

It would be almost impossible to have a climate as nearly perfect for grapes as California's and not be tempted to cultivate a variety with the reputation of the Pinot Noir. California vintners have of course yielded to this temptation, and the number of acres planted in Pinot Noir has more than quintupled in the past ten years.

Of all the world's wine grapes, Pinot Noir is certainly one of the most temperamental. Great wine can be made from it only with great fortune and effort, and even in its Burgundian homeland there are a number of vineyards whose produce is only ordinary. In California, as in other areas of the world to which the grape has been transported, the results are usually far below the best of Burgundy. Most California Pinot Noirs that we have tasted have nowhere near the fruit, finesse, softness, and rich character of a good Burgundy. Perhaps climate, exposure, and soil differences are the reasons; perhaps it is simply that our Pinot Noirs are still a few score years away from finding just the right combination of hillside and vine to produce a great wine. After all, France has quite a head start on us in adapting vines to the perfect environment.

The vast majority of California Pinot Noirs are rather thin in body and flavor—as light, tart, fruity wines they are fine; as wines with a fantastic reputation and a high price tag they are not. And now, as noted above, the grape formerly known as Gamay Beaujolais may also be used in wine labeled Pinot Noir. Their color ranges from light red to a robust ruby; some have marvelous aroma and disappointing taste, others have little aroma and good taste. The tannin content is usually low to moderate, and they are not generally the best California wines to put away for years of aging.

Exceptions do, of course, exist. The best California Pinot Noirs, while different in character from a Burgundy, can be fine wines with rich color, full body, and a complexity of flavors which will benefit greatly from a few years in the bottle. Unfortunately, only a few vintners have thus far succeeded in producing a wine of this caliber. And, in all fairness to the consumer, we must mention that our own tastings have demonstrated that wine "connoisseurs" and novices alike often prefer much less expensive wines. In one blind tasting a Gallo Hearty Burgundy outdistanced half the other entrants, all of which were Pinot Noirs.

Zinfandel

The Zinfandel grape probably originated somewhere in Europe, perhaps in Hungary or Italy, but its exact ancestry prior to its introduction to California in the mid-1800s is still unknown. In any case, it is today considered a wine unique to California.

Second only to Carignane in total acreage among California's wine grapes, Zinfandel is also one of the most potentially exciting. For years Zinfandel was dismissed as a rather ordinary varietal well suited to jugs and to blending into California Clarets, but recent vintages have produced some truly excellent and distinguished Zinfandels. Of course, with over twenty thousand acres planted in this grape the variations in style of the wine remain considerable.

A good deal of Zinfandel grown in the Central Valley and the Cucamonga district of Southern California, as well as some from the flat vineyard land of Mendocino and northern Sonoma County, still finds its way into half-gallon and gallon jugs and into generic reds. Zinfandel is also one of the principal grape varieties in many California Ports. Some of the inexpensive Zinfandels can be quite nice, particularly those from small family wineries that take great pride in the tradition of this grape, and an aged Zinfandel of this style may make a very good, everyday table wine. However, in very warm climates Zinfandel grapes do raisin rather easily. This can impart a caramelized, raisinlike aroma and taste to the wine that is not particularly pleasant.

In the cool North Coast valleys and hills Zinfandel is at its best, though here, too, a large variety of styles reflects the desires of the different wine makers. Some are light and fruity and quite drinkable when but a few years old. Others are inky-black, big in body and tannin, and require several years in the cask and many years of bottle aging to reach their peak. The best of both styles may have a distinctive aroma which has been likened to lush, ripe raspberries.

Some very exciting and unique wines of recent years have been produced from late-picked Zinfandel grapes loaded with sugar, which create wines with considerable depth, fruitiness, and a very high alcohol content.

Because of the wide variation among wines labeled Zinfandel, perhaps more than with any other variety it remains very important to pay close attention both to the particular winery producing the wine as well as to the area in which the grapes were grown.

Other Red Grape Varieties

Many other red wine grapes are used for blending purposes in California, but at least five of these occasionally find their names on the labels of varietal wines. *Charbono, Grignolino,* and *Nebbiolo* all come from northern Italy, where at least the latter two are considerably more important than they are in California. Charbono does not have a particularly distinctive varietal aroma, but it can produce a nice medium-bodied red wine that will sometimes age very well. Grignolino is tarter and fruitier and produces a lighter-colored wine, often with an orange cast, that lends itself well to rosés. Red wines can also be made from this grape, although sometimes other varieties are added to enhance the color. Nebbiolo is responsible for the Barolo wines of the Piedmont district of Italy, and in its homeland the grape produces big wines with considerable fruit and fine aging potential. In California the grape is considerably less distinguished, and what little there is of it is used primarily for blending.

The *Carignane* is the most widely planted red wine grape

in California and is a major component of many generic wines. A few wineries do varietally label this wine, although it is generally a rather ordinary red wine without great depth or character.

The *Red Pinot,* or *Pinot St. George,* as it is also called, is actually not at all a member of the Pinot family. It can produce a medium-bodied, pleasant red wine, though once again it does not generally possess a particularly distinctive varietal character.

NEW WINES FROM NEW GRAPES

The Department of Viticulture and Enology at the University of California at Davis is constantly experimenting with new grape types in an effort to improve the varietal complement of California vineyards. To date several varieties have been developed which show good promise.

The first of these, the *Ruby Cabernet,* is a hybrid of the Cabernet Sauvignon and the Carignane. The goal of the cross was to combine the character of the Cabernet Sauvignon with the productivity of the Carignane. Most Ruby Cabernets, while admittedly not approaching the greatness of the Cabernet Sauvignon, are light, fruity, pleasant red wines that are a good sight better than most Carignanes and at their best are capable of developing some complexity with proper aging.

A word of warning is in order regarding labeling practices with this grape. Some vintners choose to label their Ruby Cabernets simply *Cabernet,* and the unwary consumer may think he is purchasing a bottle of Cabernet Sauvignon. To be sure you're buying a true wine from this expensive grape check to see that the name Cabernet Sauvignon is stated in full on the label.

The *Emerald Riesling* is the result of an accidental cross pollination between a Muscadelle of California and a White

Riesling. It is a highly productive variety of high sugar content that still retains a good level of natural fruit acids. It may be grown in some of the warmer areas of California to produce a pleasant medium-dry white wine.

The *Flora* is a cross between Semillon and Traminer grapes. While only a few wineries now produce Flora as a varietal, it is sometimes used by others in blending. At its best a Flora is a pleasant, fruity, spicy white wine.

The *Gold* is a new variety that has many different grapes in its parentage, but the predominant aroma and flavor characteristics are of a Muscat nature. In the Lodi district some aromatic, slightly sweet white wine is being produced from this grape.

One of the major goals in creating these new hybrid varieties is to find grapes that will grow in the warmer districts of California and still retain enough fruitiness and acidity to produce good table wine. The results to date look very promising, and in years to come these and future varieties may do much to improve the quality of wine produced in the great inland valleys of California.

California Vs. European Wine

Every discussion of California wines these days includes a comparison between California wines and wine-making techniques and their counterparts in Europe. Each side has so many devotees and trade organizations rooting for it that it's difficult to say much of anything without stepping on someone's toes. So let's go stamp on a few feet.

The average California jug wine, exemplified by such well-known producers as Gallo and Italian Swiss Colony, is without doubt much more palatable than the ordinary, inexpensive wines that are found on most European tables. Though not great, the California wines put out in half-gallon and gallon jugs have it all over similar everyday European wines when it comes to technical quality, taste, consistency, and for that matter even price (if you consider how much more expensive things usually are in the United States).

But in all fairness to Europe, the "average" European wine is *not* typified by the 99-cent specials on Leibfraumilch, Beaujolais, or even Spanish Zinfandel (!) currently inundating American liquor stores and supermarkets. While occasionally one of these bottles may hold a wine that is indeed a bargain at such a low price, at best these are rather nondescript, worthless blends and at worse they can be out-and-out frauds. In either case, they have usually been created exclusively for the American market by shippers and importers who are more interested in making dollars than they are in making wine. Certainly it would be a mistake to consider these "bargains" truly representative of the viticultural region named on the label.

So comparisons between inexpensive, everyday wine in Europe and California are simple: the California product is usually better. But since in the present book we deal primarily with the premium wines of California, it is only proper to spend the rest of this chapter comparing them to only the premium wines of Europe, those wines from reputable producers that are clearly identified as the product of a specific commune, château, or vineyard. These are the dinner wines of Europe, not the *vins ordinaires,* and they are in much the same relation to the average European wine as premium California wines are to the bulk or jug wines of the Central Valley.

But one major difference must be noted before we proceed any further: price. While it may seem that California wines have been soaring in price for the past few years, their rise has been unspectacular when compared to the heights attained by the famous and not-so-famous wines of Europe, especially France. Five years ago you could buy a very good French château-bottled wine for $3 to $5 a bottle; today that same wine is probably selling for a minimum of $6 a bottle a year before it is even due to arrive in this country! And the most famous of the 1970 red Bordeaux wines, for example, are already being quoted to wholesalers at nearly $20 a fifth. The rise has not been so noted with certain French whites or lesser-known red wines, but when you are confronted with a choice between a wine from California and one from France, certainly your wallet will have a lot to say in the matter.

We do not want to imply that all good European wines are now beyond the range of the average consumer; many very fine wines from Italy, Spain, Germany, and the less famous regions of France are available with a little bit of looking. In fact, importers are now paying much more attention to the lesser wines of Europe and, while Bordeaux and Burgundy may be floating out of sight, the consumer should find himself with an even greater selection of wines from which to choose.

With the above *caveat* in mind, then, we shall try to discuss Europe and California without referring constantly to price; but you know that it's there.

Most of the early California wine makers brought their trade with them from Europe. The founders of Paul Masson and Beaulieu came from France; Wente, Krug, and Beringer from Germany; and Sebastiani and Martini from Italy. They were used to drinking wine named after its native district: Burgundy, Chablis, Rhine, Sauternes, so after their arrival in California they continued the practice of labeling similar wines with the names of European regions.

Today, any resemblance that once may have been found between, for example, a French Burgundy and a California Burgundy no longer exists. To understand why, it is necessary to first examine some of the laws that govern European wine-making and labeling practices.

Throughout Europe, and especially in France, the types of grapes that may go into a particular wine are limited by both climate and governmental regulations. The French use a system of labeling, called *appellation contrôlée,* that carefully delimits geographic areas, grape types, growing conditions, and alcoholic and sugar contents. All premium French wines must carry an *appellation contrôlée* and have been grown and produced under fairly exacting standards. Thus a French red Burgundy is usually made from the Pinot Noir grape, a Chablis from Chardonnay, a red Bordeaux primarily from Cabernet Sauvignon, and a Sauternes from Semillon and Sauvignon Blanc. Even the lesser grape varieties used in blending are carefully restricted. It is not surprising, there-fore, that you can expect some recognizable consistency among similarly labeled wines.

In California, wine is often made from these same fine grapes, but here the better wines are labeled with the name of the grape rather than the name of the region in which the wine was produced (although this information will appear in a secondary position on the label). Thus wine made from the Pinot Noir grape is not labeled Burgundy but is simply labeled Pinot Noir. Certainly this method of varietal labeling is at least as honest as the French system and is probably much easier to remember. The difficulty with this system is that, under present law, a wine need contain only 51 percent of a given variety in order to be varietally labeled.

Because of the American practice of labeling wines for a specific grape variety, the question of blending seems to arise much more often here than it does in discussing European wines. While many European wines are in fact produced from only one grape, others have traditionally been produced from a particular blend of grapes. Champagne, for example, is generally produced from both Chardonnay and Pinot Noir, and all Bordeaux, perhaps the most famous of the reds, are blends. In fact, while it is the Cabernet Sauvignon that is invariably identified with the great wines of Bordeaux, some of the best and most famous châteaux may contain only 50 or 60 percent Cabernet Sauvignon. Château Cheval Blanc, the most famous of the St. Emilions, contains no Cabernet Sauvignon at all, though recent plantings have included a little of this famous grape.

Why, then, is there such a fuss made in California over whether or not a wine is 100 percent varietal? Again, back to France: all the various grapes that may be grown in Bordeaux, the Cabernet Franc, Merlot, Bouschet, Malbec, are very closely related to the Cabernet Sauvignon. In fact, a St. Emilion or Pomerol, which is likely to contain only small amounts of Cabernet Sauvignon, can easily be taken by experts for a Médoc, which would generally have 60 to 80 percent Cabernet Sauvignon. In California, on the other hand, the blending grapes might not be so closely related and the resulting wine may lose much of its varietal character. Since there is no restriction whatsoever on which grapes may be blended with the primary variety, the percentage of that primary variety becomes more important.

The fact that a California varietal is made entirely from the named grape does not necessarily mean that the wine itself is superior to one that has been judiciously blended. Some very successful California Cabernet Sauvignons, for example, are blended with up to 25 percent of other varieties. Recently there has been increasing interest in the use of various Bordeaux grapes, particularly the Merlot and Cabernet Franc, and some of the resulting blends are quite good indeed.

If the best California wines are generally labeled for the variety of the grape, what then are California Burgundy, Sauterne, Chablis, Rhine Wine, and Claret? Perhaps the only general statement that can be made about these wines is that they usually bear little if any resemblance to their European namesakes. Often they are wines of lesser quality, although there are a few wineries that do produce fine wines under these labels. California wines bearing these generic (regional) names are made from a myriad of grape varieties including a few good ones and a host of inferior types, and their quality ranges anywhere from a good wine to one that is barely palatable at fraternity parties.

In Europe a Chablis is a quality dry wine made from the Chardonnay grape. A Rhine Wine may be dry or semisweet and is generally made from grapes of the Riesling family. A Sauternes is a luscious, sweet, golden wine made in the district of the same name near Bordeaux. In California, however, a white wine labeled Chablis may be indistinguishable from one called Sauterne. In fact, among the large commercial wineries it is not unheard of to stop the production line, change labels, and continue filling the bottles with the same wine.

Some grape varieties are more commonly used in California generics than others. California Burgundy often contains varying amounts of Petite Sirah, Zinfandel, and Carignane. A Chablis may contain French Colombard, Green Hungarian, and perhaps some Chenin Blanc and Pinot Blanc. But even among blends utilizing these grapes, variation can be great. And certainly there is no way of consistently distinguishing Sauterne from Chablis or Burgundy from Claret.

The practice of using European regional names in California, while historically understandable, is confusing to the consumer and at most is only vaguely relevant to the contents of the bottle. The system should be changed. Why not replace the present one with the use of California regional names, such as Napa Valley dry red or Livermore Valley sweet white, or proprietary names, like Paul Masson Emerald Dry or Christian Brothers Château La Salle? While the use of proprietary names might be on the increase, real change will remain a long way off as long as the vintner continues to feel that the European names are more commercially attractive.

Because of the great climatic variations from year to year, the vintage of a European wine is one of the most important indicators of the wine's quality. Anyone who has lived in Bordeaux knows that the city is famous for two things: wine and rain. Whenever there is too much of the latter, the former is bound to suffer. This is true in other European regions as well. Indeed, it is often necessary to sugar the grape must in Germany and Burgundy (a practice illegal in California) in order to obtain wines of an acceptable alcoholic content. Whenever the climate in these areas is good enough to make sugaring unnecessary, the wines are better.

In California, the claim is often made that every year is a vintage year. The climate of her premium grape-growing regions is more consistent, and it is said that a good wine can be produced every year. Indeed, in comparison to Europe this is true. But even given this climatic consistency, vintage dating can still be an important indicator of a wine's character.

We have prepared the following descriptions of recent vintages for the Napa Valley to demonstrate that variations do exist from year to year. Of course, no vintage chart can be perfect, for some wineries will have succeeded more or less than their neighbors in any given year. In addition, yearly variations in California are less pronounced than in many areas of Europe. It is rare that even a lesser year in California will not produce some rather palatable wines, while it would be difficult to say the same for such poor French and German vintages as 1963, 1965, and 1968.

1964: A year when rather severe spring frosts damaged many vines and reduced quantity. The grapes that remained had the benefit of a warm summer and fine weather during the fall harvest. Some very fine red wines were produced, notably some excellent Cabernets.

1965: A good year whose red wines were perhaps a little lighter and earlier-maturing than the preceeding or following vintage.

1966: A very dry spring kept the quantity of this harvest down, but weather conditions otherwise were very fine and some very good, long-lived reds were produced. Once again the Cabernets were fine and Barberas and Zinfandels from this vintage also show richness and promise of continued development.

1967: Generally lighter reds were produced this year, and this vintage must be considered a lesser one.

1968: A superb year for most red wines in the Napa Valley. The Cabernet Sauvignons for the most part have excellent flavor, breed, and elegance, as do many Zinfandels, Barberas, and even a number of the generic reds. Pinot Noir performed better than average, with the product of several vintners displaying good body and depth.

A few white wines may still be around from this vintage. Generally they were successful, with a few Rieslings and Sauvignon Blancs being particularly good although some Chardonnays were lacking in acidity.

1969:   Many of the red wines from this year are very fruity and pleasant, though lighter in style and without the long aging potential of 1968 or 1970.

The whites were quite successful, including some fine Johannisberg Rieslings. This was also the year when Napa Chardonnay seemed to come into its own, and some rich, mouth-filling Chardonnays with good acid were produced.

1970:   This year saw some of the most severe and prolonged spring frosts of recent memory, reducing the yield in some areas to ⅓ to ½ of normal. The summer was very warm, and as often happens in years of short quantity, the quality of the surviving crop was high because of excellent ripening. Many reds show promise of being quite full-bodied with a long life ahead of them.

The whites were generally good, though not outstanding, for the warmth of the summer lowered the acidity of many varieties.

1971:   A rather unusual year for California, for cool weather and rain in late spring delayed the blossoming and setting of the fruit. Cool weather at harvest time prevented some varieties, particularly the late-ripening Cabernets, from reaching optimum sugar content, and while it is too early to tell how the reds will ultimately develop, many of those tasted in the barrel seemed rather light, though with good fruit.

The cooler weather seemed to preserve the freshness and fruitiness of many of the whites, and these will probably prove to be more successful than the reds.

1972:   A year when Mother Nature seemed intent on proving her supremacy. Significant frosts occurred in the spring, and several days of intense heat in early summer caused sunburn damage, which further reduced quantity and also lowered the acidity of much of the remaining crop. Light rain in late September caused bunch rot in a few of the tightly clustered varieties, such as Chenin Blanc, but most of the early ripeners were picked without further damage. But then the rains came and lasted for over a week, catching most of the Cabernet Sauvignon still on the vine and preventing further ripening. Certainly some good wines from this vintage are available, but careful selection is necessary, and for the second year in a row California Cabernets might not achieve their full potential.

As implied above, some varieties may do extremely well in a given year while others may be left wanting. Pinot Noir and Chardonnay, for example, are two varieties that are very dependent on ideal growing conditions, and they may suffer from even slight variations.

The date on a bottle of wine makes it easier to locate a bottle that you particularly enjoyed. It is also an instant indicator of a wine's age, thus telling us how long the wine has had a chance to mature in the bottle or to oxidize on a retailer's back shelves.

Many California vintners regularly blend wine from several years to achieve a more uniform final product, and for this reason do not vintage-date their bottles. This practice certainly has merit as long as the winery has high standards and the wine maker makes judicious decisions. Often nonvintaged reds will be more mature when released, thus obviating the necessity for aging. But while blending may produce consistency, this means weakening strong years as well as raising the quality of poorer harvests. And there still seems to be no reason for not at least displaying the bottling date on the label, if only for those whites that may start to go downhill after a couple of years.

Climatic conditions are extremely important in the growing of wine grapes. One of the major factors in climate, temperature, may be conveniently measured on a scale of "day-degrees" that was developed at the University of California at Davis. Each day during the growing season that the average twenty-four-hour temperature rises above 50 degrees Fahrenheit is added to the grand total. For example, an 85-degree day contributes 35 day-degrees to the season total. The following table (reprinted through the courtesy of *Wines and Vines* magazine) compares the temperatures among several California and European wine regions.

Place	Annual Day-degrees
Fresno	4680
Livermore	3260
St. Helena (Napa Valley)	2900
San Jose (Santa Clara Valley)	2590
Bordeaux, France	2519
Beaune, France (Burgundy)	2400
Sonoma	2360
Aptos (Santa Cruz Mountains)	2110
Auxerre, France (Chablis)	1850
Trier, Germany (Moselle)	1730
Geisenheim, Germany (Rhine)	1709

As can be inferred from this chart, the Rieslings and Chardonnays of California are grown in areas quite different from Germany and Chablis, where the average season temperature is over 1000 day-degrees cooler. Also, one of our most successful varieties, the Cabernet Sauvignon, comes from Bordeaux, where the average temperature during the growing season approximates that of our own premium grape-growing areas.

On the other hand, California Pinot Noirs are often quite different from the French Burgundies produced from the same grape, although this may seem surprising since the temperature of our cooler valleys is similar to that of the Burgundy region. Of course, many factors besides temperature—soil, rainfall, and exposure, for example—contribute to a vine's environment, and differences in some of these may help explain why California wines do not always resemble their European counterparts.

Another difference between many European wines and those from California is reflected in the acid content of the grapes. In poor vintages many European wines are overly tart, or sharp, while in good years the climate is still usually cool enough to maintain good acid balance in the wine. The warmer climate of California causes many grapes to reach the winery somewhat deficient in natural acidity, and it is not unusual for wine makers to add citric or tartaric acid at the time of vinification in an attempt to boost the fruitiness of their product.

Another major difference between California and Europe is that European wineries almost universally (and often by law) specialize in only one wine type; California wineries, with very few exceptions, produce whole "lines" of wines, including red, white, and rosé table wines, Champagnes, and often fortified dessert wines as well. This, we feel, is one of the major defects in the California wine industry today. It is simply irrational to expect several different grape varieties to yield equally good results under the same soil and climatic conditions. While there does seem to be more attention given in new plantings to match grape variety with the particular microclimate of the area, the insistence on planting at least five or six varieties in a single plot of vineyard shows no sign of decreasing. Many of the new smaller wineries have restricted their field of interest to three or four grape varieties, though this decision may be dictated as much by economics as by desire. But in their wish to provide the consumer with as many attractive labels as possible from which to choose, California's larger wineries have succeeded only in producing a whole host of sometimes mediocre products instead of concentrating on the development of a few high-quality wines.

The result is often mass confusion, as when a winery produces several Rieslings, a Traminer or two, and a Rhine wine; then a Sauvignon Blanc, a Semillon, and several "Sauternes" of varying degrees of sweetness. Oftentimes a consumer, while attempting to escape one wine type that he does not like, will end up buying a very similar wine under a different label.

If viewed as an experiment to discover which varieties should be continued, the wineries' ventures would be laudable, but unfortunately there seems to be no trend toward decreasing the number of wine types being produced. Restaurants and retail stores are just as much, if not more, to blame, for they are generally more concerned with presenting a whole "package" to their customers than in offering the best quality at the most reasonable price. So the proliferation of varieties continues, and instead of selecting only the better wines from a given winery and thus having more space for the many good wines that are available, both restaurants and retail stores continue to stock their wine lists with the entire lines of a few wineries, a system that often results in fewer real choices being left for the consumer.

Most European wineries are very small by American standards, although control in many areas is gradually falling into fewer and fewer hands. But among the more traditional wineries, those that are not still family operations are usually run by small companies or cooperatives. Their small size adds a measure of consistency to the resulting product: all of the grapes often come from their own vineyards, which almost invariably surround the winery itself. The soil conditions, climate, and exposure of the vines are likely to be the same throughout the vineyard, and the relatively small amount of wine produced means that it is generally fermented, handled, and stored under identical conditions in the same building. The result is a vintage that is either all good or all bad, but is in any case consistent. Unless a particular bottle has been grossly mishandled, it is unlikely that two bottles of the same year carrying the same château or vineyard label will be very different in quality or character.

This of course does not apply to a wine possessing only a general label, such as Bordeaux Supérieur or Beaujolais, for such wines are usually blends that have been created and bottled by a shipper. Not subject to similar limitations for vineyards or capacity, they will not attain as great a degree of consistency.

When California wines receive treatment similar to that of the small, traditional European winery, they are often denominated "estate-bottled," the equivalent of the French *mise en bouteille au château* or *au domaine*. If a winery has vast land holdings, the term loses much of its significance, but at smaller wineries it may denote a wine of more consistent quality, especially in these days of limited grape availability and almost unlimited demand. And for those wineries which estate-bottle only a few wines, such a wine is often a showpiece and likely to have received more careful attention.

Many large California wineries produce more wine in one year than most French châteaux could produce in twenty. The obvious advantage of the size of California wineries is economic: large-scale operations are more efficient and therefore less expensive to run, and some of these savings are undoubtedly passed on to the consumer. Their size also enables California wineries to employ the latest chemical and mechanical techniques in their operations.

But the larger the operation, the more impersonal must be the wine-making process itself, no matter how dedicated the vintner may be to producing the best wine he can. Decisions are best made by a wine master who knows his wine intimately, who has not only analyzed it but who can draw on years of experience and tasting to determine how to bring out its best qualities. The wine that he bottles should be guided by an independent effort to achieve the best wine possible from the materials at hand and not to simply get something on the market before economic pressures become unbearable.

The larger California wineries buy grapes and bulk wine from many independent growers to meet their needs. Some of these grapes may come from vineyards on a valley floor, others from slopes of surrounding hills, some from Napa, and some from Lodi. The different growing conditions will produce grapes of varying flavor and quality, and it is impossible to reproduce conditions each year in order to obtain the much-vaunted "consistency" that many wineries claim. Particularly in today's market, where wineries often have difficulty purchasing as many grapes as they would like, the grapes brought to some wineries may simply be whatever they can get rather than the product of specific vineyards selected for their quality or character.

On the technical side, California's wine-making procedures and equipment may be somewhat more modern than those of most European wineries, but there are no major differences that affect the consumer—hardly anyone, in Europe or California, still uses his feet! California wines are generally more thoroughly filtered than their European counterparts, and very seldom will you find a California wine that is less than brilliant. When you do it is usually the product of one of the smaller wineries that bottle their wines unfiltered. Many European wines more than a few years old will begin to throw some sediment. A word of caution, however: do not reject a wine, particularly an older red, simply because there is a bit of sediment in the bottle. Most excellent red wines throw off some solid precipitates during aging, but, when properly decanted, the wine is not the least bit hurt by the experience. Sediment in a white wine is more likely to be suspect, but is not in itself objectionable, especially in a well-aged full-bodied wine.

The recent technical advances that have been made in California—mechanical harvesting and field-crushing, new presses, temperature-controlled fermentation tanks, centrifuges, etc.—have often resulted in better quality and can have an important effect on the style of a wine as well. Particularly in the whites, wine-making techniques in California have concentrated on protecting the grape juice and resulting wine as much as possible, thus preserving the fruit character of the grape. Primarily because of technical advances, California whites may be fresher, fruitier, and cleaner than some European wines. Of course, this does not always mean that the wine will suit your own taste preferences. For example, many people prefer the slightly musty, oaky character of a French white Burgundy, feeling that a Chardonnay that is merely fresh and fruity has not lived up to its potential. On the other hand, many wine drinkers today agree that the clean, fresh character of the best

California Chenin Blancs surpasses that of the sometimes clumsy Vouvrays of the Loire valley.

California reds may also be fruitier and lighter than many European wines, but here the differences reflect the wine maker's attitude toward the wine he wants to produce more than technical changes.

Some less expensive California jug wines are pasteurized or highly filtered to kill or remove harmful organisms that may remain in the wine and to prevent spoilage. These processes also destroy some useful elements that contribute to the aging process and to the development of bottle bouquet, but they do prevent a gallon jug of wine from spoiling for some time after it has been opened. However, most *premium* wines are not pasteurized and thus should be drunk soon after opening.

Price can usually be used as a fair indication of quality in European wines, since wine merchants taste their selections carefully and generally buy wine at a price commensurate with its quality. It is true that today a great many European, especially French, wines are badly overpriced and that many "name" châteaux will be expensive no matter what their quality, but within the European price system there is still a relationship between price and quality. The important thing for our consideration is that the prices for wines produced in the same region and from the same grape varieties can vary tremendously. Bordeaux wines of the same vintage appearing on the American market range from $2 to $30 a bottle, depending on the reputation of the château and the quality of the year.

In California, on the other hand, price is often a much less reliable indicator of a wine's worth. The great majority of California's varietally labeled premium wines are bunched within a dollar of each other, and a few cents' difference in price is more likely to reflect advertising costs or expansion plans rather than any real distinction in quality. Across-the-board price increases invariably represent the cost-of-living trend or rising grape prices and do not herald a jump in quality or an especially good vintage. In fact, vintage is totally irrelevant to the price of California wines (except that an older vintage will understandably cost more than a recent one). Although most vintners will readily admit in private that this year's wine may not be as good as last year's, this is never translated into a corresponding reduction in price.

In partial explanation of the continued increase in wine prices, it must be remembered that many factors influence the cost of a wine that are not directly related to the quality of the wine. Grape prices are rising drastically because of the almost infinite demand, though this situation should ease when the many new vineyards being planted come into bearing. Land and construction costs keep going up, and winery equipment—presses, fermentation tanks, oak barrels, etc.—has jumped tremendously in price in the last couple of years. Still, it's a shame that the wine's quality seems to have been left out of the accountant's calculations.

We have found that those wines that sell for considerably more ($4 and up) are generally better wines than their more economically priced brethren, but even these more often than not reflect the reputation of the grape variety or the exclusivity of the winery rather than a conscious attempt to measure a jump in quality. Because of this almost uniform irrelevance of price to quality, you, the consumer, must choose your wine knowledgeably and not be guided solely by your pocketbook.

When all is said and done, perhaps the basic difference between European and California wines is to be found in the attitudes of those who produce and drink them. While it is regrettably true that for the lesser quality European wines commercialism is on the upswing—what with roadside tasting and sales rooms and the growing practice in some areas of not vintaging wine from poor years—fine wine and wine making have been cloaked in a tradition that has long made reputation as important as sales. After all, if your own name is on the label you might take a more personal concern than if you were just working for a corporation. How much longer this tradition will continue remains to be seen, for today reputation often takes a back seat to the almighty dollar. The 1968 Lafite-Rothschild, for example, is a disgrace to what is one of the most prestigious names in the world of wine.

While in most European countries the enjoyment of the finer wines is restricted to the well-to-do, in the United States, at least since the end of the Second World War, wine making has been directed at the average consumer, not the connoisseur. This different emphasis should result in a greater range of wines and prices available to the consumer—a greater democratization, if you will, of wine drinking.

This chapter has been included to please those who insist on comparing European and California wines at every turn, as well as to provide a very brief introduction to Europe for those newly interested in wine. But while you may rightfully make comparisons of those generic California wines that still use European regional labels, we can see no reason for expecting California varietals to be simply imitations of European wines made from the same grapes. California and European wines should complement one another, not compete as though there were only one prize. California wines have their own character and distinctiveness, and that California has not become a copy of Europe should certainly be no criticism.

The Art of Tasting
and Appreciating Wine

HOW

Drinking a glass of wine can be anything from a blasé experience to an esthetic adventure reminiscent of the fine arts. The amateur may look on in awe or disbelief at the way an expert tastes wine and listen in amazement to the long flow of gustatory adjectives used to describe a glass of wine. Many questions arise: Does a "connoisseur" really know what he's talking about? How can one say so much about a bottle of wine? This chapter will answer these questions and in so doing will try to dispel some of the unnecessary mystery and suspicion that still surround the art of wine drinking.

Good wine is meant to be savored, not guzzled. This is one of the characteristics that set it apart from many other alcoholic beverages. As with all other arts, a certain technique has developed for its evaluation, and a simple tasting procedure will help you to appreciate wine and also to learn to distinguish one wine from another.

First, hold the glass to the light and note the wine's appearance and color. Experience and our remarks under "The Characteristics of California Wines" will tell you what color is appropriate for each variety of wine. Notice also if the wine is clear. Before the advent of modern technology in wine making, some of the primitive filtration techniques did not remove all the suspended particles, often leaving a cloudy, not very esthetically pleasing wine. All of the California wines available on the market today (with the exception of a few older reds) should be brilliantly clear.

The second step is to gently swirl the wine in the glass. This will help bring out the various odors that may be present. Sniff the wine to detect the aroma(s) of the grape(s) from which the wine was made and to see if there is any bouquet, which usually develops during aging. Once again, a backlog of experience is a great aid in this part of the evaluation. Experience, of course, is not necessary to determine whether you like the aroma of a particular wine, and should the fragrance turn out to be a pleasant one, this simple procedure will greatly enhance your enjoyment of the wine. Swirling and sniffing the wine will also aid in the discovery of any off-odors that may be present. Wine should have no sharp, vinegary type of aroma. Neither should there be any hint of hotness or harshness in the aroma, for this is a sign of undesirable chemical constituents (aldehydes).

The most common off-odors are sulfur dioxide, earthy, woody, green, raisiny (overripe grapes), and yeasty. And even these may not be undesirable in some wines: the *goût de terroir* of a dry Semillon or Sauvignon Blanc may be described as earthy; Champagnes often have a somewhat yeasty character; and a certain amount of woodiness is not always undesirable in red wines.

Sulfur dioxide gas is often used in California to kill undesirable bacteria during fermentation, but excessive use may result in the always objectionable lingering odor of sulfur. This is usually more noticeable in white wines than in reds and also produces a very pale, bleached color (the latter is often present even when no odor or taste is discernible). Greenness comes from unripe grapes and is evidenced by a very sharp, overly acid sensation. The opposite result, a kind of thick, raisiny sweetness, is reached when overripe grapes are used.

This seems to occur with some California Zinfandels in particular.

The third step is the tasting of the wine. If it seems that we have lingered too long over elaborate preliminaries before coming to this point, try to keep your chin up. Actually, you can learn a great deal about a wine before you even taste it. But it's true that the real proof lies in the drinking. Take a sip, and roll it over your tongue so that all the areas of taste will be reached. As you can see from the accompanying dia-

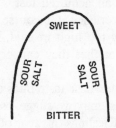

gram, each of the four basic tastes is sensed on a particular area of the tongue. Notice whether the wine is sweet or dry and whether the acid content is high or low. Pay attention to the feel of the wine on the tongue: light or heavy? If the wine is red, pay particular attention to the amount of astringency (tannin) present. Many people collect a little wine on the front of the tongue and suck air in over it. The warm air helps trap and bring out aromas that otherwise might have been missed. The most effective method is to carry out the above procedure with several sips of wine, concentrating on each sip on one particular feature. Finally, swallow some wine and note the aftertaste that lingers in the mouth and throat. The aftertaste should always be pleasant, never sharp (acidic), hot, or bitter. If you are in the process of evaluating several wines, a little bread will not only clear your taste buds but will also help absorb all that wine in your stomach (if you're in the midst of a long stay in the Napa Valley!).

White wines are generally light-bodied compared to the reds

and do not have the astringent tannin found in red wine. For these reasons, beginning wine drinkers often learn to enjoy and appreciate white wines before they are ready to move on to the red varieties. Many novice wine drinkers also prefer a sweet to a dry wine, for the sweetness masks the acidity, which is more noticeable in a dry wine. But a certain degree of acidity is essential for a correctly balanced wine; wines of low acid content often seem thin and watery and cannot stand up well with food. While this is to some extent a matter of personal preference, it is also an acquired taste, which will be appreciated with more experience. Of course, there are still many wines that are simply too high in acid, and these should not be excused by a claim that they can be appreciated only by a connoisseur.

But for those of you whose taste buds are not yet acclimated to the more tart wines, may we suggest skipping over the very dry Chardonnays or Rieslings in favor of one of the semisweet table wines. These wines are less complex, and their sugar content tends to smooth over those characteristics that the beginner might find objectionable. One such variety that has enjoyed particular favor with California vintners is the Chenin Blanc, which is generally a mellow, fruity wine.

It is generally agreed that of all the red *Vitis vinifera* (European) grapes planted in California, the one with the most character and interest is the Cabernet Sauvignon. While this medium-red, hard, full-bodied, and tannic wine is a favorite with connoisseurs, we don't advise those of you who are not yet very familiar with many wines to go out and start at the top with a $5 or $6 bottle of Cabernet Sauvignon. Those who do so may stand the chance of being disappointed with this very dry, astringent wine, and may well decide that if this is the best, then the rest of the California wines are probably not worth trying.

Wine, like most of the more interesting foods in the world, is an acquired taste, and Cabernet Sauvignon, being one of the most complex and distinctive grapes, produces a wine that can be appreciated only against a background of experience with less forceful wines. In California two of the better introductory red wines are the Zinfandel and the Gamay, which are both usually light, smooth wines, which, while not as complex as the Cabernet Sauvignon, can be very pleasant drinking experiences.

WHAT, WHEN, AND WHERE

Let us now assume the successful completion of these first steps and deal with the person who enjoys a wide variety of wines, including those that are complex and highly distinctive. It is now that the large selection of California wine types, each with its own characteristics, can be fully appreciated.

Wine and food are the best of companions; when properly chosen, each is capable of bringing out the finest qualities of the other. While wine is a bridge across which one flavor can enhance another, its versatility also allows it, when served alone, to complement a quiet evening or moments of friendly conversation. The intricate mélange of sensations that emanates from a glass of wine produces a warm glow that quickly enraptures all those who enter its world.

Just as food is available in many styles and flavors, wine, too, is available in many varieties, each with quite different characteristics. There are numerous rules, written and unwritten, that govern the selection of wine for a particular food. The simplest of these is, of course, white wine with white meat, red wine with red meat, and rosé with anything. While the "rules" do exist, we feel that you should be most concerned with fitting your own tastes. A person is more apt to enjoy a wine if he chooses what he likes and not what tradition dictates. It is not uncommon to meet a snooty waiter in a fashionable restaurant who will delight in looking aghast at your "unusual" wine selection. But if you fully understand the criteria on which you have based your judgment, you will be better able to confront the situation and avoid unnecessary intimidation or embarrassment. Although the idea is almost universally repugnant to "connoisseurs," we know one fairly experienced wine drinker who will drink nothing but a medium-sweet Chenin Blanc with steak!

There are several reasons, however, why it is a good idea to understand the "established" criteria for selecting wine. Most of these traditions are based on centuries of experimentation and therefore deserve your consideration. You may also at times entertain people who do live by the book and would like to have your selection geared to please them.

To our minds the first and foremost rule is that the wine which precedes or accompanies a meal should be as dry as your taste preferences allow. A dry wine tends to perk up your appetite and bring out the flavors of food. A wine with notice-able sweetness has the opposite effect on appetite and often does not harmonize as well with the main course. A sweet wine is really at home with dessert; it is here, with cakes or sweet fruit, that its lush flavor can best be appreciated. People who definitely prefer a sweet wine to a dry one may compromise by selecting a medium-sweet wine to accompany their meals, at least until they, too, may be converted to the drier varietals.

One motive for serving white wine with white meat and red wine with dark meat is the esthetic value of the complementary colors. Another, more important, reason is that fish and fowl tend to be light meals, consistent with the choice of the more light-bodied white wines, while steaks and roasts are more ro-bust meals and deserve the company of a rich, full-bodied red wine.

Fish, however, is more sharp than heavy. A more acidic wine helps to soften any excessive "fishiness" that may be present in the meal, and for this reason a dry, crisp white wine is usually the best selection.

The French often serve cheese for dessert, and many believe that the best red wine of the evening (if you're doing it up big and having several different wines with your meal) should be reserved for the end and served with the cheese. They feel that cheese brings out the best in a red wine and that a fine wine brings out the best in the cheese. Try this sometime and see if you agree. Here in America this rule is often forgotten or ignored, and white wines are often served with the lighter, mellower cheeses.

Veal, lamb, and ham are what may be considered in-between dishes, and here personal preference is foremost. Our own tastes run along the line of a light red wine, like a Gamay, with veal and lamb and perhaps a very dry rosé with ham. Veal and lamb are often prepared with fancy wine sauces, and in this case a bottle of the same table wine used in the cooking is a logical choice to accompany the meal.

Much is written about the selection of a "spaghetti wine" to go along with such highly seasoned Italian dishes as lasagne or spaghetti. When such a wine is recommended it is more often than not because of its Italian name (Chianti, Grignolino, Barbera) than because of any more rational criteria. Chances are that any low-priced, ordinary red wine will suffice with these meals, for while their highly distinctive seasonings add much to their flavor, they can only blunt the finesse and character of a fine Cabernet Sauvignon, Pinot Noir, or other premium wine.

Choosing the right wine in a restaurant is a task expected to be performed with an air of knowledge, dignity, and aplomb. In few other areas has the American bon vivant succeeded so well in failing. All too often he will point to or mispronounce a name on the wine list and then glance up to see whether the wine steward smiles or grimaces. In better restaurants, of course, you may simply rely on the advice of the wine steward, but trusting your wine selection to an ordinary waiter will usually buy only a name, not necessarily a good or appropriate wine.

The only way to succeed and to look stylish at the same time is to expend a little effort. Read books or articles about wine and become familiar with names and how to pronounce them. Experiment at home with various wines. Remember the varietals that usually appeal to your taste, and do not forget those that have disappointed you. When selecting a wine in a restaurant, try to match the varietal with the entree. Decide whether a red, white, or rosé would best complement the food. If in doubt, or if two people are ordering very different dishes, choosing a rosé is an easy out, though two half bottles are often a better idea. As one becomes more familiar with food and wine, the task of matching one to the other becomes easier.

In most restaurants the waiter will pour a sample of the wine for the person who ordered it before he fills every glass. This should be sniffed and sipped to be sure that it smells and tastes natural and that there are no gross technical defects. Simply not liking a wine is not sufficient reason to refuse it, but on the other hand one should not feel bound to accept a wine that reeks of sulfur.

The more elegant restaurants will often produce the cork for inspection. In this case the proper thing to do is to smell it to be sure it smells like a wine-soaked cork and to look at the bottom of the cork to see that it is moist. The latter is offered as proof that the bottle has been correctly stored on its side. We have a friend who also enjoys biting the cork and watching the waiter's eyebrows rise. While commendable in its own right, it is doubtful that such a practice will greatly enhance your enjoyment of the wine.

One should order wine at the same time as the meal so that the restaurant will have enough time to chill a white or a rosé or to decant an old red that may have thrown some sediment. A red wine should be opened at the table at least a half an hour or so before it will be drunk. (You'll have to ask the waiter to do this; unfortunately, letting a wine "breathe" is not common practice in most restaurants.) Virtually all sound red wines have enough vitality to remain open without harm for some time before drinking, and this allows the long-entombed aroma and bouquet to begin to blossom more fully. A few older reds may be so delicate as to require immediate drinking, but these are fairly rare and when ordering such a wine (also usually quite expensive) the advice of the wine steward should be followed.

Buying a bottle of wine from the local liquor or grocery store for dinner should be a simple task, but since the rows and rows of well-stocked shelves may well offer more confusion than comfort, we would like to present a few guidelines.

First, of course, you must decide what general type of wine— red, white, or rosé—is in order. This will depend on what's cooking that evening and on your personal taste.

If you settle on a white or rosé, you must next tackle the subject of dry or sweet. When shopping only for yourself, personal preference is foremost. When shopping to please others, remember that people unaccustomed to drinking wine usually prefer something with a little sweetness, while experienced wine buffs will cringe at anything but a very dry wine with their meal. In no case, however, should you serve a sweet dessert-type wine (various California "château" wines or a French Sauternes, for example) with dinner; while perhaps not quite analogous to a May-December marriage, both wine and food will suffer from such an incompatible union. While it's not always easy to tell the sweetness of a wine from the outside, you may find some indication on the front or back label, or, failing that, you can turn to the descriptions of individual wines in Part Two of this book. When buying a varietal wine, the name of the grape may also give you a clue; wines made from the Chenin Blanc, for instance, are almost always slightly sweet, while Chardonnays and California Rieslings are generally drier wines.

Red table wines should never have any noticeable sweetness, so perhaps a glance at our comments on the general characteristics of California wine types for something that sounds interesting would be the best guide for the novice wine buyer on a trek through his local liquor store. One warning, however: a Cabernet Sauvignon, though probably California's most celebrated wine, is, at its best, quite forceful and often tannic and is not usually appreciated by the beginner or those who prefer a delicate wine. Save it for a châteaubriand and someone you know will enjoy it.

California wines carry either the name of a European district —Chablis, Sauterne, Rhine, Moselle, Burgundy, Claret—or that of a grape variety. The latter are usually more expensive and, with a few exceptions, better wines. While it is admittedly more difficult to remember grape names, especially since most are of French or German origin, it is generally worth the effort.

A great deal of the shelf space of most liquor stores is devoted to bottles or jugs of wine with screw-top caps. Another sizable area is reserved for fifth-size bottles with corks. We recommend that you choose from the former when you plan on adding 7-Up to the wine for a summer cooler or when you plan on serving it at a backyard barbecue where you're sure your guests will consume gallons. California's finest wines are always sealed with a cork, and it is from among these that you will probably select most of your dinner wines.

Like anything else in life, selecting wine becomes easier as one becomes more experienced. By all means try different varieties of wine in your own home. If you like, wine-tasting parties where different types of wine can be compared are often very enjoyable as well as educational. Allow one third to one half bottle of wine (total, not of each variety!) per person, and vary the wines to be tasted according to the expertise of your guests. Half bottles are ideal and economical for this purpose. And, perhaps most important of all, jot down the name and vintage of a wine that you like or despise, for this will make it easier to select a wine for that next important meal.

Now that you've brought a bottle home, a few words on serving wine are appropriate. White wines are usually served chilled. A good temperature is 50 to 55 degrees, low enough to be refreshing but not so cold as to suppress the aroma. Medium-dry and sweet wines usually benefit from a little extra chilling. Red wine is traditionally served at cellar temperature, about 10 to 15 degrees warmer than the whites. This sometimes presents a problem in the summer, when room temperature often rises into the eighties. When this happens you should keep the wine in as cool a storage place as possible and then bring it out shortly before the meal. Some people prefer chilling their red wines, but we feel that this can only dampen the flavor.

When sediment appears in an ancient bottle of red wine it does not detract from the quality of the wine, but for esthetic reasons a clear wine is preferable. Stand such a bottle upright for about twenty-four hours prior to serving; this allows the sediment time to settle to the bottom. Wines with very heavy sediment may require several days of settling. The bottle may then be opened and the clear wine carefully poured into a table decanter. It is a good practice to decant the wine with a bright light or candle behind the neck of the bottle, so that you can stop pouring whenever the first traces of sediment appear. If some sediment does make its way into the glass the wine may taste somewhat dusty.

Finally, a couple of remarks on equipment. While wine can be drunk in anything from Baccarat crystal to paper cups to *botas,* it is usually at its best when served as elegantly—but simply—as possible. We favor the traditional tulip-shaped stemmed wineglass, whose slight inward slope at the top concentrates the aroma and whose bowl is large enough to allow swirling and sniffing the wine. And use a glass that is as clear as possible —never tinted or etched! While the latter may look beautiful on the shelf, it makes it difficult to evaluate or truly appreciate a good wine.

Corkscrews are available in every conceivable shape, size, and design, and by no means are all of them capable of easily and cleanly extracting a stubborn cork. Most premium corks are from $1\frac{3}{4}$ to 2 inches long, and you must have a corkscrew that will go all the way through. Also, be sure that the point is sharp and that the handle is smooth enough to grasp comfortably (those corkscrews that dangle from can openers should have been abolished years ago!). As long as the screw is long enough to penetrate completely through the cork, all of the various types of corkscrews—traditional, single-levered, double-winged, etc.—are equally adept at removing the last barrier between you and Bacchus' nectar.

WHY

Some people do not understand how others can treat wine with such respect or appreciation. To them it is just another beverage, another alcoholic drink. What is it that makes wine so special?

Wine can be likened to a living being. It thrives on proper care and turns against those who mistreat it. From the moment that the first tender buds appear on the grapevine in early spring until harvest time in the fall, the development of the fruit is followed with great anticipation and concern by devotees of the finished product. Spirits rise and fall with each change in the weather. Though the viticulturist is essentially at the mercy of Mother Nature, he does as much as he can to ensure the proper maturation of the fruit of his labor. When to harvest is the last critical decision before the situation is taken out of the hands of nature and turned over to man and science. At harvest time the full potential of the vintage lies instilled within the grape. From this point until it is drunk the wine will greatly benefit from proper care and may be irreparably harmed by incorrect handling.

Though science has invaded and captured much of the process of wine making, parts of it today remain very much of an art dependent on the skill of the wine master. It is he who decides when to transfer the wine from wooden casks to glass bottles. Blending is perhaps the greatest test of the wine master's skill, for the final product must be carefully balanced so as to correctly harmonize the best features of each of the components.

Almost all premium wine benefits from aging in the bottle. A very young wine that is rough and harsh will often improve with time, reach a plateau, and then slowly decline. White wines generally mature quickly, reaching their peak a year or two after they are bottled. While great white wines will last for five or more years in the bottle, the great majority of whites can (and should) be drunk relatively young without any loss of quality.

Red wines, particularly those that are full-bodied and high in tannin, age much more slowly than whites. Cabernet Sauvignon and Pinot Noir are two California reds that, when they are at their best, benefit from many years of bottle aging. When they are young these wines tend to be hard and astringent. The aging process smooths them out, softens the wine, and takes away its bite. A good Zinfandel will also benefit from aging, while Gamay is often an exception among red wines and may be drunk when it is still quite young.

It is almost impossible to overemphasize the fact that a good red wine will improve measurably with bottle aging. Unfortunately, economic factors force most California wineries to release most of their supply of these better wines within two or three years after they are fermented. These wines usually require several more years of bottle aging (and could often have used a few more months in the cask) before they will reach their peak, and the very finest will remain palatable for many years after that. The wine consumer can do himself a great service each year by putting some of these young wines away in a cool, dark place. After a few years he will be able to serve a much finer wine worth many times its original price. Being able to observe your wines, through periodic tastings, slowly mature and attain their highest quality can be both enjoyable and informative, and the feeling that one has played some part in a wine's coming of age can be very gratifying.

When storing wine, either in a specially prepared cellar or in a makeshift corner of the garage, it is important to observe several rules. Light, heat, and wide variations in temperature are harmful to wine. Try to select a storage area that is dark, has a temperature that remains fairly constant, and is as close to the optimum of 55 to 60 degrees as possible. Always store bottles of wine on their sides so that the cork remains moist; otherwise it will dry out, shrink, and allow air into the bottle. The result may be an expensive bottle of wine vinegar.

Almost all supermarkets and many liquor stores violate one or more of these rules. Bottles of wine are left standing upright and are often exposed to direct sunlight. One takes a chance when buying an improperly treated bottle of wine, especially from those stores that have a fairly slow turnover. Try to shop where wine is properly cared for; perhaps if enough people insist on this, other stores will change their habits.

It is against this background of nature, science, art, and time that one can truly realize all that goes into producing a good wine. When this knowledge is combined with the enjoyment of drinking, it is not difficult to enter and appreciate the art of a fine wine.

PART TWO

The Wineries and Their Wines

The following pages contain detailed descriptions of hundreds of wines produced by the major California premium wineries and by some smaller wineries whose reputation has placed them in competition with the better-known labels.

Writing a book that hopes to present objective descriptions of anything is admittedly a difficult undertaking, particularly when it involves such a highly personal sensation as taste. But while any method of tasting or sensory evaluation of a wine, no matter how carefully controlled, must necessarily remain somewhat subjective, it is possible to inject a measure of consistency, if not total objectivity, into an evaluation that extends over an appreciable period of time. This we believe we have accomplished.

Most of the wines discussed were tasted at least twice; many were evaluated three or four times at intervals of several weeks or months. Since there were two tasters, this provided a minimum of four samples for the great majority of wines evaluated. And, while our tastings were of course more intensive during the months in which we were actively engaged in preparing this manuscript, we have been able to draw on tasting experiences that include a comprehensive view of much of the past decade. Thus, total tastings ran into the thousands, giving us a wide range of samples for comparison purposes.

On occasion we did invite other persons, from both within and outside the wine trade, to participate in our tastings. These sessions provided us opportunities to see how particular wines impressed different people, and prompted us to note a few occasions where our opinions differed markedly from others. None of our descriptions, however, are based on group rankings, for we feel such a procedure often blurs meaningful distinctions among wines. The evaluations offered here remain solely our responsibility.

The details of a good method of wine tasting are explained in Part One. Our tastings usually began, where possible, at the winery itself and were supplemented by further tastings of bottles purchased in retail stores as well as some later sent by the wineries. While our tasting environment varied from the underground caves of Buena Vista to the well-lighted and modern tasting room of Paul Masson, we don't feel that such variations in interior décor affected our taste buds. It is also generally accepted that one's impressions vary with the time of day; to dispel whatever prejudice might result, we always made our second evaluations at a different time from the first.

Even though it is very possible that you may enjoy a wine that we found uninteresting, part of each description—body, acidity, sugar content, etc.—is given in neutral terms that are uncolored by our own likes or dislikes. These do remain tasting descriptions rather than technical analyses, for whether a wine *tastes* tart or soft is more important than the absolute acidity level. We are not attempting to guide you toward our selection of California wines, but rather to present you with enough information so that you can make your own selections. Along the way we will warn you against the disappointments that may be lurking under several well-known labels and, where appropriate, will recommend some of the lesser-known wineries that might otherwise be passed over by a consumer familiar only with the better-advertised names.

The wines are generally evaluated as to color, aroma, bouquet (if present), dryness, body, acidity, tannin (for the reds), aftertaste, and overall character. In making use of the many descriptions, you might keep the following in mind.

Color and aroma should be esthetically pleasing, and the aroma of a varietal wine should be characteristic of the grape variety used to produce the wine. Any off-odor present (sulfur, volatile acid, etc.) is a negative factor.

With a few exceptions, the wines are rated as dry, slightly sweet, medium sweet, or sweet; your preference of one type over another is entirely a matter of personal taste.

Whether or not the sugar, acid, body, and tannin of a wine are well balanced is one of the most important factors to consider when evaluating the overall impression left by a wine. For example, a sweet wine should have adequate body and acid to back up its sugar content; otherwise, the wine will taste sugary rather than rich and fruity. There should be enough acidity in a dry white wine to give it a clean, crisp taste. Too little acid means a dull wine, and too much produces a sharp, unpleasant taste. Mention is made of any wine that we feel is particularly distinguished by either its balance or the lack thereof.

A wine of good character is one that is pleasing to both nose and palate and also possesses enough individuality to distinguish it from other, similar, wines. It should be well balanced, with the distinctive aroma and flavor of the grape variety from which it is made. Hopefully, it is a wine that will evoke pleasant memories long after it has been drunk.

All of the wines evaluated in the following section have been placed in one of five categories: excellent (****), very good (***), good (**), average (*), or below average (BA). A comparative list of these categories arranged by wine type may be found at the end of Part Two. We have not attempted to identify the "best" wine within a given category, since we do not feel that a large group of wines can possibly be reduced to a numerical order of precedence. A close look at most such lists often reveals that a wine's ranking reflects mathematical averages carried out to fractions of a point rather than any noticeable difference in quality.

Two main criteria used in the rankings are how pleasant the wine is to drink and how it compares with other California wines sporting a similar label. A wine's potential character is also considered in judging young red wines, like Cabernet Sauvignon, which are normally expected to age for some time before reaching their peak. Price is also taken into account, and we have probably laid more emphasis on this factor in the second edition than in the first. After all, a $5 wine should be better than just drinkable.

Though the temptation may be to turn immediately to the end to see which wines received the highest rankings, these might not, in fact, be the ones that you will enjoy most. To be more certain that you will enjoy a wine, check its complete description as well as its comparative ranking. For, even though we may consider it excellent for its type, you may not care for that kind of wine at all.

Finally, many people have asked us which is the best winery in California. The answer is both simple and confusing at the same time: there isn't one. While some wineries do, on the average, produce better wines than others, there is no one winery that is consistently outstanding and that deserves to be unreservedly called "the best." Each winery has its own specialities, its own "best" wine, but none makes either all excellent or all bad wines. Besides, whatever winery makes your favorite wine is the "best" winery in your eyes. So get out there and start tasting!

NAPA

Perhaps the most famous of California's wine-growing regions, the Napa Valley is an area of beauty and inspiration for the wine lover. Though the hordes of weekend and summer tourists are rapidly approaching an unmanageable number, in a quiet moment the valley retains an almost European air. The large acreage of flat vineyards is reminiscent of the country around Bordeaux, while on a fall day the brightly colored vines surrounded by cloud-covered hills could pass as a scene from Alsace.

The vineyard region of Napa lies about an hour and a half's drive north and slightly to the east of San Francisco. The valley itself extends for about thirty-five miles in a gentle northwesterly crescent from the shores of San Pablo Bay to the hills above Calistoga, culminating in the four-thousand-foot-high Mount St. Helena. Several viticultural and climatic areas are included, and the highest concentration of vineyards lies on the valley floor astride state Highway 29.

On the drive north from San Francisco vines first become noticeable around the town of Oakville, where the new Robert Mondavi Winery and Oakville Vineyards are located. Two miles up the road, the village of Rutherford is little more than a dot on the map, but is famous as the home of Inglenook and Beaulieu. The charming town of St. Helena is a few miles farther north and is surrounded by many well-known names, including Louis Martini, Charles Krug, Beringer, and Christian Brothers. Except for a few local variations, this central area falls into region II on the viticultural temperature scale, similar to Bordeaux.

Beyond St. Helena the valley narrows and enters perhaps its most picturesque stretch. New wineries, such as Freemark Abbey and the white monolith of Sterling, as well as the longer-established Kornell Champagne Cellars, receive visitors here. The area remains relatively cool and well-suited for grapes, although as the northern end of the valley is approached the climate becomes warmer and the land more heavily planted in older, heavy-bearing vines rather than the delicate premium varietals. Of course, with the tremendous interest in wine today many of the older vines are being replaced with more valuable premium varietals, although whether these vines will prosper in the warmer climate is questionable.

The valley is surrounded on both sides by mountains which are generally cooler than the valley floor. To the west the Mayacamas range separates Napa from Sonoma, and contains many beautiful vineyards planted to Chardonnay, White Riesling, and Gewürztraminer, as well as some selected areas where Cabernet Sauvignon does well. The white wines from these hills reflect the cooler temperatures and are often lighter and fruitier than those from the valley below.

Vineyards extend right to the foot of the hills on the east side of the valley, but then the rather precipitous rise leaves only a few accessible areas. Among the few areas which have been planted are Howell Mountain and Pritchard Hill, where the new Chappellet Vineyards is located.

One of the newest and potentially most exciting areas in Napa lies at the foot of the valley in what is called the Carneros region. Here the winds from nearby San Pablo Bay have a cooling influence, and the climate seems well-suited to such early-ripening grape varieties as White Riesling, Chardonnay, and Pinot Noir, varieties that often lose much of their distinction when planted in the warmer areas farther north.

Beaulieu Vineyard

Founded by Georges de Latour in 1900, Beaulieu has gained wide recognition over the decades as one of the best premium wineries in California. Much of Beaulieu's success is due to André Tchelistcheff, wine maker from 1937 to 1973 and one of the most respected enologists in California. He, in turn, has been very ably assisted by Dr. Richard Peterson, who holds a doctorate from the University of California and, with Mr. Tchelistcheff's retirement, has become head wine maker. In 1969 Beaulieu was purchased by Heublein, Inc., which also owns the United Vintners umbrella that includes Inglenook and Italian Swiss Colony. Thus far it seems that Beaulieu's tradition of quality and limited production is being maintained, and the only policy changes of note are the steadily rising prices of Beaulieu wines—although these days everyone else is becoming more expensive, too.

Beaulieu's excellent reputation is founded primarily on the Cabernet Sauvignon, and, indeed, the winery does an excellent job with California's best red wine grape. Unfortunately, Beaulieu's other wines do not rise to the heights of the Private Reserve Cabernet, and the familiar BV label cannot serve as a blanket recommendation of every wine. The Sauternes and Riesling varieties are particularly ordinary, although the Chardonnay has steadily improved in recent years. The reds are a bit more consistent, and they should retain the elegant, well-balanced style of the Cabernets. In a fine vintage all of Beaulieu's wines should certainly be good ones, but it would be nice to see a price structure that actually reflects the relative quality of the wines rather than simply the reputation of both winery and grape variety.

All BV wines are vintaged, a practice we would certainly welcome in other California wineries, and all have the nearly unique feature of an informative back label which clearly names each grape variety present in the wine. The winery is located in Rutherford and is open for both tours and tasting, the latter including a good representative sample of wines which are changed each month. The atmosphere is very pleasant, and the employees have been both friendly and fairly well informed.

A new visitor's center is due to open in 1973, with a restaurant, shops, and a post office in addition to the Beaulieu facilities.

Dry Sauternes   Light yellow with a light fruity-woody aroma, this is a slightly alcoholic wine of moderate body and light to moderate acidity. The *1971* has little Semillon character, though it's not unpleasant.   (*)

Haut Sauternes   Made from Semillon, Sauvignon Blanc, and Muscadelle de Bordelais, with the first predominating. While previous years have been well balanced and quite successful, the *1969* was no better than the average California sweet Sauternes-type wine. With light to moderate body and acid, it is a little less sweet than Château Beaulieu but has little flavor and a rather green nose and taste. For the money, still a better buy than the more expensive Château Beaulieu.   (*)

Château Beaulieu   A sweeter, less fruity wine than the Haut Sauternes, the Château Beaulieu generally retains some of the woody-earthy character of the Sauvignon Blanc grape in both aroma and taste. The *1970* is typical, with light to moderate body, moderate acid, and a simple sweet taste.   (*)

Chablis   A blend of Chenin Blanc, Melon de Bourgogne, Pinot Blanc, and Colombard grapes. This has consistently been an above-average generic, fresh and clean. The *1971* is typical, with light to moderate body, moderate acid, and a crisp aftertaste. A bit short on flavors, but still quite pleasant. (**)

Pinot Chardonnay Often disappointing in the mid-1960s, recent vintages have shown marked improvement. The *1969* (**) was a fairly full wine with good acid and some ripe fruit character in both aroma and taste, though it could use more complexity. The *1970* is probably the best Beaulieu Chardonnay to date. It is an elegant, spicy wine of moderate body and acid and a complex peppermint-alcoholic nose. Some overtones of oak are also present, and a couple of years of bottle age until the mid-1970s will round out the flavors. (****)

Riesling From Sylvaner grapes, this has generally been a good wine, though it varies from full-bodied to fairly light. The *1971* is dry and well balanced, with light to moderate body and acid and a fruity aroma. (**)

Johannisberg Riesling Not a particularly exciting wine, usually off-dry and a bit heavy and awkward. *1969* (**) had a very nice flowery aroma, moderate body and light to moderate acid, and some Riesling character, while *1970* was a bit harsh and alcoholic, with little fruit or flavor. (*)

Beaurosé Produced from Gamay, Grenache, and Cabernet Sauvignon grapes. Dry, with light to moderate body and acid, the *1970* (*) had a slightly bitter aftertaste. *1971* was fresher, fruitier, and more tart, with a fruity citrus aroma. (**)

Grenache Rosé Generally dry, tart, and pleasant, although the *1971* is less successful than previous vintages. The aroma is only vaguely characteristic of the flowery Grenache and the aftertaste is a bit rough. (*)

Burgundy Generally a well-made wine (from Gamay and Mondeuse grapes), of which *1969* is typical: light to moderate in body and tannin, moderate acidity, fairly fresh and fruity. Good flavors that generally do not need additional bottle age. (**)

Burgundy Special Bottling 1968 Medium-dark red with a rich coconut-mint-oak nose, this is certainly one of the best generics produced for some time in California (though its price is higher than that of the average varietal). With moderate body, tannin, and acid and deep fruit flavors, it is quite good now and should continue to improve through the mid-1970s. (***)

Gamay Beaujolais Very successful when first introduced in 1968, this wine has slipped a bit since then. Light red in color with a strawberry aroma, the *1970* had fairly light body, low tannin, and light to moderate acidity which left it in the very fruity Beaujolais style. *1971* was more tart and its fruitiness a bit more intense. (**)

Pinot Noir Often blessed with a rich, distinctive aroma, Beaulieu's Pinot Noirs tend to be a bit short on flavor. *1968* (***) was an exceptional year, for the wine was moderate in body, acid, and tannin and possessed the full, rich character that a Pinot Noir should have. Smooth and drinkable from the beginning, it should nevertheless improve through the mid-1970s. *1969* was a drop back to normalcy, and the wine was rather thin and ordinary, with a tart fruitiness rather than rich flavors. At this level of quality, it is clearly overpriced and overpraised, though it may improve with age. (*)

Cabernet Sauvignon Usually released when about two and a half years old, this is generally one of California's better Cabernets. Often characterized by a minty-berry nose and elegant in style rather than big and powerful, there is nevertheless noticeable variation in vintages. Among the more recent, *1965* and *1967* were good, light, fairly tart wines, while *1966* had more body and character, with well-balanced flavors that will develop very well for at least ten years. *1968* (***) is similar to the 1966, with a developing

Cabernet nose, light to moderate body, and moderate acid and tannin. Probably one of Beaulieu's best regular Cabernets, and superior to some Private Reserve bottlings. *1969* was less successful, though it is a good Cabernet of light to moderate body, tannin, and acid with a delightful minty nose that comes out after breathing for an hour or so. Less future than the 1968. (**)

Cabernet Sauvignon Private Reserve   Kept separate from the regular Cabernet and given an extra year of barrel aging and sixteen months of bottle aging before being released, the Private Reserves have long been recognized as representing the finest red wines in California. Again elegant rather than overpowering, the best will be near the top in any competition. There is less variation than with the regular Cabernets, though *1962, 1964* (when only Private Reserve was produced), *1966,* and *1968* were particularly outstanding in the past decade. *1967* (**) is one of the few disappointments; while not a bad wine, it is rather simple and not up to Private Reserve standards. Moderate in body and acid, with light to moderate tannin and a fruity, portlike aroma. The *1968* sold as a "future" for over $10 a bottle, and while the price must be attributed to auction fever, the wine itself certainly lives up to its reputation. Dark red with a characteristic minty aroma, it is a well-balanced wine of moderate body, tannin, and acid that will be one of California's best. Already pleasant, but try it again in 1980. (****)

Beringer Bros.

In 1970 the Nestlé Company, of Swiss chocolate fame, purchased the Beringer Bros. Winery from surviving members of the founding family. Established in 1876, Beringer is symbolic of much of the history of the California wine industry, and in earlier years it enjoyed an excellent reputation. By the 1960s the quality and marketing status of Beringer was slipping, and the new owners have a formidable task to rebuild the winery's fame.

Already some changes are evident, with more planned for the near future. The large, old cooperage is being replaced by new fifty-gallon American oak barrels, and new standards call for red wines to be aged in wood for two years and in the bottle for one year before they are released. Considerable money has been spent in remodeling and renovating the visitor reception facilities, including the beautiful old Rhine House and the thousand-foot limestone tunnels that have long made Beringer such a popular tourist attraction. The tours remain very enjoyable and include a tasting of several wines. The producing winery is in the Los Carneros region of Napa and is not open to visitors, although plans call for the construction of new facilities to be ready for the 1974 crush. These will be located in St. Helena, just across the highway from the Rhine House.

Current production is about 800,000 gallons, about half of which is in the less expensive line of Mountain wines. Fifteen hundred acres of vines are owned or leased by Beringer including 250 acres in Yountville and 400 acres in Sonoma's Knight's Valley.

It is still too early to reach any firm conclusions about the direction that Beringer wines will take under their new owners. Several of the whites are nice wines with good varietal character, though none could be called outstanding. The red wines currently on the market are on the tart side, but these still largely represent blends of wines made before the sale.

Certainly Beringer's wine maker, Myron Nightingale, brings with him an excellent reputation that suggests that he and his assistant, Steve O'Donnell, should produce some fine wines. The infusion of new money and a fresh outlook at Beringer has promise of reviving a fine old name, and is indeed an opportunity for big business to prove that, in selected instances, it can benefit the California wine industry.

Dry Sauterne A wine of some Sauvignon Blanc-Semillon character, but the taste is a bit heavy and alcoholic. Dry, with light to moderate body and acid and a woody aroma. (*)

Fumé Blanc 1970 Produced from Sauvignon Blanc grapes and finished dry. Lots of good flavor and aroma characteristics of the grape. Medium-yellow color with medium body and light to medium acidity. Some oakiness in the taste with just a touch of harshness in the aftertaste. (**)

Chablis Usually in the high average or low good category, this has been a fairly clean, fresh wine of some fruit but weak flavor. The most recent sample followed this pattern, with a vinous aroma and light to moderate body and acid. Grapes used include Chenin Blanc, Green Hungarian, Sylvaner, and occasionally Sauvignon Blanc. (**)

Pinot Chardonnay Usually pleasant, but without great depth or complexity. The *1971* has a light apple aroma, light to moderate body and acid, and a fairly smooth aftertaste. Could really use more Chardonnay character, though it is quite drinkable. (*)

Grey Riesling A dry wine with a little spice in the aroma and flavor. Light to medium body and acid, with a touch of harshness in the aftertaste. Otherwise pleasing. (**)

Johannisberg Riesling The *1971* is a typical, fairly dry Napa Riesling that is a bit alcoholic and slightly rough, but nevertheless well made. Light to moderate in body and acid, with a very nice flowery-anise aroma and good Johannisberg character. (**)

Chenin Blanc A slightly sweet, fairly crisp wine of light to moderate body and acid and an intriguing taffylike aroma. Not outstanding, but pleasant and possessing good varietal character. (**)

Vin Rosé From Gamay and Zinfandel grapes, this is a wine of medium-pink color and a fruity strawberry aroma. Light to medium in body and acid with a dry, though slightly heavy, finish. Fairly good fruit. (*)

Burgundy A tart, simple wine with light to moderate body and tannin and moderate acid. Well balanced, with a fruity aroma, and a bit better than average. (**)

Pinot Noir 1969 A very ordinary wine with thin flavors and little varietal character. Light to medium in body, acid, and tannin, with a light, fruity aroma. Disappointing for a Pinot Noir. (BA)

Cabernet Sauvignon 1969 Medium-red color with a fruity Cabernet aroma. Light to medium in body, with moderate tannin and acidity. A good wine, a bit tart when young, but one that should smooth out by the mid-1970s. (**)

Zinfandel Fruity in the aroma, but rather tart. Light to medium in body and tannin, with moderate to high acidity. Not unpleasant, though the acidity will be too high for some. (*)

Barenblut Originally a light wine from Grignolino and Pinot Noir, other red varieties are now supplementing this proprietary blend. A tart wine with light to moderate body and tannin and rather simple flavors. Not unpleasant. (*)

Grignolino Light to medium red in color with a slightly fruity woody aroma. Light in body and tannin with light to medium acidity, this is a smooth wine, though it could use more character. (*)

Chappellet Vineyard

Since its completion in time for the 1969 crush, the cathedral-like winery and setting of Chappellet have made it one of the most talked about new wineries in California. Owned by former Los Angeles corporate executive Donn Chappellet, the triangular winery rises out of 100 acres of young vines which include about 50 acres of Cabernet Sauvignon and lesser amounts of Chardonnay, Johannisberg Riesling, Chenin Blanc, and some Merlot. Located on Pritchard Hill in the eastern slopes above the Napa Valley, the vineyards gradually rise from the winery to the Chappellet home, which commands a magnificent view of the vineyards themselves, the Conn Dam reservoir, and the valley beyond.

Donn Chappellet and wine maker Philip Togni produce only four varietals, and quantities are currently so limited that they often disappear within weeks of being released. The first vintage for all but the Chardonnay was 1968, although the year does not appear on the label since the grapes were crushed at another winery. All whites are fermented dry, and the Chenin Blanc in particular has been a big, alcoholic wine that to our tastes could use more fruit and character. The Riesling is delicate, elegant, or thin, depending on the prejudices of your own palate. Both the Chardonnay and Cabernet Sauvignon are aged in French oak barrels, at this point it appears that these will be the leading wines of Chappellet. In future vintages, the Cabernet will probably contain up to 25 percent Merlot, while all other varietals are 100 percent.

Chappellet *looks* like a premium winery. Both vineyards and winery are immaculate, and the exposure and slope far above the valley floor should be conducive to extracting maximum quality from the grapes. The desire to make fine wines is evident, but those we have tasted do not yet reflect the full potential of Chappellet Vineyard. As the very young vines mature, the grapes should gain depth and complexity, and the future is certainly promising.

A mailing list is being established to keep consumers in touch with the latest developments at Chappellet, but the winery is closed to casual visitors. Those interested in meeting Mr. Chappellet and seeing the winery are requested to write in advance, and arrangements will be made when possible.

Chardonnay   *1970* was the first vintage for the Chardonnay, and since the vines were only four years old, it is at best difficult to judge how ensuing vintages will turn out. The wine itself is quite light, as might be expected, but it has good Chardonnay flavors and adequate fruit and acidity. Assuming that as the vines mature the resulting wine will become fuller and more complex, the Chardonnay may well become the best of Chappellet's whites.   (**)

Johannisberg Riesling   At its best (and if not overchilled), this wine may have a light flowery-melony aroma that is very pleasant. The *1971* is typical of past vintages in its light to moderate body and acidity and rather weak Riesling character. Dry, it needs more fruit and flavor to accompany its delicate style and high price.   (*)

Chenin Blanc   The early Chenin Blancs were dry, woody, and lacking in fruit, but the most recent vintages show some improvement. *1970* produced a fairly soft wine with some oak character and a fruity aroma, though one that still could use more fruit. *1971* was similar, dry, just a bit rough, though not unpleasant.   (*)

Pritchard Hill Chenin Blanc   This is a secondary label employed by Chappellet for wines not up to the standards of the premium label, though thus far only the Chenin Blanc has been bottled as Pritchard Hill. The current bottling also contains some Johannisberg Riesling and Chardonnay press wine. The *1971* has a pleasant melon nose, fairly light body, and light to moderate acid. Dry, it is tart with good flavors and a slightly bitter aftertaste.   (*)

Cabernet Sauvignon   Medium red with a very nice minty-spicy nose, the *1968* has light to moderate body and acid and moderate tannin. Young and undeveloped at present, it shows very good promise. Big in flavors, and future vintages should be even better. (***) The *1969* is the fullest of the first three vintages and will receive extra bottle age before release, while the *1970* that we tasted in the barrel should produce a well-balanced wine similar to 1968.

Charles Krug Winery

Charles Krug is one of the few large California wineries that have succeeded in maintaining consistently high quality despite a list of nearly twenty varieties of table wines. Only 40 percent of the winery's production is sold under the premium Charles Krug label; most of the rest is sold in jugs under the "CK" brand, and a small percentage is marketed under the inexpensive "Mondavi Vineyards" label.

Krug has not expanded its volume in the past few years, although it has more than doubled its former vineyard holdings until they now total approximately 1500 acres, nearly all in the Napa Valley. As these come into bearing, greater production may be expected. A centrifuge has been added to clean up young wines, and most Krug wines spend some time in small American oak barrels. The Chardonnay, Pinot Noir, and Vintage Selection Cabernet Sauvignon are aged in sixty-gallon French oak.

In several years of drinking and tasting we have never come across a "bad" Krug wine, one that we would place in the below-average category, and perhaps that is one of the best compliments we can offer. Several Krug wines are noteworthy, and certainly the Gewürztraminer, Moscato di Canelli, and Vintage Selection Cabernet Sauvignon generally rank near the top of their respective groups. The rest of the line is seldom exciting, but most are above average and few have been disappointing. Certainly the Charles Krug label is one of the most reliable among California's larger premium wineries. Although only the Chardonnay is vintaged among the whites, they have been relatively consistent over the past several years. Still, a vintage date would be helpful, if only to protect you from buying an older wine that has oxidized on a retailer's shelves.

The winery in St. Helena is open every day of the week for tours and tasting. The tour has been quite informative, and the Krug guides have always been friendly and knowledgeable. During much of the year the tasting room is very crowded and selection is limited to three wines, two of which are almost invariably the best-selling Chenin Blanc and Vin Rosé. Those of you who wish to combine touring with more extensive tasting should try to visit the winery on a winter weekday, when the less harried guides may be willing to open additional varieties.

Dry Sauternes   Dry with a fruity, slightly grassy aroma, this wine has some Semillon character but is a bit rough. Moderate body and acid.   (*)

Sauvignon Blanc   The best aspect of this wine is its characteristic spicy, almost rich, cigarlike aroma. Sweet, with light to moderate body and acid, it has good varietal character but tastes sugary rather than fresh.   (*)

Dry Semillon   Light yellow with a spicy, slightly characteristic aroma, this wine has some character but seems flat because of a lack of fruit acidity. Light to moderate body. Not as good as previous batches.   (*)

Chablis   Light to medium yellow in color with a vinous aroma. Light to medium in body and acid, dry, and a little fuller and fruitier than most California Chablis.   (**)

Chardonnay   Always a good wine, the *1969* and *1970* vintages have been even better. Similar in style, both have moderate body and acid and a touch of oak spiciness in aroma and taste. Excellent varietal character and a fine example of what a fairly large winery can do with the Chardonnay grape. Will keep for several years.   (***)

Grey Riesling   An off-dry, spicy wine that is very succesful for this grape. Light to moderate body and acid, very slightly *pétillant* when first opened, and with a pleasant flowery-spicy aroma. (**)

Sylvaner Riesling Light to medium yellow with a dull, slight pineapple aroma, this is a dry, pleasant, ordinary wine. Light to moderate body and acidity and fairly fruity. (*)

Johannisberg Riesling A typical slightly spicy California Riesling nose, moderate body and acidity, and a hint of sweetness leave this a fairly simple wine that is nonetheless quite pleasant. Very slight *pétillance*. (**)

Traminer Less distinctive than the Gewürz, the most recent bottle tasted was dry, slightly *pétillant,* and light to moderate in body and acid, with a slight spiciness in the taste. A high average. (*)

Gewürztraminer Medium yellow with a distinctive flowery-spicy aroma and sometimes a slight sparkle. Off-dry, this is a wine of good varietal character, moderate body, and a level of acidity that generally leaves it soft rather than crisp. Consistently pleasant. (**)

Chenin Blanc Continues to be a good wine that is sure to be a crowd pleaser. A well-made wine with a pleasing fruity aroma, light-yellow color, and a refreshing finish aided by slight effervescence. Medium sweet, with light to medium body and moderate acidity. (**)

White Pinot Fairly ordinary in the past, the current White Pinot is a dry wine of good body and acid. While probably not to everyone's taste, the melon-oak aroma is pleasant and strong varietal character is in evidence. (**)

Moscato di Canelli Light yellow in color with a delightful, flowery nose, this is a fresh, crisp wine with fairly light body and moderate acidity, definitely on the sweet side. Perked up by a slight sparkle, it is one of California's most successful sweet white table wines. (***)

Vin Rosé Orange-pink with a fruity-pineapple nose, this wine is generally produced with a slight sparkle. Light to moderate in body and acid with a touch of sweetness, it is simple but pleasing and retains good fruit.   (**)

Burgundy   Only an average wine in *1967* (*), the fine harvest in *1968* produced a surprising generic of light to moderate body, tannin, and acid and very good, somewhat rich flavors. Fruity and fairly smooth, it is undoubtedly the best Krug Burgundy in recent years.   (***)

Gamay Beaujolais   Formerly labeled *Gamay* and produced from the Napa Gamay grape, the name was changed in 1969, reflecting the decision that the Napa Gamay is the true Beaujolais grape. It has been a tart, fruity picnic-type wine of light to moderate body, and the *1969* follows this style. Simple, but quite pleasant.   (**)

Pinot Noir   Never a particularly interesting wine, the *1969* is typical: light to moderate in body, acid, and tannin; the flavors are fairly simple and not distinctive. Fruity aroma, but with little varietal character. While not unpleasant, it sells for the same price as the Cabernet Sauvignon and has never been as successful a wine.   (*)

Claret   Light to medium red with a fruity-woody aroma, this is an ordinary light-bodied generic. The *1968* was fairly tart, though not unpleasant.   (*)

Cabernet Sauvignon   In recent years the regular Cabernet has been a wine of good character and some potential, though it has never achieved great complexity or depth. The *1967* was a bit fuller than most, with moderate body, acid, and tannin, and a characteristic sagebrush nose. Though still a good wine, the *1968* was disappointing in that it did not reach the heights of several other Napa Valley Cabernets of that vintage. It has a fruity, slightly minty aroma, and light to moderate body, acid, and tannin. Well balanced and with potential for improvement through the mid-1970s, it will nevertheless not be memorable.   (**)

Cabernet Sauvignon Vintage Selection   Generally released when about five years old, the vintage-selection wines have consistently ranked among the best of California's Cabernets. In past years, the *1960* and *1964* were particularly outstanding, with deep flavors, often perfumed bouquet, and a life span of at least two decades. *1963* and *1965* were also very good, while the *1962* was unfortunately disappointing, as its character was rather thin and little was left to improve with age. There was no *1967* produced, since the wine did not come up to vintage-selection standards, but the *1966* is superb. Medium red with a warm, peppery-anise nose, it is a big wine of excellent character and good developing flavors that should improve through the late 1970s. Highly recommended. (****)

Zinfandel Krug's Zinfandels have often been quite nice, fruity wines when young, but they tend to lose this youthful charm rather quickly. The *1968* (*) was ordinary, thin, and tart by early 1972, though the younger *1969* still had a pleasant fruitiness later in the year. Nothing special, but well balanced with light to moderate body, acid, and tannin. (**)

Christian Brothers

Founded in 1882 to make wines for their own use, the Christian Brothers winery has now grown to an annual production of over 6 million gallons of wine and brandy. A multimilliondollar building program was launched in the fall of 1971, and a new winery and visitors' complex should be completed in South St. Helena by 1975. The Brothers also own 1500 acres of vineyards in the Napa Valley.

Considering the staggering number of table wines produced, the Christian Brothers do a better than average job of creating good and generally quite drinkable wines. Both whites and reds are soft and pleasant, though they often lack great distinction or complexity. The whites have been a bit more consistent than the reds, and it is often the "lesser" varieties that are more successful, perhaps because the lack of character in such wine as the Chardonnay and Johannisberg Riesling is disappointing. The Chenin Blanc has been consistently good, as have the rosés and several of the generics.

The reds are aged for two to five years in various sizes of oak and then given several months of bottle age before being released. The result is generally a fairly smooth, well-aged wine that does not need extended bottle age to become drinkable. While not as consistent as the whites, they are generally equal to or a bit above the level of other large California wineries. In addition, their prices have remained relatively reasonable.

The average Christian Brothers wine is dedicated to the average American consumer who prefers a soft, smooth wine (often with a touch of sweetness) that he does not have to worry about aging. While Christian Brothers wines are not the most distinctive in California, the goal of producing good, drinkable wines has certainly been achieved.

All Christian Brothers wines are nonvintaged blends, as they feel that greater consistency can be achieved in this manner. Variations do nonetheless exist, but at least a useful bottling code may be found on the back label which may help you to locate additional bottles of a wine that particularly pleased you. The code consists of five numbers, the first two representing the month, the third the year, and the last two the day the wine was bottled. Thus 06214 was bottled June 14, 1972.

Two Christian Brothers wineries are open to the public. The Mont La Salle Vineyards, midway between Napa and Sonoma, is a beautiful winery surrounded by acres of vines high in the Mayacamas Mountains, while the wine and Champagne cellars are housed in an impressive graystone building just north of St. Helena. At both locations informative tours and tasting are available, and virtually all the wines may be sampled. Your hosts are generally friendly and ready to answer questions.

Dry Sauterne Generally a dry wine with an aroma showing some Sauvignon Blanc character. Easy to drink, with light to medium body and acid, though light in flavor. (*)

Sweet Sauterne Slightly sweet with light to medium yellow color and a fruity aroma. A simple, not unpleasant wine. (*)

Haut Sauterne Medium sweet, with light to medium body and acid. Without the complexity of the finest sweet wines, though many will still enjoy this one. (*)

Sauvignon Blanc Light to medium yellow in color with a pleasant, fruity varietal aroma. Slightly sweet, with fairly good balance and flavors. A nice wine. (**)

Chablis Consistently a fairly good generic, the latest batch is dry with light to medium body and acidity. Fairly pleasant, though simple, with a slightly fruity aroma. (**)

Pinot Chardonnay Light yellow with a soft, fruity aroma. Pleasant, with light to moderate body and acid, but only slight Chardonnay character. (*)

Rhine Light yellow with a pleasant fruity nose, this is a good generic wine. Light to moderate in body and acid, dry, and slightly *pétillant*. (**)

Riesling Light to moderate in body and acid, this is a clean, dry wine of little distinction with a slightly flowery aroma. (*)

Johannisberg Riesling Light to medium yellow with a typical slightly fruity California Riesling nose. Light to moderate body, light acidity, dry. Soft and ordinary. (*)

Grey Riesling Light yellow with a slightly fruity aroma, this is a dry, fairly soft wine of light to moderate body and acid. Pleasant but rather neutral in flavor. (*)

Chenin Blanc A pleasant wine with a light spicy-flowery aroma, light body, and light to moderate acid. Off-dry, the flavors are delicate but fresh and fruity. Well balanced. (**)

Pineau de la Loire This is Christian Brothers' estate-bottled Chenin Blanc, and it is fuller and sweeter than the regular bottling. It is a soft, medium-sweet wine with a good fruity nose, though to some it may seem sugary. Some variations have been noted, but it has always been a well-made wine since its introduction in 1970.   (**)

Château La Salle   Made from Muscat de Frontignan grapes, this is a sweet wine that has varied from fresh and complex to heavy and sugary. Unfortunately the latest batch is in the sugary category, with light to moderate body and not quite enough acid. Distinctive perfumed apricot aroma, but a bit cloying unless you like very sweet wines.   (*)

Vin Rosé   Dry with a fruity Gamay aroma, light to moderate body and acid. A well-made wine with good fruit and smooth flavors.   (**)

Napa Rosé   A medium-sweet wine with slight *pétillance,* this is a clean wine with good fruit and well-balanced body and acid. Slightly fruity aroma and medium pink in color.   (**)

Burgundy   A blend of several grapes, including Gamay, Zinfandel, and Petite Sirah. Consistently a good wine of medium-red color, light to medium body and tannin, and moderate acidity.   (**)

Gamay Noir   A fairly full Gamay with a rich, woody-minty aroma. Light to moderate in body and acid with moderate tannin, this wine could use a couple of years of bottle age and should be a very pleasant wine of good character.   (***)

Pinot Noir   Though a bit inconsistent in the past, the current bottling is a well-made wine of light to moderate body, tannin, and acid. Fairly soft with good fruit and varietal character, it is not a great wine, but is certainly pleasant.   (**)

Pinot St. George   One of the two estate-bottled wines of Christian Brothers, this is an unusual varietal bottled to our knowledge only by Christian Brothers and Inglenook (as Red Pinot). It is a soft, easy-to-drink wine, but to our tastes it has little distinction or varietal character and does not merit its premium price tag. Light to moderate in body and tannin with moderate acid, it is a good red but nothing special.   (*)

Claret   Light to medium red with a vinous aroma, this is a well-balanced everyday red of light to moderate body, acid, and tannin. There has been some variation among different batches, but the wine is generally in the high average category.   (*)

Cabernet Sauvignon   Generally light to moderate in body, tannin, and acid, with recognizable Cabernet character. The most recent batch had a distinctive green olive aroma and rather simple flavors. Usually well aged and smooth, though a couple of extra years won't hurt.   (**)

Cabernet Sauvignon Brother Timothy Selection, Bottled, 1967   A nice wine that is fuller in body and shows more aging potential than the regular Christian Brothers Cabernet. Medium red in color and with a fruity, vanilla aroma, and moderate body, acidity, and tannin. A typical Napa Valley Cabernet which should age well until the mid-1970s.   (**)

Zinfandel   A pleasant, fruity wine of light to moderate body and tannin and moderate acidity. Fairly simple, but fresh and with good flavors. Usually needs no further bottle age.   (**)

Freemark Abbey Winery

While the planting program for Freemark Abbey's 100 acres of vineyards was begun in 1960, the winery did not offer its first wine until 1967. While the wines of the first couple of years had occasional problems, the most recent vintages have shown that Freemark is capable of producing very fine wines.

Indeed, under wine maker Jerry Luper, with Brad Webb as consultant, Freemark Abbey has already acquired a considerable reputation.

All wines except the Johannisberg Riesling are aged in sixty-gallon French Nevers oak barrels; the Johannisberg is put into large American oak tanks. The result is that Freemark Abbey wines have noticeable oak character which contrasts to the fresh, fruity style of many other California vintners. Even the Chardonnay often requires a year or two of bottle age before it reaches its peak, though its rich flavors can also be appreciated when it is young. A relatively small winery, Freemark Abbey has reached its maximum production of 50,000 gallons annually, although additional land is already owned should the winery decide to expand in the future.

As is shown in the individual descriptions that follow, Freemark Abbey should clearly be included in the higher echelons of California's premium wineries. Concentrating primarily on four varietals, the wines are distinctive and well made; they are also relatively expensive, but worth investigating.

The winery itself is located two miles north of St. Helena in a very picturesque stone building that houses a well-known candle factory and gourmet shop on its upper floor. Informal tours are offered to those interested in seeing the small but efficient operation, but no tasting is available. The people at Freemark are honest and friendly, and if you take the trouble to walk down and chat you should receive a warm reception.

Pinot Chardonnay Generally full-bodied with distinctive Chardonnay flavors, in 1969 and 1970 the wine also achieved just the right balance of oak and fruit, while *1967* and *1968* were less successful. The *1969* (****) has moderate body and acid, and the nose is a mélange of fruit (peaches?) and spicy oak character. Very well balanced, the flavors are spicy and distinctive, reflecting both varietal and oak character. *1970* is just a touch lighter, but very similar in character. The fresh apple aroma and flavors need a couple of years to round out and develop, but even now the wine is very fine. (****)

Johannisberg Riesling In the big, dry California Riesling style rather than the delicate German manner. Two lots were released in *1969: Lot 91* had a fresh, flowery aroma and dry finish, while *Lot 92* was fuller and had a touch of *Botrytis* flavor, though it was dry and a bit harsh in the mouth. *1970* was again a big, dry wine which to our tastes could use a bit more fruit and finesse. (**)

Pinot Noir An unexciting, nonvintaged Pinot Noir composed of 75 percent 1967 and 25 percent 1969 was the first of this variety offered. The *1968* (***) has a soft maraschino aroma and fairly light body, acid, and tannin, but the flavors are complex and show good varietal character. Well balanced and delicate, rather than powerful or rich. *1969* was less good, as the delicacy of the 1968 is not balanced by complex flavors. Light-bodied with light to moderate acid and tannin, it does retain good varietal character. (**)

Cabernet Sauvignon The *1968* has developed into a rich, well-balanced wine with good fruit, and moderate body, tannin, and acid. The deep, oatmeal aroma is very nice, and certainly this vintage has a longer future than the softer *1967*. The *1969* has a characteristic mint-sagebrush nose, and its slightly lighter body probably reflects the 12 percent Merlot that has been blended with it. Drinkable now, but potentially a better wine than the 1968, for the flavors are quite full and rich. Both vintages should reach their peak in the late 1970s. (***)

Petite Sirah Current plans call for this wine to be made every other year, in very limited quantities. The *1969* was a very full, black, peppery wine that certainly showed intense varietal character. With lots of tannin and a long road ahead of it, it won't appeal to everyone, though we enjoyed its strong flavors. The *1971* tasted in barrel echoed the deep, peppery style of the 1969, and it will probably be a wine to put away for your children's wedding or graduation.   (***)

Heitz Wine Cellars

Joe Heitz is one of the most respected vintners in the Napa Valley, and quite a number of new wine makers have put in some time as apprentices at the Heitz winery. He was wine maker for several years at one of the larger California wineries and is a former professor of viticulture and enology at Fresno State College. Mr. Heitz began making wine under his own label in the early 1960s, and soon purchased a handsome store winery just off the Silverado Trail several miles east of his St. Helena tasting room. These facilities were expanded in 1973 with the completion of a new building adjacent to the 1898 cellars. Production is currently about 25,000 gallons annually, though if all goes well this will be gradually increased to a maximum of 100,000 gallons.

Heitz has a full range of cooperage available, including redwood holding tanks, large oak casks, and over six hundred small oak barrels, mostly French. Among the whites, both the Pinot Blanc and the Chardonnay have always had some oak character, and of course the reds also spend time in the sixty-gallon barrels. While Mr. Heitz does have thirty-eight acres of vines planted primarily with Grignolino, most of the grapes for his wines are purchased from independent growers in Napa. These vineyards include some of the best in the state, and many Heitz labels carry the name of the specific vineyard from where the grapes came. This policy enables you to follow the product of a given vineyard from year to year and also gives deserved recognition to the growers themselves.

With the exception of the 1968 Pinot Noir and occasional

disappointments in the other varietals, Heitz wines are generally quite good and seem to have achieved greater consistency in the past few years. The whites are big and flavorful and exhibit good varietal character, and the Cabernets usually show good breed and excellent potential. Vintage variations do exist, although they are not always reflected by differences in price. The major varietals have always been expensive, and thus while many Heitz wines are very fine, they are often competing with wines that sell for a couple of dollars less.

The tasting room on Highway 29 at the south approach to St. Helena is open every day, and selected bottles of the less expensive varieties may be sampled.

Chablis   Consistently one of the best generic whites in California, this is a dry wine with a clean, flinty aftertaste and well-balanced flavors. Light to moderate in body with moderate acidity, it is a tart, refreshing wine often with a pleasant, slightly spicy aroma.   (***)

Pinot Blanc   Until 1971 this wine was produced from old vines on Fred McCrea's Stony Hill property, but then the vines were uprooted to be replanted in Chardonnay. These *McCrea Vineyard* bottlings have been big, full-flavored wines of excellent character that are often better than many Chardonnays. *1969* (***) followed this style very successfully, while the last vintage, *1970,* is a bit lighter and elegant rather than powerful. Not as complex as previous years.   (**)

Heitz Pinot Blanc grapes now come from the *Lyncrest Vineyard,* and the first wine so labeled is the *1970.* It does not have the depth of the McCrea wines, though it remains an above average wine of some character. Light to moderate in body and acid with a hint of oak in the aroma.   (**)

Pinot Chardonnay   Recent Heitz Chardonnays have been quite good, although whether they merit their high price tag is debatable. They are also designated by vineyard, "U.C.V." referring to Napa acreage owned and farmed by the University of California, and the "Z" wines coming from a vineyard owned by Zinfandel Associates. The *1969 Lot U.C.V.-91* was quite disappointing and not up to former vintages from this vineyard. Moderate in body and acid but a bit rough and rather weak in flavors. (*) *1969 Lot 2-92-Z* (***) was much more typical of a good Heitz Chardonnay: big and well balanced, it has a spicy-pepperminty nose and good fruit. Needs a couple of years of bottle age to smooth out the rough spots, but it has good depth. The *1970* wine from the same vineyard, *Lot Z-02*, is quite similar, though perhaps a bit softer and fruitier.   (***)

Alicia (*a nectar of Chardonnay*)   Produced only in 1967 and selling for $27 a bottle, this wine is unavailable now, but so much has been written about it that we felt compelled to give you our impressions as well. Produced from Chardonnay grapes that were attacked by the noble *Botrytis* mold, it is a sweet, fairly big wine that does not, however, capture the richness or intensity of the great sweet wines of Germany or Sauternes. It is a well-made wine with pleasant ripe fruit character in the taste and a fairly deep Chardonnay aroma, but it does not have outstanding complexity or interest. The price was outrageous no matter how rare the wine.

Johannisberg Riesling   The 1968 through 1971 Johannisbergs have been consistently fine wines, very similar in style. Both *1970* and *1971* produced dry, flavorful wines of strong character, though they were a bit lighter than previous years. Both have a spicy-fruity aroma, well-balanced acidity, and a very slight roughness in the aftertaste that will smooth out with a few months' bottle age.   (***)

Grignolino Rosé   An unusual varietal of deep-pink color and a pleasant floral aroma. Dry, the *1971* was quite tart, with fairly light body and moderate acid. The flavors are rather weak and disappointing.   (*)

Burgundy   Again a good generic, though not as consistent as the Chablis. The most recent blend tasted was well aged, with a fruity aroma and light to moderate body, tannin, and acid. Smooth and pleasant. Like the Barbera, this was purchased from another winery. (**)

Pinot Noir   This varietal is subject to rather wide variations, and it is difficult to generalize about it. The *1963* (***) was a big, rich wine and certainly one of the best in California, while a *nonvintaged* (**) blend released in 1970 was much lighter and tarter, though it did retain a very nice fruity aroma. The *1968* was disappointing, as it is rather weak in flavor and lacks potential despite the noticeable tannin present. Light to moderate in body and acid, it is a not unpleasant wine with a slightly musty-woody nose, but it is overpriced. (*)

Ruby Cabernet   A wine of medium-red color and a pleasant spicy-citrus-fruity aroma. With light to medium body and moderate acidity and tannin, this is a good wine with the potential of improving with several years of bottle age. (**)

Cabernet Sauvignon   Often an excellent wine, and in recent years quite full-bodied and tannic when young. The first wine, designated *Lot 62-65,* was a very fine, elegant wine with fairly subtle flavors, while the *1965* was a bit weaker in character except for a striking peppermint aroma. *1966* (****) is big, rich, and full, with deep fruity flavors and the potential to improve through the late 1970s, though right now the tannin is rather overpowering. The *1967 Martha's Vineyard* is similar and has the characteristic minty-green olive nose of Heitz Cabernets, but it is slightly less powerful and complex than the 1966. It has good fruit, and will probably mature by the mid-1970s. (***)

Barbera   Purchased from a large Sonoma winery and sold under the "Heitz Cellar, Sonoma" label, this nonvintaged wine generally has good varietal character and a rich, berrylike aroma. Fairly mature and smooth, it has moderate body and acid and light to moderate tannin. Well selected. (**)

Grignolino   From Heitz's own vineyards, this is a fairly light, tart, fruity wine with an intense peppery nose. Well made and interesting, with more character than the rosé. Non-vintaged.   (**)

Zinfandel Lot 63-69   A wine with some Zinfandel character and a slight woodiness in the nose. Light to moderate in body and tannin with moderate acidity, it has fair character, though the tartness may be a little strong for some palates.   (**)

Inglenook Vineyards

Covered with ivy and nestled against a sleepy Napa Valley hillside in Rutherford, from the outside it looks as if little has changed at the Inglenook winery since the Finnish sea captain Gustave Niebaum founded it in 1879. But the decade of the 1960s was a tumultuous one for Inglenook, with two changes of ownership and a severalfold increase in production. In 1964 Inglenook was sold to United Vintners, the large organization that produces Italian Swiss Colony, Petri, and several other California wines. Then in 1969 Heublein, Inc., purchased a majority interest in United Vintners and thus control of Inglenook.

Big business has clearly gained the upper hand at Inglenook, as production has now risen to 1,000,000 gallons annually. Sales of Inglenook wines were up 117 percent in 1972 over 1971, and the Heublein wine auctions have led to full-page magazine ads proclaiming that Inglenook is the most expensive wine in California. The wineries of Inglenook and Italian Swiss Colony are involved in a consolidation of operation (at Rutherford), although future expansion is indefinite at the time of this writing.

The clearest result of all this activity is that there are a lot more Inglenook wines than formerly. The *Vintage* line, which is produced at Rutherford from North Coast Counties grapes, accounts for about one half of Inglenook's total production. The less expensive *Navalle* line, which carries the Inglenook label although the wines are made at Asti in northern Sonoma County, also accounts for a very large share of the Inglenook sales record. (These are discussed in Part Five, on jug wines.)

The premium "estate-bottled" Inglenook wines are still produced from Napa Valley grapes, and many of these come from the considerable acreage owned by members of the United Vintners organization, whose vineyards are considered part of the Inglenook Estate. The wine-making facility at Inglenook naturally includes the most modern equipment for handling both red and white wines. The reds are generally aged in thousand-gallon German oak casks which impart minimal oak character to the wines, though small American oak casks are also being purchased.

Inglenook has long been justly famous for its Cabernet Sauvignon, and this varietal has continued to rank among California's best in a good vintage. Some older Inglenook Cabernets we have had an opportunity to taste have been very fine, although the aging potential and quality of the Cabernet does vary from year to year. Still, the reputation enjoyed by Inglenook's Cabernet Sauvignon remains well deserved.

As is true for other California wineries, however, the glory of the Cabernet does not reflect equally on the rest of the wines produced by Inglenook. While the reds are generally well-made wines of better than average character, the whites are almost as consistently ordinary and overpriced. The Riesling varieties have been particularly disappointing, while the Dry Semillon is perhaps the only white that has always shown good varietal character. The less expensive *Vintage* wines are about average for California generics, and again the reds are better than the whites.

While some of the wines are certainly good, you should make your selections carefully and not expect everything labeled Inglenook to be automatically a fine wine. It is clear that the

Inglenook name and the publicity attached to Cabernets which
have sold for hundreds of dollars a bottle are being used to
sell wines which otherwise might command a much lower price.
This is particularly true of the Navalle wines, which have no
legitimate connection with either Napa Valley or the traditional
methods of wine making at Inglenook.

The winery building at Inglenook is quite picturesque, set
back from the highway and protected by a moat of vineyards.
The tasting room is very comfortable, and all varieties except
the Cabernet Sauvignon, Pinot Noir, and Chardonnay are generally available.

Dry Semillon　Consistently a wine of good varietal character,
the Inglenook Semillons have a distinctive woody-grassy
aroma and a characteristic earthy taste. The *1970* was quite
dry, with light to moderate body and acid.　(**)

Pinot Chardonnay　Recent vintages have been highly ordinary, though they are rarely unpleasant. Both *1970* and
1971 were wines of light to moderate body and moderate
acid; the former was already showing its age in late 1972,
while the latter had a bit of green oak character. Some Chardonnay character, but undistinctive and overpriced.　(*)

Grey Riesling　Similar to the Sylvaner in style and roughness,
though the *1969* was a bit better. With a slightly oily oak
nose, it is dry, light to moderate in body and acid, and has
a slightly alcoholic taste.　(*)

Sylvaner Riesling　One of the slower-selling varietals and not
one of the best. The *1969* is dry, with light to moderate
body and acid and a spicy aroma. It is bothered by a rather
rough aftertaste that has also been present in previous vintages.　(BA)

Johannisberg Riesling　A bit inconsistent, but usually the best
of Inglenook's Riesling varieties. The *1971* has a fresh,
flowery aroma and a soft, pleasant finish. Off-dry with light
to moderate body and acid, it is a well-made wine even
though it is without great distinction.　(**)

Traminer The slightly spicy aroma heralds some Traminer character, but the *1971* is rather neutral in flavor. With moderate body and light to moderate acid, it is soft and drinkable. (*)

Chenin Blanc Usually pleasant if simple, but the *1970* does not have the freshness of other California Chenin Blancs. Slightly sweet with light to moderate body and rather low acid that results in a somewhat watery wine lacking fruit and flavor. (*)

White Pinot A dry Chenin Blanc that lacks fruit. While the wine is occasionally a bit fresher and more pleasant, the *1970* is rather bland, with light body and acid. (*)

Gamay Rosé Formerly *Navalle Rosé* until the lower-priced Navalle line was introduced, this has been a very fruity, dry rosé with a candy-apple or strawberry aroma. The *1971* slipped a little, as its light body and character did not live up to the aroma. Slightly rough. (*)

Gamay Made from Napa Gamay grapes, this is fuller and less fruity than the Gamay Beaujolais. The *1969* is not overly distinctive, but its light to moderate body, acid, and tannin are well balanced. Soft, ripe fruit aroma and good flavors that may gain from a year or two of bottle age. (**)

Gamay Beaujolais A light, tart, fruity wine, exactly what one would expect of a California Gamay Beaujolais. *1968* had light to moderate body and tannin with moderate acid and a fresh, fruity taste. *1969* was very similar, though a bit lighter. (**)

Pinot Noir The *1968* was typical, with light to moderate body and tannin and moderate acid and rather weak flavors. Little Pinot Noir richness. *1969* was a touch better, with a pleasant musty-fruity aroma, but it still lacked the character and depth that you should expect from the expensive Pinot Noir. (*)

Cabernet Sauvignon Traditionally one of the Napa Valley's best Cabernets, the regular bottling is 100 percent Cabernet and is generally released when about four years old. We have often preferred the stronger character of the regular to that of the cask bottling. Usually quite good, the *1963* was outstanding, while *1964* was very disappointing considering the reputation of the vintage. The next three years were very similar: *1965* was a bit unbalanced when young, but should develop very well. *1966* saw a wine of moderate body, acid, and tannin with good varietal character that needs another few years of age. *1967* was one of the most successful Cabernets of this vintage in the Napa Valley, though it was a bit lighter than the 1966. Medium-dark red with an undeveloped slight vanilla nose, it has good fruit and will develop complexity and roundness through the late 1970s.   (***)

Cabernet Sauvignon Cask Bottling   Generally a bit softer and at its best more elegant than the regular, due to the 15 percent Merlot that is blended with the Cabernet Sauvignon. Not always worth the extra money asked, *1963, 1965,* and *1967* were all a bit disappointing, though they were still good wines. *1964* was superb, and *1966* (***) was also a fine wine, with well-balanced minty flavors. The *1967* is a nice wine, but its light to moderate body, tannin, and acid do not seem likely to produce a wine of great interest or complexity. Best feature is its fruity-cocoa aroma, though potential is limited.   (**)

Zinfandel   Always a fairly tart wine, with a good berry-grapey aroma. The *1968* (*) was simple and a bit harsh, while the *1969* had better balance and good Zinfandel character. Will improve for two to three years and lose some of the woody flavor now present.   (**)

Charbono   Varietally labeled only by Inglenook and with just a touch of Barbera also present. While *1966* and *1967* were pretty ordinary, *1968* returned to form. Moderate in body, tannin, and acid, it is a good wine that needs two to four years to overcome the slight tannic bitterness present. *1969* was typical of this vintage in being lighter and fruitier. Its minty flavors also need a couple of years to develop. (**)

Red Pinot Though unavailable for quite some time in 1972 and 1973 as the wine had not developed enough to be released, this varietal is still being produced by Inglenook. The fairly full-bodied *1967* is one of the best of recent years, though its rich aroma and flavors have already become quite soft. Should continue to gain complexity for a couple more years. (**)

"Vintage Bottled" Wines

Chablis A dry, slightly fruity wine of light to moderate body and acid. *1970* had a slightly rough aftertaste, though it is not unpleasant. (*)

Rhine *1970* is distinguished from the Chablis by a green-fruity character in aroma and taste. Ordinary, off-dry in the mouth but with a dry, slightly alcoholic finish. (*)

Vin Rosé Not vintaged, but priced in the "vintage" class. Never particularly distinctive, the most recent bottle tasted had a heavy raisiny-woody nose and flavor that was not very pleasant. Dry and dull, with moderate body and light to moderate acid. (BA)

Burgundy In the past this has been the best of the line, and the *1970* continues the tradition of a soft, fruity, drinkable wine. Quite light in body, the flavors are nonetheless pleasant. (**)

Zinfandel The *1969* is very similar to the Burgundy, with light body and light to moderate tannin and acid. Quite drinkable, with some varietal character, though not a deep or complex wine. (*)

Louis M. Martini

An Old World concern for quality has remained an integral part of the Martini winery, still owned and operated by the Martini family that founded the winery in 1934. Despite its size, the winery is a personal concern much more reminiscent of the smaller California wineries than of Almadén or Paul Masson. In 1972, Louis Martini was named the American Society of Enologists' Man of the Year, providing yet another example of the esteem in which he is held by his fellow wine makers.

The wines of Martini fit well into the pattern that the Italian origin of the winery might suggest: robust, straightforward, and tart. Particularly successful, and consistently good buys, are the Barbera and Zinfandel. With the possible exception of the Pinot Noir, the reds are generally good honest wines that will improve greatly with several years bottle age. If you'd like to see what an older Martini wine is like, the Private Reserve and Special Selection wines (offered primarily at the winery) are generally well chosen and worth the extra price asked for a well-aged wine.

While the Folle Blanche and Gewürztraminer have been distinctive and very pleasant, the rest of Martini's whites are ordinary and generally indistinguishable from the mass of California's other premium white wines. Often tart and a bit rough, they lack the fruit, freshness, and varietal distinction that should characterize a good white.

A new tasting room is now open every day to accommodate visitors, and tours are also available. The complete line of Martini wines may be sampled, and your reception should be both friendly and fairly informative.

Dry Sauterne   Light-bodied with light to moderate acid, this is a very ordinary wine that has been characterized by a rather rough woody aftertaste. Palatable, but consistently disappointing. (BA)

Chablis   In the past ranked in the high average or good category, this has been a dry, light, well-balanced wine, clean and crisp but with no great distinction. (*)

Pinot Chardonnay   Generally weak in varietal character or distinctiveness, though inoffensive. *1970* (**) was a bit better than other vintages, with good fruit and well-balanced character, while *1971* was a bit weak in fruit acidity and had little flavor to balance the touch of oak in the taste. (*)

Rhine   An off-dry wine with a touch of Muscat character in aroma and taste. Light body, light to moderate acidity. Not as good as the Chablis. (*)

Riesling   Pale yellow with a light fruity aroma, this is a fairly light-bodied wine with light to moderate acidity and inoffensive character. Dry. *1971* is similar to previous years. (*)

Sylvaner   Generally similar to the Riesling. Apparently a slow seller, available vintages are often behind other whites. The *1969* tasted in late 1972 was a bit old and rough, with light to moderate body and acid and a dry finish. (*)

Johannisberg Riesling   Usually characterized by a nice flowery aroma, with some character and a dry finish. *1970* (**) produced a pleasant wine of light to moderate body and acid; *1971* was very simple and seemed to have a hint of sweetness. (*)

Gewürztraminer   Always characterized by an enticing, spicy-flowery aroma, this has been one of the most consistently successful Martini whites. Both *1970* and *1971* produced off-dry wines of light to moderate body and acid, though the flavors of the *1970* (**) are disappointingly weak after the delightful aroma. The *1971* is soft and pleasant. (**)

Dry Chenin Blanc   The *1970* is typical, with light to moderate body, moderate acid, and a slightly fruity Chenin Blanc aroma. *1971* was a bit lighter; crisp but ordinary, it could use more fruit. As the name suggests, it is dry.   (*)

Folle Blanche   This is a very dry, very tart wine whose appeal may be limited, but whose reasonable price has always made it attractive. The *1970* (**) was clean, light, and tart, while the *1971* had a bit more fruit and character to balance its dry tartness. The only varietal Folle Blanche currently produced in California, and definitely worth trying.   (***)

Gamay Rosé   Generally dry and pleasant, with noticeable Gamay character in nose and flavor. *1971* had light to moderate body and acid, a nice light pink color, and a clean, fresh taste.   (**)

Burgundy   Rather heavy fruity nose, light to moderate body and acid, and moderate tannin. Slightly sweet in the finish, this wine will benefit from another year or two of bottle age. Some complexity.   (**)

Pinot Noir   While some of the Special Selections may be a bit fuller and richer, this has generally been a fairly light, tart wine that has not caught the intensity of a good Pinot Noir. The *1969* was a particularly light, Gamay-style wine; though pleasant enough on its own, it was disappointing for what should theoretically be a full, rich wine.   (*)

Cabernet Sauvignon   Again, the Special Selection wines are often superior wines at moderate prices, and surely represent some of the best bargains in Cabernet Sauvignons today. Long-lived, most will not reach their peak for ten to fifteen years. The regular Cabernets have had good varietal character and some potential, though rarely do they rank in the top echelon. All need at least five years' bottle age.

The *1967* was a bit sharp when young, with light to moderate body and moderate acid and tannin, but it had straightforward Cabernet character. As with Krug, *1968* was a bit disappointing considering the success of other Napa vintners in that year, but the wine has good fruit and character, with moderate body, tannin, and acid. Reasonably priced, it might be one to put away and speculate on for a few years. (**)

Zinfandel Martini's Zinfandel has always been handled as a premium varietal, and the results have been consistently above the California average. Often rough when young, almost all Martini Zinfandels will improve with a few years of bottle age. The *1968* (***) was, like the Barbera, very successful. With light to moderate body and tannin and moderate acid, it has good fruit and will develop well through the mid-1970s. The *1969* was similar, though not quite as complex as the 1968 and with less future. (**)

Barbera A consistently good, moderately priced wine that can, at its best, become a soft, rich wine of considerable complexity and interest. Generally on the tart side with light to moderate body, the best recent years have been 1964 and 1966. The *1968* (****) is perhaps the finest of the decade, with moderate body and acid, good berrylike aroma and flavors, and excellent potential for development through the late 1970s. A fine example of the heights to which a Barbera may rise. *1969* was less good, with moderate acidity and light to moderate body and tannin. Still pleasant, but without the depth or staying power of the 1968. (**)

Mayacamas Vineyards

Mayacamas is a small, picturesque winery located 2400 feet high on the slopes of Mt. Veeder, a former volcano in the midst of the Mayacamas Mountains that separate the Napa and Sonoma Valleys. The winery was revitalized in the 1940s by Jack and Mary Taylor, who continued to operate it through the 1960s with the aid of wine maker Robert Sessions. In 1968 the property was purchased by its present owner, Mr. Robert Travers.

Accessible only by a veritable jeep trail, the winery and vineyards are in a beautiful bowllike setting surrounded by trees, mountains, and sky. Some 35 to 40 acres of land are planted in Chardonnay and Cabernet Sauvignon, with eventual plans to expand to 100 acres. As many of the vines are young and production in this area is low, additional grapes are now purchased from other Napa vineyards to attain a current production of ten to fifteen thousand gallons annually.

Some fine wines are produced at Mayacamas, although a few recent vintages have been fraught with the technical problems that sometimes beset a small winery. The Chardonnays have been especially promising, with the latest vintages capturing the fruit present in the wines of the late 1960s and adding the complexity of oak. The Cabernet Sauvignons have been less consistent, although the 1969 and 1970 show good promise in their youth. The winery has also received much well-deserved praise for the 1968 Late Harvest Zinfandel.

Visitors to the winery are asked to write or phone ahead for an appointment and may be assured of a very friendly reception.

Chardonnay   In recent vintages always a good wine, the *1967* was especially notable for its apple fragrance and good fruit. The *1968* and *1969* (*) had less fruit, but good varietal flavor and character, although unfortunately some bottles of the 1969 acquired a displeasing sulfurous aroma. The *1970* is a fine Chardonnay with medium-yellow color, a fruity apple aroma and an oily-oaky bouquet with good flavors and depth. It will last through the mid-1970s. (***)

The *1971*, tasted in the cask, appears similar to the 1970; it is developing good flavors and should be another fine wine.

Chenin Blanc   The *1971* vintage is the last one planned for this varietal at Mayacamas. The wine has a fruity, melon-like nose, is fairly dry, and has a light, fresh, tart flavor. (**)

Cabernet Sauvignon   Both *1966* and *1968* (*) were disappointing, the former for lack of balance and the latter for an unpleasant sulfurous nose. The 1968 does have good character underneath the aroma, and if the off-character dissipates, the wines may be better in five to ten years than it now appears. *1967*, on the other hand, is a good wine with complexity and more body and aging potential than most Napa Valley wines of this vintage.

The *1969* Cabernet is still rather young, with an undeveloped nose and closed-in flavors. It does have good fruit, body, and tannin and the promise of developing complex Cabernet flavors. Try it again in the late 1970s. (***)

The *1970*, tasted after two years in medium-sized oak, already shows a pleasant green-olive, sage aroma, medium body, and good acid and tannin. It is an impressive wine that, if development continues smoothly during its additional year in small oak, seems destined to have a long future.

Late Harvest Zinfandel 1968   Unfortunately largely inaccessible to the average consumer, this wine has created such interest that we feel it merits some discussion here. The grapes were picked at 27 degrees Balling, not counting the contribution of some raisined grapes, and when fermentation was over the alcohol had risen to a very unusual 17 percent. (This strength is several degrees higher than wine yeast is supposed to be capable of reaching, and special label approval was required from the government.) The wine is well balanced and smooth and its full body is accompanied by good acid and a deep round fruitiness. So powerful and rich that it probably has to be drunk by itself, the wine is enjoyable now, though its complexity and relatively undeveloped nose indicate good aging potential, too. It certainly should remain excellent for ten to fifteen years if the deep fruitiness persists. It is unfortunate that a few wine merchants exploited the wine's uniqueness by pushing it to ridiculously high prices.

Oakville Vineyards

Oakville Vineyards was created in 1968 with the purchase of the 280-acre Bartolucci plantings in the central Napa Valley. The vineyard holdings have since been augmented by several hundred acres owned by some of the Oakville partners, and in 1972 Oakville purchased the 1600-acre Inglenook Ranch from the John Daniels estate. Only 110 acres of the ranch are currently in vines, but future plantings can be expected. Thus all Oakville wines will be produced from the winery's own grapes, even though production is expected to grow from about 60,000 gallons in 1972 to 250,000 gallons by 1975.

Managing partner of Oakville is Bud van Loben Sels, who,

along with wine maker Peter Becker, has been the driving force behind the winery. The winery building itself is presently adjacent to the Oakville tasting room and gift shop on Highway 29, though it is not generally open to the public. The whites are fermented in stainless steel, while the reds undergo fermentation in fiberglass-lined concrete tanks. All the reds are aged for some period of time in sixty-gallon French Nevers oak, though of course the length of time varies with each variety.

The first vintages of Oakville Vineyards have certainly been successful, and the wines are generally distinguished by their strong varietal character. The whites tend to be forceful, rather than delicate, as evidenced by the big character of the dry Sauvignon Blanc. Consultant Karl Werner, formerly wine master for the celebrated Schloss Vollrads in the German Rheingau region, takes particular pride in this wine, and you will surely be tasting similar wines from Oakville in the future. The reds also show very good breed, although the Cabernet Sauvignon is the only truly outstanding wine at present.

The people in the tasting room are very friendly and fairly knowledgeable, and most varieties may be sampled. A small picnic area is available, and the gift shop is well supplied with more than a loaf of bread to accompany your jug of wine.

Our House White Produced from Sauvignon Blanc, a few other varieties, and some press wine, *Lot 71* is a dry, clean, slightly alcoholic wine of good body. A good, everyday wine, though not that inexpensive. (**)

Sauvignon Blanc Oakville's first wine from this grape was a slightly sweet *nonvintaged* wine with a bit of Muscat de Frotignan added to enhance the perfumed aroma. Light, crisp, and quite pleasant. (**)

A definite change in style was heralded by the *1971 Reserve,* which is a fairly full-bodied, very dry wine with characteristic earthy flavors and aroma. A strong-flavored wine, with good varietal character, that is austere rather than fruity. (**)

Future vintages should resemble the style of the 1971, though a small amount of sweet Sauvignon Blanc may also be made.

Chenin Blanc *1971* produced an off-dry wine with light to medium body and acid and good fruit. Not deep or complex, but pleasant and well made. Could use a bit more character in the nose. (**)

Gamay Rosé A very fruity wine from Napa Gamay grapes, the *1971* is dry and well balanced with a pronounced berry aroma. Fairly intense flavors, with more character than many other rosés. (***)

Our House Red A straightforward, everyday red primarily from Carignane and Mondeuse grapes. More character than the average generic, while not overly exciting. Light to moderate in body, tannin, and acid. (**)

Napa Gamay The *1969* (***) was a fairly big Gamay with interesting flavors and good potential, though it was less fruity than the *1970*. The latter has a woody-cinnamon aroma, light to moderate body and tannin, and moderate acid. It has good character, but needs two to three years to smooth out. (**)

Cabernet Sauvignon Oakville's best wine to date. In *1968* both a regular and Reserve were bottled. The *regular* (***) is a well-balanced wine of moderate body, tannin, and acid with a very good spicy-sagey-minty aroma. The *Reserve* (****) has a bit more depth, but otherwise is similar. Both have excellent character and should be aged until the late 1970s. No 1969 was produced, but the *1970* is worth waiting for. An intense, powerful wine with complex flavors and lots of body and tannin, it is already a fine wine

but will not reach its peak until the 1980s. Excellent
fruit. (****)

Zinfandel Both *1970* and *1971* have good varietal character and light to moderate body and tannin with moderate
acidity. The 1970 had a delightful raspberry aroma;
the 1971 is not quite as intense, but still retains good
fruit. (**)

Robert Mondavi Winery

The Robert Mondavi Winery crushed its first grapes in 1966,
and, despite a somewhat shaky start during the first couple
of years, by 1968 it had clearly joined the ranks of the best
California wineries. Production has increased to several hundred thousand gallons annually, but thus far quality has also
continued to improve.

The interior of the Mondavi winery, one of the most in-
novative California wineries, includes centrifuges, a new rotating fermentor, and of course the most modern presses,
filters, and temperature controls that are familiar sights
throughout the wine country. Mr. Mondavi's goal is to have
all the equipment necessary to handle each of his wines with
individual attention, without worrying about the physical or
technical limitations that may plague less complete operations.

While the importance of wood character and oak aging for
certain varieties is clearly recognized, great attempts are made
to protect the young wine from oxidation and foreign matter
in the juice. The result of these procedures has generally been
the production of very fresh, fruity wines that retain a pronounced grapey character. Although excessive "cleaning up"
of wines may often rob them of much of their distinctiveness,

Mondavi has thus far been successful in maintaining an excellent balance between cleanness and varietal character.

The winery, in the style of a Spanish mission and located in Oakville on Highway 29, is surrounded by vineyards that stretch to the nearby hills. The tours are informative and the tasting facilities excellent. During the crowded summer months only three wines are poured for tasting, but at more peaceful times a larger variety may be available.

As the descriptions that follow indicate, the wines of Robert Mondavi are among California's best, and all carry premium prices as well. It is important not to confuse the Robert Mondavi Winery with "Mondavi Vineyards"; the latter are lower-quality, lower-priced wines produced by the Charles Krug Winery. The confusion stems from the fact that the Mondavi family now owns Krug, while Robert Mondavi left Krug to found his own winery, which is completely separate from the Krug operation.

Fumé Blanc While several other wineries have adopted "Fumé Blanc" as a synonym for Dry Sauvignon Blanc, the name was originated by Robert Mondavi to describe a wine in the style of the dry French wines of the upper Loire River. This has been a consistently outstanding wine of its type: very dry with the earthy taste and aroma of the Sauvignon Blanc grape, the wine retains good fruit and a clean, pleasant aftertaste. Both *1970* and *1971* produced wines of light to moderate body, moderate acidity, and excellent varietal character.   (***)

Chardonnay This variety has been steadily improving since the relatively ordinary *1967* and *1968* vintages. The *1969* was a fairly soft wine, with a very nice apricot aroma and a touch of oak in the taste. The *1970* is similar, just a bit more tart, and is reminiscent of a French Meursault.   (***)

Riesling Always very pleasant and fresh, the *1971* follows suit as an off-dry wine of light to moderate body and acid.

A nice luncheon wine, well balanced and clean, with a good fruity aroma. (**)

Johannisberg Riesling   The *1971* is similar to preceding vintages, a light, clean wine with slight sweetness and a distinctive flowery aroma. Light yellow in color with light to medium body, medium acidity, and good fruit. (***)

Traminer   *1970* and *1971* were both a bit better than previous years, producing fresh, slightly spicy wines of light to moderate body and acidity. Dry, with a flowery nose. (**)

Chenin Blanc   Light yellow with a flowery varietal aroma, both *1970* and *1971* produced medium-sweet wines of light to moderate body and acid. Very good fruit, well balanced, and with fresh varietal character. (***)

Gamay Rosé   A dry rosé generally characterized by a strong candy-apple aroma, light to moderate body, and moderate acidity. The *1970* (***) was clean and fruity, while the *1971,* though still good, was a bit rough and not as fresh as previous vintages. (**)

Gamay   Produced from Napa Gamay grapes, this is a light, Beaujolais-style wine of low tannin and moderate acidity. Tart, clean, and fresh, the *1971* is a fine wine that is lighter and livelier than other Napa Gamays, though previous years have not always been as successful. (***)

Pinot Noir   After disastrous beginnings in *1966* and *1967,* the *1968* (**) Mondavi Pinot Noir had moderate body and possessed good character, some complexity, and a well-balanced hint of oak. *1969* was like a full Gamay: pleasant, light, tart, and fruity, with some Pinot Noir character. (**)

Cabernet Sauvignon   As for other Napa Valley vintners, *1968* (****) was a banner year for Mondavi's Cabernet, a complex wine of rich aroma and flavors that should improve through 1980. Previous vintages have been lighter and less distinctive, though a 1966-bottled unfined was quite successful. *1969* (***) was similar in style with moderate body, tannin, and acid and a very nice minty-vanilla nose, though it lacks just a bit of the intensity and potential of the 1968.

Souverain Cellars

Vines were first planted on the Souverain property in 1871, but Souverain itself was started only in 1943 by Lee Stewart. In mid-1970 the winery was sold, and a larger facility has been built to replace the small cellars on Howell Mountain. At the time of this writing expansion plans are still in a state of flux, so we have decided to defer a discussion of the current status of Souverain until the Appendix at the end of this book, where a more complete look at the new Souverain Cellars will be found.

In the past, Souverain's whites have been generally quite successful and well above average for California; they are clean and pleasant, and nearly all evidence good varietal character. The reds are fairly light and either tart or sharp, depending on your own preferences. They have not been as well balanced as the whites, except for the 1968 Cabernet and 1970 Zinfandel, which may well be the best reds Souverain has produced in recent years.

Chablis   Dry, clean, and tart, the *1970* is a typical Souverain Chablis. With light to moderate body and moderate acid, the flavors are a bit weak but still pleasant and show some character.   (**)

Pinot Chardonnay   A bit better in recent years, this is generally a fairly full white with some oak character and good fruit. *1969* (**) was a bit rough when young, though the wine was well balanced and had good Chardonnay character. *1970* was a bit lighter in body, but the flavors remain full and similar in style to the 1969. The aroma is particularly intense, and the wine should be at its peak in 1973–75. (***)

Riesling   Made from Johannisberg Riesling press wine and Flora, the *1971* was just a little bitter in taste. Fuller and drier than the Johannisberg, but rather clumsy and with little distinction. (*)

Johannisberg Riesling   Often one of the best in California, although 1971 did slip a bit. The *1970* (***) is typical, with a fresh, flowery Riesling nose, light to moderate body, moderate acid, and a touch of sweetness. Very pleasant and clean. *1971* was a bit weaker in all categories, but otherwise similar in style. Still a good wine, but overpriced and not up to previous years. (*)

Pineau Souverain   Both the Chenin Blanc and White Pinot have been discontinued to be replaced by this dry Chenin Blanc labeled in the French style. The *1970* was not terribly exciting, although the honeydew-melon character of the aroma shows good varietal character. Light to moderate body, moderate acidity. (*)

Flora   A hybrid varietal which is a cross between Semillon and Traminer, this has been a consistently pleasant wine. The *1970* is medium sweet, with well-balanced light to moderate body and moderate acid. The aroma is fruity, almost honeylike, and the flavors are interesting and smooth. (**)

Green Hungarian   Rather uneven in character, with *1970* being the most successful vintage to date. Light to medium in body with moderate acid, this is a very clean, lively wine with just a hint of sweetness. Aroma is fresh, fruity, and quite pleasant. (**) *1971* is similar, with a spicy aroma but a bit less character. (**)

Burgundy A blend of Grenache, Petite Sirah, and Zinfandel that often is quite successful. The most recent batch had a rich, oaky nose and very good fruit. Light to moderate in body with moderate tannin and acid, it should continue to improve for a few years. Much above average for a generic. (***)

Cabernet Sauvignon Generally in the light style, elegant when good and thin when less successful. Both *1966* and *1967* (**) had good fruity Cabernet character, and they were on the tart side. Little aging potential, but pleasant. *1968* was head and shoulders above the others and already has a complex black currant-minty nose and developing flavors. Still on the tart side, but with moderate body and tannin, which will lend themselves well to further aging. Very good fruit. (****)

Zinfandel *1967, 1968,* and *1969* (BA) were all fairly thin and sharp. *1970* is markedly better, and hopefully future vintages will follow its pattern. Still fairly light, the moderate tannin and acid are in better balance and good berry-like Zinfandel character is evident in both aroma and taste. Should develop through 1975. (***)

Spring Mountain Vineyards

In many ways Mike Robbins, who owns Spring Mountain, has built his winery backward. In fact, a winery building is not scheduled to be completed until 1974, although a few vintages of Spring Mountain will have already come and gone by then. But whichever way Spring Mountain was started must have been the right way, for its first wines were truly outstanding and probably represent the most successful introductory wines of any of the new Napa Valley wineries. Unfortunately the second vintage was not as successful, though the desire and effort necessary to produce fine wines clearly remain.

Spring Mountain has eighty-five acres near St. Helena planted to Cabernet Sauvignon, Chardonnay, and Sauvignon Blanc, but it is only with the 1972 vintage that these vineyards will be supplying a large proportion of the grapes the winery requires. Eventually all Spring Mountain's grapes will come from its own vines, and production is anticipated to rise from 8000 to 9000 gallons in 1972 to a maximum of 25,000 to 30,000 gallons by 1980. Until the vines are mature and the wine-making facilities complete, grapes and wine have been bought from other wineries: the 1967 and 1969 Sauvignon Blancs were crushed by Wente, while the Chardonnay and Cabernet Sauvignon were fermented in Joe Heitz's cellars. Mr. Robbins and wine maker Chuck Ortman have then aged, blended, and finished the wines, with much of the work being done in the basement of the Robbinses' beautifully restored Victorian house just north of St. Helena. The Cabernet Sauvignon is aged for about one and a half years in Nevers oak, while the Chardonnay and Sauvignon Blanc are in Limousin, the former in new oak for six months, the latter in once-used barrels for perhaps three or four months. All the wines do have well-balanced oak flavors and thus need some bottle age to reach their peak.

The wines all show excellent varietal character, and the "line" will be limited to the three varieties discussed above. Certainly Spring Mountain has gotten off to an auspicious beginning, and we wish Mr. Robbins continued success.

No tasting or tours are available, though the wines enjoy fairly good distribution despite their limited quantities. Any questions or requests for information should be directed to Mr. Robbins.

Sauvignon Blanc   Two wines were actually produced in
   1967 (***) (which are identified as *Lot W-67-L* and *Lot*

W-67-N), one aged in Limousin oak and the other in Nevers. Both were big wines, with elegant, slightly earthy flavors and a clean, dry finish; the Limousin had a touch more complexity, and future vintages will be aged only in this oak. No *1968* was produced, and the *1969* also had good varietal character. Softer and less distinctive than the 1967, it could perhaps use a little more acidity and fruit. Still, quite pleasant. (**)

Chardonnay   1969 (****) was the first vintage, and it was one of the finest in a year which saw several very good Chardonnays being produced. Moderate in body and acid, its spicy-fruity oak character is distinctive, yet refined and well balanced. The aroma is particularly pleasant, with a spiced-apricot character. The *1970* is below the 1969 in quality, though the price has remained as high. The aroma is still pleasant and rather spicy, but body, acidity, and flavors are all less complete. Soft and drinkable, but without depth or complexity. (**)

Cabernet Sauvignon   The first "vintage" was a blend of 1968 and 1969 labeled *Lot H-68-69*. (****) A big wine with excellent Cabernet character and deep, rich fruit flavors. While the aroma is already developing a minty-cocoa complexity, this wine should really be aged until at least 1975 and probably longer to achieve its full potential. The *1970* is also quite good. With moderate body and fairly high tannin and acid, it, too, needs several years bottle age to round out its good sagelike Cabernet flavors. (***)

SONOMA

Vines were first brought into Sonoma County in the early 1800s by the Spanish fathers, who established the last of their chain of California missions in the little village of Sonoma. In the 1850s Colonel Agoston Haraszthy brought cuttings of European vines to the area and founded his own winery on the grounds of what is today Buena Vista, and Sonoma has remained an important viticultural area since that time.

Sonoma County is some sixty miles in length, and includes within its boundaries many different vineyard regions. Perhaps the most famous area is that immediately surrounding the historic town of Sonoma, which includes two well-known wineries, Sebastiani and Buena Vista. Vines have also long been planted in the beautiful Valley of the Moon, just a half hour's drive north of Sonoma along Highway 12, and today several small wineries continue the wine-making tradition of this area.

The county's largest acreage of vines lies north of Santa Rosa in a long stretch of warm, fertile countryside that extends through the towns of Healdsburg, Geyserville, and Cloverdale. This area was originally settled by many Italian families, who continued to make wine in much the same way as they had in their native country. These wineries became known for sturdy red wines that spent many years in large redwood cooperage and for rather harsh whites whose alcohol content and lack of acidity reflected the warmth of the climate. Today the visitor to northern Sonoma may explore wineries that range from the ultramodern plant at Windsor to the small stone and wood buildings of Nervo and Foppiano, where wine making continues much as it has for the past fifty years. The northern-most part of the county is dominated by the large winery of the Italian Swiss Colony at Asti, which provides the traveler with a view of yet another style of wine production.

The Russian River cuts across the middle of Sonoma County, and here and there along its banks or tucked back in the hills are a few small vineyards, while a larger concentration of vines may be found in a picturesque setting adjacent to Korbel at Guerneville.

The wineries of Sonoma County are more widely scattered than those of the neighboring Napa Valley, but for the wine enthusiast who has enough time on his hands the area is well worth visiting. The peaceful, tree-lined country lanes wind past gnarled old vineyards that have been supplying grapes to generations of California wine drinkers. The varietal composition of the vineyards is unusual, with over 8000 of the county's 13,000 acres of bearing vines planted to Carignane, Zinfandel, Petite Sirah, French Colombard, and Palomino (Golden Chasselas). This reflects a time when the number of premium varietals made in the county were few, and the vast majority of wine was either sold as country red or white from the tasting rooms of small family-run wineries, or else sold in bulk to large wineries, where it was then blended into jug wine.

Today recent plantings of Cabernet Sauvignon, Pinot Noir, and Chardonnay approach three thousand acres, and vineyards are appearing in many different regions. Dry Creek Valley, a few miles west of Geyserville, is rapidly filling with vines, while to the east of Geyserville, along Highway 128 in Knight's and Alexander Valleys, many acres of prune orchards have been uprooted and replanted with grapes. If care is taken in the selection of these new areas, the premium varietals now being planted should do well.

Buena Vista Winery

The Haraszthy Cellars, as Buena Vista is sometimes called, traces its lineage back to the 1860s and Colonel Agoston Haraszthy himself. Located in a eucalyptus grove just outside of the city of Sonoma, the famous limestone aging tunnels of Buena Vista complement the very picturesque setting.

The musty-woody aroma that has characterized Buena Vista's wines in the past has been toned down in more recent vintages, though it still appears occasionally in the reds. Most of the red wines also have a fair amount of tannin, so adequate bottle age is a must to bring them to their peak. The whites still tend to lag behind other wineries in retail sales, and you should be certain that they have been well cared for before buying one of the older vintages.

Although presently owned by the Young Brothers supermarket chain of Southern California, Buena Vista has remained relatively small, and we are sure that the concern for quality we noted several years ago still exists. Recent tastings of Buena Vista wines have, however, often been disappointing, particularly in the whites. For example, the 1971 Gewürz Traminer Cabinet, long one of our favorites, was not a good wine, nor was the popular Green Hungarian. The reds are much more consistent, and some fine Cabernet Sauvignons, Zinfandels, and even Pinot Noirs have been produced.

However, a strong ray of hope for the future improvement of Buena Vista wines is present in the form of a newly planted six hundred acres of vines in Carneros region on the Napa-Sonoma county line. Under the direction of Rene Lacasia, the most modern techniques of vineyard development are being employed, and there has been an honest attempt to match grape varieties with the particular microclimates and soils that exist in the gently rolling vineyard. The first plantings will begin bearing in the mid-1970s, and it will be interesting to see if any change in the style or quality of Buena Vista wines will be apparent.

Buena Vista offers no formal tour of the winery, although descriptive photographs encourage the visitor to wander through the aging cellars. (Be sure to bring a sweater, as the tunnels are often quite cool and damp.) The tasting room is a rather dimly lit cave which resembles a souvenir-selling catacomb and is an experience in itself. A representative sample of Buena Vista's wines is available for tasting, but the guides, while they are very friendly, may be uninformed about the company's wine-making practices.

Chablis   Dry, with light to moderate body and moderate acid, this is a tart, drinkable everyday wine.   (*)

Chardonnay   This has usually been a fairly good wine of some varietal character, but without great complexity or fruit. The *1971* does have a light, fruity green-apple aroma and a pleasing, if not overly, distinctive flavor. Dry, with light to medium body and moderate acidity.   (**)

Johannisberg Riesling   The *1971* is typical of past Johannisbergs, with a light-yellow wine, a fruity citrus aroma and fairly light body and acid. Dry, with little Riesling character.   (*)

Gewürz Traminer   This is the dry companion to the Gewürz Traminer Cabinet. In the past it has been a pleasant spicy wine of good character. The past two vintages have, however, been considerably less successful. The *1970* suffered from premature oxidation and loss of fruit. (BA) The *1971* is a bit fresher, with light to medium body and acidity, but still lacking good varietal flavors.   (*)

Gewürz Traminer Cabinet   In the late 1960s this was generally a very successful medium-sweet wine that retained the spicy-fruity character of the Gewürz grape. Recently, however, the sugar has remained while much of the character has faded, and the *1971* was a particularly disappointing, weak, sugary wine. (BA)

Green Hungarian While a couple of previous vintages of this variety have been pleasant and fruity, the *1971* is flat, flavorless, and dull, with none of the little character that Green Hungarians usually possess. Dry. (BA)

Cabernet Rosé 1971 Consistently one of Buena Vista's best wines, this is a dry, fairly tart wine of good character, with light to moderate body and moderate acidity. Light to medium pink in color, it has a delightful pearlike aroma. (***)

Zinfandel Rosé 1971 A new wine, light, tart, and dry, but a bit lacking in character. Pleasant fruity nose and good medium-pink color. (*)

Burgundy Generally light to moderate in body with moderate tannin and acid, often needing a couple of years of bottle age. This wine has ranged in the past from good to average, with the most recent sample tasted, the *1967* being fairly ordinary. (*)

Pinot Noir 1968 Cask Bottling Buena Vista often does an above-average job with this difficult grape, and 1968 was no exception. Good fruity nose, with moderate body, acid, and tannin. Needs a couple of years' bottle age, but should be pleasant. (**)

Cabernet Sauvignon Often fairly light and undistinctive, the most recent wine ("cellared and bottled by" Buena Vista) has moderate body, tannin, and acid and has very good character and potential. It already possesses a distinctive sagebrush-olive nose and rich, developing flavors. (***)

Cask bottlings of Cabernet Sauvignon are also available,

and these are generally good, with potential to improve for several years.

Lachryma Montis 1967   The "tears of the mountain" is a special Cabernet Sauvignon, though that varietal designation does not appear on the label. It has a full, minty aroma and light to moderate body, acid, and tannin. Not very deep, but it should develop through the mid-1970s.   (**)

Zinfandel   Sometimes a bit rough when young, this is generally a wine of good character and aging potential. The *1968 Cask 160* (***) was particularly good, with well-balanced, big flavor and good fruit. The regular *1968* and *1969* are a bit lighter, but both have a good berry-spicy character and should be very pleasant in three to five years. Of the two, the 1968 had more character, while the 1969 was a bit tarter. Both are good wines.   (**)

Barbera, Cask 149   Medium red with a good fruity-minty nose, this is a characteristically tart Barbera with light to moderate body and moderate acid and tannin. Should improve for two to four years.   (**)

Korbel Winery

Located just off the Russian River near Rio Nido, Korbel was founded in 1862 by three "bumbling" brothers who hit upon wine making after they had tried practically everything else, including growing tobacco. Until recently Korbel was known primarily for its Champagnes, but after the Heck brothers took over in 1954, they became interested in producing table wines as well. The first of these were offered for public sale in 1965, and Korbel now produces a full range of four whites, a rosé, and three red table wines (along with several dessert wines and, of course, Champagne).

Tours of the winery are given at 1 and 2:30 P.M., and, while they are interesting, the guides appear to know little beyond their memorized speeches. A large, well-furbished tasting room harbors a rather sparse wine list; contrary to previous policy, tasting is now limited to three table wines and one Champagne. While the wines are varied from day to day, the "three only" policy is apparently strictly enforced.

Korbel's wines have been uneven in the past few years, though none has ever risen above the "good" category. No one variety has been consistently good or bad, and the tasting notes that follow are based on our most recent samplings of Korbel wines. Certainly they are not up to the reputation of Korbel's sparkling wines, and their main effect has been to expand the number of labels available to the consumer without contributing any distinctiveness.

Dry Sauterne   Dry, with light to medium body and acidity and good balance. Fairly flavorful for a generic; with a clean finish and a pleasant aroma. (**)

Chablis   Light yellow in color with a vinous aroma. A dry wine with light to medium body and acid; very ordinary. (*)

Grey Riesling   Weak in color, aroma, and flavor. Dry, with fairly low acidity. Though without technical faults, this wine does not possess the character of other Grey Rieslings. (BA)

Chenin Blanc   Light to medium yellow in color with a grassy, slightly woody aroma. Off-dry, and with medium body and light to moderate acid. Heavy and sluggish, without adequate fruit. (*)

Château Vin Rosé   Despite its "château" nomenclature, this wine is fairly dry and quite light in body and, though without character, does not have the harshness that marred the

wine several years ago. Light orange-pink in color, with a
flowery aroma.   (*)

Burgundy   Medium red with a ripe fruit nose, this is a fairly
tart, pleasant wine with a slightly rough aftertaste. Light
to moderate body, tannin, acid.   (*)

Pinot Noir   Medium red in color with an undistinguished
aroma. Light to medium in body, with moderate tannin
and acidity. Awkward and dull in flavor, with little Pinot
Noir character.   (BA)

Cabernet Sauvignon   Medium red with a characteristic sagebrush nose, light to moderate body and tannin, and
moderate acidity. A fairly tart wine of good Cabernet character. For drinking now rather than for laying away.   (**)

Sebastiani Vineyards

One of the two long-established wine names in the Sonoma
Valley, Sebastiani is a large winery whose label is familiar
to all California wine drinkers as well as to many outside the
state, for its distribution and production enable Sebastiani to
reach many markets. A complete line of wines is produced,
including several generics as well as most of the premium
varietals.

Grapes come from two hundred acres of bearing vineyards
owned by the winery and from local growers who have been
supplying the Sebastianis for years. Looking to the future, an
additional two hundred acres have been planted in the Schell-
ville area a few miles from Sonoma.

The white wines still have little to offer in the way of
character or distinction, and even the Green Hungarian and
Gewürztraminer were disappointing in 1971. Hopefully this

will be just a temporary lapse for these formerly successful varieties.

The reds, however, have been showing well recently and have more depth and finesse than those that were available several years ago. Bottle-aging facilities have been expanded from 1.2 to 3 million bottles, with the goal being to offer large supplies of reds aged at least two years longer than most other California wines. The recently released 1967 varietals are quite successful and show promise that this system may provide the consumer with some nice mature wines. Cabernet Sauvignon, Pinot Noir, Barbera, and a selected Burgundy are aged three and a half to four years in large redwood, and six months to a year in newly acquired fifty-gallon American oak barrels. The small cooperage has probably helped recent wines attain greater character and balance.

Most varietals will now be vintaged, and the formerly confusing bin-labeling system has been revised. Bin numbers now reflect consecutive bottlings of a wine from the same year and will no longer be used on nonvintage and white wines. Thus the bottlings of 1970 Zinfandel are labeled Bins 1, 2, 3, etc.

The Sebastiani tasting room has recently been remodeled, with stained-glass windows and beautiful oak-cask carvings by Earle Brown adding considerably to the warm interior. All varieties are available for tasting, the reception is friendly, and the winery is well worth visiting during a trip to historic Sonoma.

Chablis　In the past not the most successful generic, *1971* is noteworthy for a sulfurous aroma that did not dissipate after several hours. Dry, light yellow in color, with light to medium body and low acidity. From Semillon, Sylvaner, Colombard grapes.　(BA)

Pinot Chardonnay　Consistently a well-balanced wine without faults, though without adequate varietal character. *1971* has light-yellow color, a vinous aroma, and light to moderate body and acid.　(*)

Sylvaner 1969 is a neutral wine with a slight peachlike aroma, light to medium body and acid, and a dry finish. (*)

Johannisberg Riesling In the past on the heavy and woody side, the *1967* is the first vintage bottling of this wine and is an improvement. It reached peak maturity in 1972 with a deep pearlike aroma, a hint of sweetness, and light to medium body and acid. (**)

Kleinberger Riesling Produced as a varietal only in *1969*, this is a fresh, fruity, clean wine with a flowery aroma. Light to medium in body and moderate in acid. A nice wine, though overpriced. The vineyard has now been replanted, and this wine will probably be available again around 1975. (**)

Gewürztraminer Finished medium sweet, this has ranged from a pleasant spicy wine to one of only average character. *1971* has a flowery aroma, light to medium body and moderate acidity. Though certainly not unpleasant, it is disappointing for its lack of varietal character to balance the sweetness. (*)

Chenin Blanc 1971 is similar to past vintages and has a pale-yellow color and a spicy-sage aroma. Medium dry, light in body, and light to moderate in acid. A pleasant wine, though it could use a touch more balance between sweetness and fruit. (*)

Green Hungarian In the past this has been a successful and pleasant wine, but *1971* is definitely disappointing. Dry, with little color and no aroma, the taste was flat and dull. (BA)

Vin Rosé 1971 is similar to, though probably a little smoother than, prior vintages, and is a dry, fairly pleasant and fresh rosé. Fruity aroma, with light to moderate body and acid. (**)

Grenache Rosé A medium-sweet rosé with dark-pink color

and a simple, undistinguished flavor. Light to medium in body and acid, with slight harshness in the aftertaste. (*)

Burgundy Produced from Zinfandel, Petite Sirah, and Carignane grapes, the latest *nonvintage* has good color and a pleasant spicy aroma. Medium in body and acidity, with light to moderate tannin, it is a smooth wine with more complexity than most generics. (**)

The first vintaged Burgundy is a *1967* and this is a rather big wine for a Burgundy. A nice, complex flavor with fruity aroma, light to medium body and tannin, and moderate acid. (***)

Gamay Beaujolais Since 1968 when the winery began producing this as a fairly light wine meant to be drunk young, the wine has been very pleasant with good fruitiness. The *1971* has a nice raspberrylike aroma, light to medium body, acidity, and tannin and is well balanced. (***) In 1972, some of the harvest was bottled when only a month old in the style of a "new Beaujolais." Labeled *Nouveau,* it is a pleasant, light-bodied red wine whose freshness would go well with a picnic or light lunch. (**)

Pinot Noir The *nonvintaged* wines have been without great character (*), with the exception of *Bin 121,* which was from the 1964 vintage and was released with good aged flavors and fairly full style for a California Pinot Noir.

The *1967* has light-red color and light to medium body and tannin and, while a fairly drinkable wine, shows less class than the other vintaged reds. (*)

Cabernet Sauvignon The *nonvintage* (*) has generally been a wine of average Cabernet character. The latest bin is similar, and has a minty aroma, light to medium body, and moderate acid and tannin. A stronger, more complex wine than this is the *Bin 32,* which, though not so labeled, is from the 1966 harvest. This wine has a deep aroma with slight redwood bouquet, medium body, and moderate to high acid and tannin. It is a powerful wine with potentially good flavors that needs until 1975–78 to smooth out.   (**)

The *1967* has light- to medium-red color and a distinctive Cabernet nose. Well balanced, with medium body, acid, and tannin, this is a pleasant wine, softer than the 1966, but still requiring three to five more years of bottle age to reach its peak.   (***)

Zinfandel   Often wines of good character and pleasant, berrylike aromas. Several bins were bottled in *1970,* and all were quite successful, with light to moderate body and acid and moderate tannin. *Bin 2* was perhaps the best, and it has a delightful strawberry nose.   (**)

Chianti   From the same grapes as the Burgundy, but with a higher percentage of Carignane. The *1970* is a tart, simple wine with good color and a vinous aroma.   (*)

Barbera   The *nonvintage* has consistently been a good wine with a pleasant berrylike aroma and an orange cast to the color indicating some age. The latest bins have been similar to prior ones, with light to medium body and tannin and moderate acidity producing wines of good flavor and fruit.   (**)

The *1967* is quite nice, with good color, a full, fruity-berry aroma, and developing bouquet. This is a powerful wine with good fruit, medium body and tannin, and moderate high acid. It should age well through the mid-1970s.   (***)

Windsor Vineyards-Sonoma Vineyards

In 1960 Rodney Strong opened a small wine-tasting room in Tiburon, selling wines that he had selected in cask from other producers under the Tiburon Vintners label. Today, Windsor Vineyards is a publicly owned corporation with national distribution (known as Sonoma Vineyards outside California), over 1000 acres of premium vines already planted in Sonoma County, and sales that should surpass the $5 million mark. Rodney Strong remains as chairman of the board and wine maker, presiding over a new, cruciform winery complex in Windsor that also includes a data-processing system to handle Windsor's tremendous volume of mail-order sales and the winery's own printing plant. Three fourths of Windsor's sales are through direct orders from consumers, most of whom also take advantage of the personalized label service available.

The most modern equipment and wine-making techniques are in use at Windsor, and all red wines are now aged for at least some time in fifty-gallon barrels. Windsor wines are not vintaged, though occasionally selected lots are offered as special bottlings.

As you will see from the descriptions that follow, Windsor wines are, with a couple of exceptions, outstandingly ordinary and are distinguished from the average California wine primarily by their personalized labels. None of the wines we tasted were unpleasant; most were fairly light and simple, and the reds generally need minimal, if any, further aging when released.

The prices of Windsor wines are comparable to those of other large California producers, so the direct-sales process has not resulted in significant consumer savings. The original tasting room–retail outlet in Tiburon is still open, and tasting is of course also available at the new Windsor facility. The atmosphere in both is pleasant and relaxed, and the winery is certainly worth seeing when you are in the northern Sonoma area.

Chablis   Light yellow with a fresh, vinous aroma; this is a fairly light, tart wine of simple, but pleasant character. Dry and clean.   (**)

Chardonnay (*made and bottled by Windsor*)   A typical, slightly apple nose introduces this straightforward wine of good Chardonnay character. Light to moderate body and acid. Not complex, but clean and with some fruit. A good buy. (**)

Chardonnay (*Special Selection; produced and bottled by Windsor*)   Medium yellow with a spicy nose and slight oak overtones. Moderate in body and acid, but fairly soft. Good varietal character. (**)

Grey Riesling   Light yellow, slightly spicy nose. Light to medium body and acid, off-dry. Light, innocuous, without character. The slight detectable sweetness is different from the finish of most California Grey Rieslings. (*)

Johannisberg Riesling   Dry with light-yellow color and a distinctive, fresh fruity Riesling nose. Light to medium body and acidity, rather steely finish, and ordinary flavor. (*)

Chenin Blanc   Pale yellow in color with a very nice spicy-apricot aroma reminiscent of Muscat. Off-dry, with light to moderate body and acidity. Pleasant. (*)

French Colombard   Pale yellow with a fresh, vinous aroma, this is a tart, dry wine, light to moderate in body and acidity. (*)

Vin Rosé   Medium pink with a spicy, fruity nose, this can be one of Windsor's best wines for the money. Dry, with light to moderate body and acidity, it is just a bit rough, but clean and well balanced. (**)

Grenache Rosé   Medium pink with a slightly off vinous nose, this wine has good fruit but is otherwise quite ordinary and very simple. Dry and light to moderate in body and acid. (*)

Burgundy   This is quite a good wine, particularly for a generic. With light to moderate body and moderate acid and tannin, it is fairly tart, a bit young, and has good flavors. (**)

Petite Sirah   Medium red with a dull, fruity aroma. Light to moderate in body, acid, and tannin, the taste is ordinary and future development questionable.   (*)

Gamay   Light to medium red color with a fruity, oatmeallike nose. Rather light in style, especially in the finish which disappears quickly. Light to medium tannin and acid.   (*)

Cabernet Sauvignon   Light to medium red in color with a fruity, slightly Cabernet aroma. Light to medium in body, acid, and tannin, this is a pleasant wine, though one without great character.   (**)

Zinfandel   Light to medium red with a minty-vegetable nose, this is a typical, traditional California Zinfandel: simple, fairly pleasant, but with no depth. Light to moderate body and acidity, moderate tannin.   (*)

MENDOCINO

Mendocino lies just to the north of Sonoma County. Although grapes have been planted here for a number of years, summer temperatures are fairly high and until recently the region was thought best suited for growing ordinary wine grapes destined for jug wines. For some twenty miles between the Sonoma County line and the city of Ukiah, U.S. Highway 101 travels alongside many acres of prolific vines, planted primarily to Carignane, Petite Sirah, Zinfandel, and French Colombard. Many of these grapes supply the Guild cooperative winery at Ukiah, as well as Italian Swiss Colony's winery at Asti, in northern Sonoma.

In the past decade attention has been focused on Mendocino as a premium grape-growing region. The small family-run wineries of Fetzer and Parducci, as well as Guild itself under the premium Mendocino Vineyards (now Cresta Blanca) label, proved that the area's Zinfandel and Petite Sirah, when handled in other than mass-production methods, could produce fine wine. Prior to 1960 there was virtually no Cabernet Sauvignon, Gamay Beaujolais, Chardonnay, or White Riesling and very little Pinot Noir to be found, but since then over a thousand acres have been planted in these varieties. While much of the countryside is probably too warm, in selected hillside areas they may do well.

Today Mendocino County is clearly an expanding viticultural region, and it should certainly be included in any wine tour through California. It is the new home of Cresta Blanca, and Weibel has built a producing winery and tasting room near Ukiah. Several small wineries are in the area, and with the continued interest in California wines the number of vintners should continue to grow.

Cresta Blanca Winery

The original Cresta Blanca Winery of Livermore was founded in 1882 by Charles Wetmore and soon gained an international reputation for fine wines, winning the Grand Prix at the Paris Exposition in 1889. The winery prospered in the ensuing decades, surviving Prohibition by making sacramental and medicinal wines. In the postwar period, Cresta Blanca became famous for its Premier Semillon, a lush, Sauternes type of wine produced from grapes affected by artificially induced *Botrytis cinerea,* the noble mold. By the 1960s, however, the winery entered a period of relative decline, and its table wines gradually disappeared from most retail shelves and restaurant lists.

In 1970, the Cresta Blanca name was purchased by Guild Wineries and Distilleries, though the Livermore winery itself remained in the hands of the former owners, Schenley, Inc. The name has been transferred to a previously owned Guild winery near Ukiah (formerly known as Mendocino Vineyards) and, despite an extensive publicity campaign, the present "Cresta Blanca" bears little relation to the winery of that name founded in the late nineteenth century. The only exceptions are that wine maker Roy Mineau has remained with the company and they do have an option on the Livermore grapes of the old winery. The present emphasis is on the Mendocino area, but Champagnes and dessert wines continue to be made in Fresno, and the winery itself may well be moved at some future date. A few wines carry the *Mendocino* appellation; the others are designated only as *California,* while the small print on the label employs the winery's business office address in San Francisco.

The new Cresta Blanca is thus a far-flung operation, in part continuing the work of Mendocino Vineyards, partially encompassing other areas of California. Production is currently around 100,000 gallons annually, and plans call for expanding this figure by 25 to 50 percent for the next few years.

Sixteen table wines are offered, and their quality varies more than that of any other California winery. They presently include some wines formerly in the Schenley-Cresta Blanca inventory; others are Mendocino Vineyards wines under a new label; still others have been purchased from various wineries and finished by the new Cresta Blanca. The whites are generally quite disappointing, lacking varietal character and often deficient in acidity. While perhaps some of this can be blamed on the problems that naturally arise in a "new" winery, we certainly hope that this trial period will end soon.

The reds also vary, but they are on the whole a bit more successful than the whites. Indeed, the Mendocino "specialties" of Petite Sirah and Zinfandel can be quite good, and the Gamay Beaujolais should also do well if the past performance of Mendocino Vineyards is a fair guide. All the reds are aged for at least two years in wood (redwood and/or oak) and, while they are usually quite drinkable when released, many will continue to improve with additional bottle age.

The management of Cresta Blanca is separate from other Guild operations, but one goal is obviously to provide a showcase for Guild North Coast Counties growers. If the wines of Cresta Blanca were in fact limited to those varieties that have proven best suited to the Mendocino area, the results would probably be quite creditable. At the present time, however, the winery is clearly overextended, and the wines have suffered. The few successful varieties have shown that Cresta Blanca has the potential for fine wines; we can only hope that the future will bring noticeable improvement in the rest of the line.

Both tours and tasting are available at the Ukiah winery.

Sauterne   This is a flat, slightly sweet wine whose main distinction is a noticeable grassiness in aroma and taste. Some woodiness is also present.   (BA)

Chablis   Pale-yellow color, with a light, vinous aroma. Light to medium in body and acid, dry, ordinary.   (*)

Pinot Chardonnay   Light yellow in color, the only substantial characteristic of this wine is its nice green-apple aroma. The taste is flat and flavorless, leaving a very disappointing wine of light to moderate body and low acidity.   (BA)

Rhine   Pale yellow with a light fruity nose and fairly light body and acid. Off-dry, a bit rough, ordinary.   (*)

Grey Riesling   Light to medium yellow with a slightly fruity vinous aroma, this is a fairly neutral wine of light to moderate body and acid. Dry and pleasant enough, it has little character.   (*)

French Colombard   Light to medium yellow with a fruity aroma, this is a soft, off-dry wine that, while it is not particularly distinctive, nevertheless leaves a pleasant, clean impression. Very drinkable, though it could use more fruit.   (**)

Green Hungarian   Though most Green Hungarians have little character, this one surpasses them in blandness. Dry, pale in color, light body and acid, and with an unpleasant chemical aroma.   (BA)

Grenache Rosé   An unusually big rosé with dark-pink color and a strong haylike aroma. Dry, with moderate body and acidity and some tannin, it is more like a slightly harsh light red and has little Grenache fruitiness.   (*)

Burgundy   Light to moderate in body, acid, and tannin, this is an average California red with neither faults nor virtues. Some wood character that may smooth out, but no great potential.   (*)

Petite Sirah   When first released this was a good wine of fine potential, but later batches were not quite as distinctive. Light to moderate in body, acid, and tannin, with some spiciness in the nose.   (**)

Gamay Beaujolais   Light to medium red with a wood-coconut nose, this Gamay is woodier and less fruity than most. Light to moderate body, tannin, and acidity, with rather simple flavors. Other bottles were lighter and fruitier.   (*)

Cabernet Sauvignon   Clearly in the style of an older red, this is a tart, slightly rough wine of some character but little potential. Woody nose, light to moderate body and tannin, and moderate acid.   (*)

Zinfandel   Like the Petite Sirah, the first released batch of this wine was quite good, with deep berrylike flavors. Unfortunately, the next batch was very disappointing, with little character and a rather rough, unpleasant finish.   (*)

Grignolino   Light red with a fruity aroma, this is a fairly pleasant, light, wine of adequate fruit. Simple, light-bodied, light to moderate in acid, and with almost no tannin.   (*)

LIVERMORE VALLEY

The Livermore Valley is an hour's drive to the east, and slightly to the south, of San Francisco, across the Diablo Range of the Coast Mountains. The warm climate and gravelly soil of the area attracted wine growers in the mid-1800s, and since then the valley has been a well-known wine region. Some of the initial vines were cuttings of Sauvignon Blanc and Semillon brought from Château d'Yquem, the most famous château of the Sauternes area of France. This initial choice was a good one, for these grapes took well to the soil and climate, and over the years some fine Livermore Sauvignon Blancs and Semillons have been produced.

Additional varieties, both red and white, have been planted, but the two white Bordeaux varieties remain the most successful. Petite Sirah is also doing well, perhaps reflecting the fact that its native home in France's Rhone Valley is another area of intense summer heat.

Over the years the names of three wineries—Wente Bros., Concannon, and Cresta Blanca—became synonymous with the Livermore Valley. Today the area is rapidly expanding, and the land is of prime value to real estate developers. Cresta Blanca has changed owners and moved to another home, leaving the former two to carry on the tradition. A great number of vines have been replaced by homes, and Wente

Bros. has planted several hundred acres in Monterey County to ensure its future supply of grapes. But Concannon is expanding its own vineyards at the winery, and as sales of and interest in California wines continue to increase, the future of Livermore as a wine-growing region seems secure, at least for the moment.

Concannon Vineyard

Vying for Livermore Valley honors with Wente Bros., Concannon's reputation is founded particularly on its Sauvignon Blanc, Petite Sirah, and Cabernet Sauvignon. While the wine list includes quite a few wines, only six varietals are produced, and this relative concentration on just a few grape varieties has certainly been successful in the case of the three just mentioned. All three are consistently above average, and in a good year they can compete in any company. Concannon's production has remained in the 100,000-gallon range, and there are no present plans to add new varietals.

The rest of the wines are generally not as good, though they have improved considerably from a rather low ebb in the mid-1960s. The limited bottlings occasionally released of certain varietals have been particularly impressive, whether in the very dry Sauvignon Blanc or a very pleasant fortified Muscat de Frontignon.

At the winery itself, located on the outskirts of Livermore and almost across the road from Wente, guided tours are available only during the week. A simple but practical tasting room, however, is open Monday through Saturday, and almost all the wines may be sampled. The current hosts are quite friendly, and some effort is made to assist you in finding the wine you will like, as well as to answer any questions you might have.

White Dinner Wine   Light to medium yellow with a slightly fruity nose, this is a not unpleasant dry, everyday wine of light to moderate body and acid. A bit rough in the after-taste.   (*)

Dry Sauterne (Dry Semillon)   Not as good as the Sauvignon Blanc, but generally a wine of some varietal character. *1970* (*) was not as pleasant as should be expected, but the *1971* has a characteristic earthy-fruity aroma and dry, earthy aftertaste. Body and acid are light to moderate, but the overall impression is a bit sluggish and alcoholic.   (**)

Sauvignon Blanc   Certainly Concannon's best white varietal and often one of the finer examples in California of a dry, earthy Sauvignon Blanc. *1971* is typical: with an earthy aroma, moderate body, and light to moderate acid, it is a dry wine of little finesse but good Sauvignon Blanc character.   (**)

   In exceptional years a *Limited Bottling* Sauvignon Blanc is also available, and the two most recent releases (*1968* and *1971*) have been very fine wines worthy of special recognition. The *1971* has a fresh, spicy-earthy-woody nose and excellent varietal character. Elegant rather than power-ful, it has moderate body and acid and dry, complex flavors. A bit more fruit acidity would make it perfect, but it re-mains one of the best wines of its type currently avail-able.   (***)

Château Concannon   A typical sweet California Sauternes-type wine: fairly light, sugary, and ordinary. *1971* had a slightly green aroma reminiscent of both Semillon and Muscat, but was otherwise undistinguished.   (*)

Chablis   An average wine of light to moderate body and acid and a slightly spicy aroma and taste. Fairly pleasant and dry, from Chenin Blanc, Folle Blanche, and Pinot Blanc grapes.   (*)

Moselle   From Johannisberg Riesling, Sylvaner, and Chenin Blanc grapes, this is a pleasant, off-dry wine that could use more flavor. *1971* is typical, with light to moderate body and acid and a nice flowery aroma, but very neutral taste.   (*)

Johannisberg Riesling   A fairly big, dry Riesling often lacking the finesse and distinctiveness that we feel should characterize this variety. *1971* is a bit heavy and alcoholic, with moderate body and light to moderate acid. Not a bad wine, but overpriced and disappointing.   (BA)

Vin Rosé   Made primarily from Zinfandel grapes, this is a dry wine of fair fruit, just a bit heavier and less distinctive than the Zinfandel Rosé. Still a good wine for the money.   (**)

Zinfandel Rosé   Always very dry, the *1971* has dark-pink color and a pleasant fruity aroma. This is a well-made wine of some character and slight anise flavors, though it could use a bit more fruit.   (**)

Red Dinner Wine   Medium red with light to moderate body, acid, and tannin, some batches of this wine have been bothered by technical faults like sulfur or aldehydes. Other bottlings have been fairly smooth, everyday drinking wines.   (*)

Burgundy   Made from Carignane, Durif, and Grand Noir grapes, the current bottling is quite pleasant and fruity, with light to moderate body, tannin, and acid. A good generic that may even improve with a little bottle age.   (**)

Petite Sirah   Concannon was one of the first wineries to produce this varietal and has been fairly consistently successful with it. *1968* (**) was well balanced, with good fruit and aging potential for about five years. *1969* is similar, though a bit lighter and more tart, with pleasant spicy flavors and good potential.   (**)

Cabernet Sauvignon   Released only as a limited bottling, often a couple of years older than other California Cabernets. In recent years, *1965* was quite good, while *1966* was quite tart and disappointingly thin in flavor. *1967* (**) has a green olive-woody aroma and some potential, though it will probably never develop great depth or complexity. Still, it has good Cabernet character and is much better balanced than the 1966. *1968* is the best since 1965, and its moderate body, acid, and tannin promise better development. The aroma is quite fruity, and the wine should reach its peak in the mid-1970s.   (***)

Wente Bros.

Legend has it that the warm sun, cool nights, gravelly soil, and premium grape varieties of the Livermore Valley blend together to produce some of California's finest white wines, and perhaps the winery most responsible for this idea has been Wente Bros. But the Livermore Valley has not been immune to the advances of tract houses, and Wente now has 500 acres of vines in the Arroyo Seco region of Monterey County as well as the 800 acres remaining in Livermore. The days of the small country winery are clearly in the past and production has now expanded to 600,000 gallons a year.

The excellent reputation enjoyed by Wente's white wines in former times cannot obscure the fact that, while many wines remain good, none could today be called great. The distinctive Dry Semillon has long been a very good wine for the money and the aromatic Blanc de Blancs is still quite nice, but the other whites, even though they often retain good varietal character, have little of the depth or complexity that one expects of a fine wine.

The sulfur problems that plagued Wente's whites for a while

seem to have been generally overcome; now it is the reds that suffer this particular affliction. When first introduced the five reds were light, inoffensive, and sometimes pleasant, but recent vintages have produced tart, thin wines of little or no varietal character or distinction. The prices have remained reasonable, but this cannot excuse inferior wines.

A few Wente wines remain sound, honest wines that may offer a good bargain when compared to the rising prices of other leading California wineries. But the improvement we have looked for in recent years has simply not taken place in many instances; we can only hope that it does lie somewhere in the future.

A well-designed tasting room is open at the winery every day but Sunday, and all varieties are cheerfully served. Tours are also available.

Sauvignon Blanc Generally possessing some varietal character, this has nevertheless been a disappointing, overpriced wine in the past. *1971* produced a better wine, dry, with light to moderate body and acid and the distinctive earthy aftertaste of the Sauvignon Blanc.   (**)

Dry Semillon Often better than the more expensive Sauvignon Blanc, this is a characteristically dry, earthy wine that will probably be appreciated by those who already enjoy the strong flavors of this grape. Both *1970* and *1971* had light to moderate body and acid, light-yellow color, and some fruit. Quite dry.   (**)

Château Semillon A sweet wine that generally retains Semillon character (it also contains some Sauvignon Blanc). The *1969* (**) had a well-balanced fruity taste and light to moderate body and acid. The *1970* was hurt by less acidity and a tinge of sulfur in the aroma, and the overall impression was sugary rather than fruity.   (*)

Chablis Made from Pinot Blanc and Chenin Blanc, this wine has occasionally captured the fruit and freshness of the latter. Generally, however, it is a dry, ordinary white of light to moderate body and acid.   (*)

Pinot Blanc   Never an outstanding wine, this is nevertheless often pleasant, with light to moderate body and acid. Dry with a slightly fruity aroma, the *1970* (**) had some character, while the *1971* was a bit more tart, yet neutral in taste.   (*)

Pinot Chardonnay   In an off-year the Pinot Blanc may well be as good as Wente's Pinot Chardonnay, and rarely is there enough difference to justify the premium price of the latter. The *1970* (**) was one of Wente's best efforts, with a spicy-oak nose, light to medium body and moderate acid. Good varietal character. *1971* is not as good, as both aroma and flavor are a bit weak. Light to moderate body and acid. Overpriced.   (*)

Grey Riesling   Still Wente's best-selling wine, this is at best a soft slightly spicy wine with light to moderate body and acid. Never overabundant in character, its relative blandness will probably appeal more to the novice wine drinker than to those who want a fresher, cleaner wine.   (*)

Johannisberg Riesling Spätlese 1969   Though Wente does not normally produce a Johannisberg, this is a special bottling from their Arroyo Seco vineyards in Monterey County. The grapes were harvested late after having been attacked by some *Botrytis cinerea,* a rare occurrence in California. The resulting wine had a full flowery Riesling nose and well-balanced light to moderate body and acid. Medium sweet, the flavors were pleasant and complex, with some of the lush, oily fruitiness associated with both *Botrytis* and fine German Rieslings.   (***)

Blanc de Blancs   Produced from Chenin Blanc and Ugni Blanc grapes, in the past this has been one of California's most successful medium-sweet wines. Current batches are a bit less rich and fruity, though still quite pleasant. With light to moderate body and moderate acid, both aroma and taste are fresh and clean, with good fruit.   (**)

Rosé Wente From Grenache and Gamay grapes, this is a fresh, dry rosé with well-balanced body and acid. Occasionally a slight sparkle is present. Medium pink in color, with a pleasant, fruity aroma. (**)

Burgundy At this time perhaps Wente's best red. Medium red with a good, spicy nose, the light to moderate body, acid, and tannin are well balanced and the taste clean and pleasant. (**)

Petite Sirah A new wine for Wente, the *1969* had noticeable sulfur in the aroma and taste when first released. This did dissipate with time, leaving a wine of light to moderate body, acid, and tannin with a slightly rough aftertaste. Some spicy Petite Sirah character, but a bit disappointing. (*) The *1970* was released with a sulfurous aroma, but this dissipated, leaving a fruity, woody nose and a young, pleasant wine with some potential. Light to medium in body and acid and moderate tannin.

Gamay Beaujolais Very inconsistent, this wine is always light-bodied and generally quite tart. The *1969* (BA) was rough and slightly gassy, while the *1970* is more pleasant, with better fruit and a smoother finish. (*)

Pinot Noir Consistently a light wine with relatively high acidity, the *1969* follows the Wente pattern. It is simply a light, tart, red wine with no distinguishing characteristics. (BA)

Zinfandel Similar in style to Wente's other reds, the *1968* is a light-bodied, tart wine of little character with a musty, grassy aroma. While not actually unpleasant, it does not reach the standards of the average premium California Zinfandel. (BA)

SANTA CLARA, MONTEREY, AND SAN BENITO

The Santa Clara Valley, about an hour's drive due south of San Francisco, was once a thriving agricultural area that each spring would blossom into a sea of brightly colored fruit trees and vines. The valley is the original home of the two premium wine giants, Paul Masson and Almadén, as well as the site of many small family-run operations. But with the growth of San Jose and the south bay region, suburbia has spread through the land and vineyards and orchards have been uprooted in favor of tract houses. Many of the small wineries in the northern part of the county have closed, while the larger ones have planted vines farther to the south in Monterey and San Benito Counties.

In the hills and mountains that border the west side of the valley a few wineries remain, and some new acreage of vines may even be found. Ridge, Martin Ray, and the Novitiate of Los Gatos are above the activity of the valley below, and are reminders of the pastoral peacefulness that once was there.

Southern Santa Clara still includes considerable vineyard acreage, and while the climate here is somewhat warmer than that a few miles to the north, some good varietals are produced. Several small wineries are nestled around the towns of Morgan Hill and Gilroy, and the roadside tasting room and winery of San Martin is a familiar sight to travelers. To the east of Gilroy, in the Hecker Pass region, may be found a number of small wineries, many of which specialize in jugs of country red, white, and rosé. The countryside here is typically Californian, with rolling golden hills studded with oak trees, and both the scenery and friendliness of the wineries makes this a worthwhile area to visit.

When it became obvious that land valuation and taxation was rendering the Santa Clara Valley unsuitable as an agricultural area, the wineries looked elsewhere for land. Guided by research of the Department of Enology and Viticulture of the University of California at Davis, vintners discovered several valleys in Monterey and San Benito Counties, where the proximity of the sea and the funneling of cool air between the mountains produced the temperatures necessary to grow premium varietals. The land is fairly dry, but the need for water can be met by sprinkler irrigation.

Almadén made the move first, planting several thousand acres near Hollister and Paicines, in a valley bounded by the Santa Cruz and Gavilan ranges of the Coast Mountains. Paul Masson and Mirassou planted their vineyards in the Salinas Valley, near Soledad, and Livermore's Wente Bros. planted vines a little further south in the Arroyo Seco area. By 1972 almost 10,000 acres had been planted in Monterey County and nearly 5000 in San Benito County. Practically every premium varietal is in evidence, and in years to come this new viticultural district will be supplying a good proportion of America's premium table wines.

The young vines are prospering, and to date some excellent wine has been made from the new plantings. The whites have been most successful, particularly the Rieslings, Traminers, and Chenin Blancs. The reds have done less well, and a pronounced green-vegetable character is noticeable in some of the Monterey wines. However it is much too early to draw any firm conclusions about the success, or lack thereof, of individual varieties, for as the vines mature certain types will undoubtedly develop better than others. Hopefully future plantings will concentrate on these successful varieties rather than continuing the present practice of planting a few hundred acres of almost everything.

Almadén Vineyards

California's largest producer of premium wines is Almadén Vineyards. Originally located in Los Gatos in the heart of the Santa Clara Valley, Almadén has been forced by urban sprawl to expand its operations to other areas and now has over 8000 acres of vineyards in Alameda, San Benito, Monterey, and Santa Clara Counties. Over half of these are in the Gavilan mountain range in San Benito, which Almadén claims comprise the largest single planting of premium wine grapes in the world. A full line of table, dessert, and sparkling wines is produced, and all are widely available throughout America.

Almadén's white wines continue to show fairly good varietal character, although in recent tastings they seem to have slipped a bit from previous years. The Gewürztraminer, Pinot Chardonnay, and Johannisberg Riesling remain the most successful, though the latter could use more character and complexity. The recently introduced Blanc Fumé (another name for Sauvignon Blanc) is also good, though it seems somewhat redundant to continue to offer a Sauvignon Blanc and a Dry Semillon Sauterne since the three wines are similar in style. While many of Almadén's wines are varietally distinguishable, putting more emphasis on fewer wines might improve both quality and distinctiveness.

The Grenache Rosé was the first commercially successful American rosé, and it continues to be one of the largest-selling California varietal wines. While not unpleasant, its high sales are probably due more to wide distribution, advertising, and the rosé-goes-with-anything syndrome than to any inherent excellence.

The reds are distinctly disappointing and generally offer nothing that cannot be found behind a whole host of other California labels at similar prices. They are relatively light-bodied and possess little varietal character, and some are even unpleasant.

A few selected Almadén wines are estate-bottled and given a vintage date, although those we have tasted have not been significantly better than the regular nonvintaged varietals. In any case, distribution of these wines is presently fairly limited, and the vast bulk of Almadén wines continue to be of the nonvintaged variety. While we have noticed a few marked variations, these nonvintaged blends are generally consistent from one year to the next.

Almadén's home winery in Los Gatos is now open to visitors only by special arrangement. Reflecting the southward expansion of the winery, a delightful tasting room is now located on the village plaza of the mission town of San Juan Bautista.

Blanc Fumé Light to medium yellow with a distinctive, earthy-woody aroma, this has the dry, earthy taste associated with the Sauvignon Blanc grape. Light to moderate body, moderate acidity, and good character, though more for the connoisseur of forceful wines than for the novice. (**)

Sauvignon Blanc Less successful in all departments than the Blanc Fumé, this is a lighter wine with at best average varietal character and little to recommend it. Off-dry. (*)

Dry Semillon Sauterne The third of Almadén's Sauterne types has a good earthy aroma, but is rather weak in flavor. Light to moderate in body and acid, it has a touch of sweetness despite its "dry" nomenclature. (*)

Chablis A dry wine with light-yellow color and a light vinous aroma. Tart, ordinary, but not unpleasant. (*)

Pinot Blanc This is a pleasant wine of light to moderate

body and moderate acidity. The nose is slightly spicy and the flavors good, though the finish is just a bit rough. (*)

Pinot Chardonnay Light to medium yellow with a good, spicy, slightly oaky nose and good flavors. Light to moderate body and moderate acid leave this a somewhat tart wine, simple but with good varietal character. (**)

Sylvaner At best an ordinary wine, with light to moderate body and acid, a light vinous aroma, and neutral taste. Dry. (*)

Johannisberg Riesling Although this has traditionally been one of Almadén's finer whites, with a nice flowery Riesling nose and a light, fruity flavor, the most recent sample we tried was disappointing with little varietal character. Hopefully this is a temporary lapse, and the wine will return to its former performance. (**)

Gewürztraminer Light to medium yellow with a distinctive, spicy-fruity aroma. Light to moderate in body and acidity, this is a wine with a touch of sweetness that is soft rather than fresh and crisp. Good varietal character, could use more fruit. (**)

Chenin Blanc Light to medium yellow with a soft, slightly grassy nose, less pleasant than previous bottlings. Light to moderate body and acid, but sluggish rather than fresh and fruity. Off-dry. (*)

Grenache Rosé Medium pink-orange with a characteristic, fruity aroma. Dry, with light to moderate body and acid, this is a pleasant wine, but it could use more fruit and character. (*)

Mountain Nectar Vin Rosé Light-orange color with a Grenachelike aroma. Medium sweet, with light to medium body and acidity. A bit of harshness to the finish. (*)

Burgundy Light to medium red with a pleasant aroma, light to moderate body, and moderate acid and tannin. A bit rough, though not bad for a generic, better than the Chianti. (*)

Gamay Beaujolais   Over the past few years this wine has varied from disappointing to very pleasant and fruity. The most recent batch has a nice, typical Beaujolais-style aroma, light body, and light to moderate tannin and acid. The aftertaste could be fresher and cleaner. (*)

Pinot Noir   Light to medium red with a slight vegetable nose and taste. Light to moderate body, acid, and tannin. A consensus last place in two days of comparative Pinot Noir tastings. (BA)

Cabernet Sauvignon   Very disappointing in years past, this wine has improved but still has a way to go to equal the better California Cabernets. The aroma is nice, with evidence of varietal character and a slight woody bouquet. Quite light in body, with light to medium tannin and moderate acidity. The flavor is weak and disappointing. (*)

Zinfandel   This is a rather thin, tart wine with a very neutral taste that captures neither the fruit nor the character of many other California Zinfandels. No technical flaws, but not up to the average California standard. (BA)

Chianti   Light red with a vinous nose, this is a light, tart wine of ordinary character. (*)

Grenoir Original   First released in 1972, this is a slightly sweet, light-colored red made primarily from Grenache grapes. Light to medium in body and acid with very little tannin, its mellow finish will be enjoyed most by those who don't really like red wines. (*)

Llords & Elwood Winery

Though a winery will be completed in the Napa Valley sometime in the mid-1970s, at the present time the vast majority of Llords & Elwood wines are purchased in bulk from other wineries and then finished and aged in cellars in the San Jose area. It is this aging and blending that gives the wines their character, for Mike Elwood and his son Richard have succeeded in imparting a distinctive style to the five varietals they produce.

The first Llords & Elwood table wines appeared on the market in the early 1960s, following their very successful dessert wines, and their circle of admirers has gradually grown since then. Certainly the dedication to the production of quality wines is evident, and on the whole Llords & Elwood remains well above the California average. While our most recent tastings have resulted in a slight fall for some of the varietals, this reflects the increasing level of competition in California as well as what might have been a disappointing *cuvée* or two in recent years.

Llords & Elwood wines are not vintaged, but are identified by a *cuvée* number as well as the date of bottling. Approximately one *cuvée* is produced per year, and they are assigned in ascending order (thus *Cuvée PN 7* is an older wine than *Cuvée PN 8*).

Chardonnay   Past *cuvées* of this wine have been disappointing compared to the other Llords & Elwood wines. The recent *Cuvée 5* was available for a short period of time but was then withdrawn from the market when the winery discovered a minor technical flaw.

Johannisberg Riesling   Generally medium-sweet wines of lush, full character rather than being fresh or tart, some may find the Johannisbergs a bit sluggish and heavy. *Cuvée JR 4* (*) was particularly disappointing, but *JR 5* (**) has a pleasant, cinnamon character that is closer to the full-flavored wines of the past.

Rosé of Cabernet   This is a big, fruity wine that retains some Cabernet character along with noticeable sweetness in the taste. *Cuvée R 6* is a bit heavy, with moderate body and acidity, but it is well balanced and has distinctive fruit. (**)

Pinot Noir This is the most consistently successful of the Llords & Elwood wines, though its deep fruity character is quite different from many other Pinot Noirs. The distinctive aroma is rich, almost portlike, and the moderate body, acidity, and low to moderate tannin combine to leave a smooth, round wine of distinctive character. *Cuvée PN 7* would rate only a "good" as it is a bit lacking in complexity and depth, but the current *PN 8* returns to form as a soft, fruity, almost "sweet" wine that most wine drinkers will find quite pleasant. (***)

Cabernet Sauvignon Softer and fruitier than many California Cabernets, at its best this is an elegant wine with soft, complex flavors. Recently *Cuvée CS 5* (*) was surprisingly thin and simple, compared to earlier releases, while *Cuvée CS 6* (***) has an intriguing chocolate-mint nose, light to moderate body, and moderate acidity and tannin. Less smooth than previous *cuvées,* it has more potential and should become an elegant wine in the late 1970s.

Mirassou Vineyards

The name of Mirassou has been familiar to California vintners since the winery was founded in 1854, but it was only in the 1960s that the fifth generation of Mirassous has decided to offer their label to the general public. Their large bulk wine business continues, but production of the premium wines has greatly increased in the past few years. Mirassou now has over 1400 acres of vineyards, 300 in the Santa Clara foothills, a small planting near Gilroy, and approximately 1000 acres in Monterey County. The latter vineyards were planted only in 1961 and, while the winery will remain in San Jose, wines from Monterey are handled separately and awarded the *Monterey* appellation. Those wines from both areas are denominated *Monterey-Santa Clara* rather than the usual *California* employed by most wineries when their grapes are from more than one county.

In addition to being one of the pioneers in the Monterey area, Mirassou was one of the first wineries to employ mechanical harvesting and field crushing on a regular basis. The goal of these new techniques is to protect the grape from oxidation as much as possible; thus the freshly picked grapes are immediately crushed and stored under an inert blanket of nitrogen before making their journey to the Santa Clara winery to complete fermentation. The resulting wine should ideally capture all the freshness and fruit of the grape, and the 1970 Chenin Blanc is certainly an excellent example of the potential for such modern methods.

While in the past we found many Mirassou wines well above average for California, recent vintages have been much more uneven, perhaps reflecting the continued expansion that Mirassou has been undergoing. While most Mirassou wines still exhibit good varietal character, there is quite a bit of variation from year to year, and today it is difficult to generalize about their quality. When at their best the wines are clean, fresh, and fruity, and they offer good examples of wines that are both very fine and distinctly Californian. They may also be quite disappointing, however. Many of the 1969 reds, for example, had a strong asparagus-vegetable aroma that we found very unpleasant.

Since 1966, several Monterey County wines have been separately designated as *Harvest* or *Limited Bottlings,* and the number of each successive harvest appears on the label. Often fuller wines with more oak character and longer aging potential, these wines do not seem afflicted by the inconsistency of the regular line, although variations do of course exist among vintages. The Chardonnay in particular has been quite successful, and the 1969 Dedication Pinot Noir is surprisingly distinctive.

The Mirassou tasting room is a very pleasant place where nearly all Mirassou wines may be sampled. Visitors are always greeted warmly and your hosts are ready to engage in serious or not so serious conversation with connoisseur and novice alike. Sales pressure is practically nonexistent, and on the whole Mirassou remains one of the most enjoyable and relaxing wineries in California to visit.

Chablis   Generally a good, clean generic made from Pinot Blanc and French Colombard grapes. The *1970* (**) is dry, with light to moderate body and moderate acid. *1971* is one of the rare disappointments, with a curious, spicy aroma and rather unpleasant taste.   (BA)

White Burgundy   With the 1971 vintage, this wine has replaced the varietally labeled Pinot Blanc. It is now made from this grape and Sauvignon Blanc. The *1970 Pinot Blanc* (**) was a dry, crisp wine with a good fruity aroma and some character. The *1971 White Burgundy* is a bit fuller-bodied and has a touch of oak character from the three months it spent in Limousin barrels. Dry, well balanced, and with good fruit.   (***)

Pinot Chardonnay   Generally a good wine, fairly light but with some Chardonnay character. The *1969* was unfortunately marred by sulfur when first released, but later tastings left a better impression. Light to moderate in body with moderate acidity, some apple character, but not one of Mirassou's more successful vintages.   (*)

Monterey Riesling   Now produced primarily from Monterey Sylvaner grapes, this has replaced the regular Sylvaner. The *1971* is fairly dry, with good fruit, light to moderate body and acid and a fresh aroma. Probably best while it's still young and refreshing.   (**)

Johannisberg Riesling   Though previous years have been a

bit more distinctive, both *1970* and *1971* were fairly ordinary. Off-dry and light to moderate in body and acid,
the wines are not unpleasant but do not have the character
that you should expect from this premium varietal.   (*)

Chenin Blanc   One of Mirassou's most successful whites,
fresh, fruity, and noticeably sweet. The *1970* (****) is a
California classic, both because it is a very fine wine and
also because it was the first machine-harvested and field-
crushed wine marketed. Very well balanced, the wine has
excellent varietal character and good body and acid to keep
the sweetness from being cloying. Elegant and great for
drinking all by itself. The *1971* is definitely less successful,
though it is still a pleasant wine, medium sweet, with light
to moderate body and moderate to high acid.   (**)

Petite Rosé   From Petite Sirah and Grenache grapes, this
was a delightful wine when it appeared in 1968. Recent
vintages seem to have slipped a bit, though hopefully this
is just temporary. The *1970* (**) was medium pink with a
sweet-fruity nose, though it is dry and crisp on the palate.
Good fruit and freshness. *1971* lacks fruit and had some
off-odors, though the taste is not unpleasant.   (*)

Burgundy   The former system of "cask" bottlings has been
replaced by vintaged Burgundies which are primarily Petite
Sirah, with some Zinfandel and Gamay Beaujolais. The
1968 (**) is quite pleasant, with light to moderate body
and tannin and moderate acidity. Will age for a few years,
but good when young. *1969* was similar, with a touch of
oak in the nose and a bit more depth of flavors. Well above
average and with a mature taste, it will last for several
years.   (***)

Petite Sirah   Generally quite fruity and often with some aging
potential. The *1968* (**) was typical, with light to moderate body and acid and moderate tannin. The almost sweet
fruit flavor is pleasant, and it will improve for three to five

years. The *1969* is an unwelcome departure from earlier vintages, as it could use more acid and is bothered by a very unpleasant asparagus-vegetable aroma. (BA)

Gamay Beaujolais The best are well-balanced, light, fruity wines in the French Beaujolais style that can be very pleasant, but the *1969* (*) is high in acid and the wine is sharp rather than tart and fruity. *1970* smells like it is straight from the fermenting tank, though its light, tart, strawberry-like character will probably not appeal to everyone. Better balanced than the 1969, but still tart.   (**)

Cabernet Sauvignon Vintages over the past decade have ranged from excellent to below average, so it is difficult to make any general comments. *1964* was superb, and no other year has touched it yet. The *1968* (**) has light to moderate body, acid, and tannin and a pronounced oaky nose. Not great, but with fair fruit and some room for future development. The *1969* has the same strong asparagus aroma that characterized the Petite Sirah, and to our tastes it is an unpleasant wine. (BA)

Zinfandel Fairly consistent, with a pleasant fruity varietal aroma. The *1968* (**) is medium red, with light to moderate body and moderate acid and tannin. More aging potential than other vintages, but pleasant when young. The *1969* is lighter and higher in acid with a slight grassy character in aroma and taste.   (*)

Harvest Selections

Gewürztraminer Fairly consistent and possessing the characteristic fruity-spicy aroma of the grape. Both *1970* (**) and *1971* (***) have just a hint of sweetness, though the finish is dry. The 1970 has light to moderate body and moderate acid, while the 1971 is a bit softer. Not outstanding, but wines of good character.

Pinot Chardonnay Quite successful, with the spicy character of Limousin oak. Generally needs two to three years' bottle age to round out and develop complexity. The *1969* (***) is the best recently, with complex flavors, good acidity, and strong Chardonnay character. *1970* (**) was aged longer in oak but doesn't quite have the complexity and balance of the 1969. *1971* has a spicy-oaky nose, light to moderate body and acidity, and should develop into a fruity, elegant wine.　(***)

Pinot Noir　The first harvest in *1966* was a wine of good varietal character and some richness in taste, though it does not match the complexity of the Cabernets. *1967* (*) was less good and shows signs of premature aging in both color and nose. Not unpleasant but very simple. No *1968* was produced, and in *1969* a special bottling was dedicated to wine maker Max Huebner. This is a fine wine, well above average for California Pinot Noirs. Elegant rather than big, it has a spicy aroma and fairly soft flavors. The body is moderate, but both tannin and acid are low enough to leave a round, subtle wine that probably needs only two to four years to mature.　(***)

Cabernet Sauvignon　Characterized by a distinctive bell-pepper aroma, the Harvest Cabernets have been consistently better than the regular bottlings. The *1966* has only light to moderate body but very full flavors, while the *1967* (***) is bigger, with moderate body, tannin, and acid and strong green-pepper flavors. *1968* has produced perhaps the best balanced wine, with a complex coconut-pepper-oak nose and good aging potential. Elegant rather than powerful, but still with good body and tannin. All three wines should improve for seven to ten years.　(***)

Zinfandel　Bigger than the regular Zinfandels and aged in four-hundred-gallon American oak casks. The *1966* (**) has fairly complex flavors but only light to moderate body, tannin, and acid, which probably reflects the youth of the vines. Good fruity nose and some potential. The *1967* has more of everything and should be a better wine in time.

Well balanced, with a very nice minty-spicy nose and good varietal character.   (***)

Paul Masson Vineyards

One of the largest of California's premium wineries, Paul Masson offers a prime example of the application of modern American technology to the age-old art of wine making. Fermenting is done in temperature-controlled stainless steel. Red wines receive about three years of age in huge 6000- to 24,000-gallon redwood tanks, and then an additional six months to a year in fifty-gallon recured whiskey barrels of American oak. Most whites never see a wood cask and are held in glass-lined tanks until bottling. Everywhere, the Masson working motto, "Wine is food, think sanitation," is practiced. While this may well be a scene more for an engineer than for a romanticist, it is one way to provide the public with the large quantities of wine demanded in today's market.

Faced with the inevitable urban metastasis throughout the once beautiful Santa Clara Valley, Paul Masson turned its eyes southward in the 1960s to Monterey County in search of new land. The result is the Pinnacles Vineyard near Soledad, where thousands of acres of grapes have been planted. A new winery is also in operation for the crushing, fermenting, and initial storage of Masson wines. All bottling is still done at the Saratoga Champagne Cellars, however, and the wines are transported there in special tank trucks.

Paul Masson wines do not have the individuality or finesse of many of California's better varietals, though they probably typify the average California wine available throughout the country. The whites are generally innocuous, and it is sometimes difficult to tell one from the other even though the labels are different. The slightly sweet Emerald Dry has been the most consistent, with the Rhine Castle and Chenin Blanc also occasionally achieving some distinction. The reds often have more character but less consistency; in particular, some are well aged and smooth while other batches might be young and rough. The Cabernet Sauvignon is never great but almost always good, while the other varieties vary greatly. Especially disappointing has been the decline of the inexpensive Baroque in recent months.

In 1972 Masson introduced five apparently specially selected varietals from the Pinnacles Vineyard. We tasted these wines several times in blind tastings, and they were uniformly disappointing. The whites in particular had an off-character and frequently were less pleasant than the regular bottlings. None of the varietals were distinctive enough to command their higher prices, and we seriously question the introduction of these wines at their present low level of quality. The wines are not vintaged, but the first number of the *cuvée* number designates the year in which the blend was created.

Masson has been a pioneer in the use of proprietary names, such as Rubion or Baroque, a practice which we would certainly encourage. Most of these wines are of average or better quality, and some fine blends have been created in the past.

Three wineries are operated by Paul Masson, although the Champagne Cellars at Saratoga is the only one open to the public. Slide-illustrated tours and a complete and modern tasting room are well done, but unfortunately the formerly unlimited tasting has now been replaced by a representative sample of wines. The original winery (founded by Paul Masson himself) high up in the Santa Cruz Mountains is open to those who subscribe to the classical and jazz concerts offered on summer weekends. Here you may enjoy some fine music and have a breathtaking view (smog permitting) of the Santa Clara Valley below.

Dry Sauterne   Light yellow with a fresh, dry aroma, this is an off-dry wine of light to moderate body and acid. Slightly rough aftertaste.   (*)

Chablis   Pale yellow with a faint vinous aroma, this is a soft wine of light to moderate body and acid. Little character, but with some fruit, and the price is right.   (**)

Pinot Blanc   Light yellow with a light fruity aroma, this is a fairly soft, simple wine with a slightly spicy taste. Light to moderate in body and acid, it could use more fruit.   (*)

Pinot Chardonnay   Light yellow with a light, slightly fruity aroma. This is a pleasant, fairly tart wine with light to moderate body and moderate acidity, but the taste is quite simple and does not exhibit great Chardonnay character.   (*)

Rhine   Never very good, the most recent batch had strong sulfur in the nose and weak, watery flavors. Off-dry, with light body and acid.   (BA)

Rhine Castle   Light yellow with a flowery Muscatlike fragrance, this is quite a sweet wine that is a bit sugary due to inadequate acidity. Flavors are quite fruity, and many novice wine drinkers will enjoy it.   (*)

Emerald Dry   Light yellow with a pleasant, slightly spicy nose, this is a very drinkable, light, tart wine. Slightly sweet with a touch of *pétillance* and clean finish.   (**)

Riesling   Light to medium yellow with a slightly fruity, slightly vegetable nose. Off-dry and fairly soft, with light to moderate body and acidity.   (*)

Johannisberg Riesling   This wine is very similar to the Masson Riesling: light to moderate in body and acid, the taste is fairly soft and ordinary, the aroma slightly fruity. Dry.   (*)

Chenin Blanc   A new wine from Masson, the Chenin Blanc has some varietal character but rather ordinary flavors. Slightly sweet with light to moderate body, moderate acid, and a slight grapefruit-citrus nose.   (*)

Vin Rosé Sec   Dry and ordinary, this is a light, slightly tart wine with a fruity-citrus aroma. Clean, with some fruit.   (*)

Pink   A pleasant, sweet apricot-Muscat aroma introduces this medium-sweet wine. With fairly light body and acid and a slight *pétillance,* this is a pleasant wine, unfortunately lacking in flavors. Very drinkable, for those who prefer a medium-sweet rosé.   (*)

Burgundy   A rather thin wine with a musty-vegetable character in the aroma. While drinkable, not one of California's better generics.   (*)

Gamay Beaujolais   In the high average or good category, this is a fairly light, tart wine with good fruit and a fresh taste. Characteristically fruity aroma, simple but pleasant.   (**)

Pinot Noir   A fairly fruity wine of light to moderate body and tannin and moderate acid. Tart, not unpleasant, but with very little Pinot Noir character.   (*)

Cabernet Sauvignon   While there have been several variations over the past few years, this is generally a wine of medium red color with an herbaceous, woody Cabernet aroma and light to moderate body, acid, and tannin. Simple but with noticeable Cabernet character, this can be counted on for a good, honest wine that may improve for a year or two in the bottle.   (**)

Baroque   When first released this was a well-balanced, fairly fruity wine of good character, but recent batches have been disappointing. It is now a light, tart, simple wine with no faults, but none of the interest or complexity of earlier blends. Gamaylike in style.   (*)

Rubion   Light-medium red in color with a fresh, fruity aroma. Light-bodied with low tannin, the acidity is light to moderate and leaves a tart, strawberry-tasting wine in the style of some light California Zinfandels or Gamays.   (*)

Pinnacles Selection Wines

Pinot Blanc Cuvée 992   Light to moderate in body and acid, this is an ordinary wine rendered unpleasant by a skunky-grassy character that permeates both aroma and taste. (BA)

Pinot Chardonnay Cuvée 951 At best an ordinary wine and certainly disappointing for a premium Chardonnay, this one finished last in two separate Chardonnay tastings. Light to moderate in body and acid, it also has some of the grassy character of the Pinot Blanc. (BA)

Johannisberg Riesling Cuvée 972 This is a dry, crisp wine with light to moderate body and moderate acid. The slightly flowery aroma does not possess the overwhelming grassy character of the other Pinnacles whites, but the wine is rather neutral in flavor and overpriced. (*)

Pinot Noir Cuvée 824 Currently the best of the Pinnacles wines, this *cuvée* has a definite aged character and some complexity. The soft, rich aroma and taste may actually be a bit oxidized, but the wine retains good fruit and has a soft, round finish. Light to moderate body and tannin, moderate acid, and good Pinot Noir character. (**)

Cabernet Sauvignon The first *cuvée, 843,* had an interesting fruity nose and some character, but it was a bit tart and unbalanced. *Cuvée 942* was fairly light and thin in flavor, though it does exhibit Cabernet character. Still, both are disappointing and lacking distinction. (*)

San Martin Winery

San Martin is well known to highway travelers between San Francisco and Los Angeles, as roadside signs for miles around beckon the passing motorist to stop and taste some wine at the winery's home in San Martin, just south of San Jose. Similar tasting rooms have been opened in San Jose, Monterey, and Gilroy, and these are responsible for a sizable proportion of

San Martin's sales. A family-owned winery since 1892, San Martin recently reached an agreement with the Houston-based Southdown Land Company to form a new corporation. Southdown will contribute 1650 acres of newly planted vineyards to add to the 1000 acres remaining in the hands of the Felice family.

As might be expected from a winery producing just under fifty table, dessert, sparkling, fruit, and berry wines of every description, the quality of the table wines is a bit inconsistent. The fairly sweet Malvasia Bianca and the Cabernet Sauvignon remain the most consistent wines, while the others have bounced around from below average to good in the past few years. Most remain near-average, though varietal character is often weak, and the wines' appeal lies in their drinkability rather than their distinctiveness.

While it might be fun to stop by and sip a little wine in the course of your journey, the surroundings at the San Martin tasting rooms are not conducive to any serious wine tasting. Visitors are ushered in groups every fifteen minutes or so to the tasting bar, where their glasses are rapidly filled and refilled with about ten different wines to the accompaniment of a nonstop spiel by the "host." The samples poured are very small and are served in appropriately tiny plastic wineglasses. While the self-created influx of tourists may justify these mass-oriented techniques, the rapidity with which the wines are served coupled with the inadequate samples offered make it impossible to attempt an evaluation of the wines based only on your ten-minute visit.

Hostess Semillon   A medium-sweet wine with a fruity-vanilla bean aroma that is soft and drinkable, but with only minimal Semillon character. Light to moderate in body and a bit low in acid.   (*)

Chablis   A pale, dry wine of light to moderate body and acid. Not unpleasant, but very neutral in taste with a merely vinous aroma.   (*)

Pinot Chardonnay   Medium yellow with a nice spicy-oak aroma and good varietal character, but unfortunately the taste is very ordinary and lacks depth. Light to moderate body and acid and lacking in fruit.   (*)

Rhine Wine   Though formerly fairly pleasant, the most recent bottle tasted had a harsh alcoholic aroma and dull, oxidized taste. Slightly sweet, with light body and acid.   (BA)

Hostess Emerald Riesling   Pale in color, this is a medium-sweet wine of light to moderate body and acid. The most recent bottling was ordinary and a bit rough, not as fresh-tasting as some previous batches.   (*)

Sylvaner   A rather strong alcoholic aroma and taste leave this a heavy, dull wine rather than a fresh, fruity one. Dry and a bit flat.   (BA)

Malvasia Bianca   A medium-sweet wine with the flowery orange-blossom aroma typical of the Muscat family of grapes. One of San Martin's most popular wines, it has good acid and good fruit to balance its sweetness, though some may still find it too perfumed or flowery. If you want a wine in the sweet style, this one's probably worth a try.   (**)

Vin Rosé   A medium-sweet rosé with a strawberry jam-citrus aroma and taste. Light to moderate in body and acid, but with a rough aftertaste and rather heavy, dull flavors.   (BA)

Grenache Rosé   An almost tasteless rosé, dry, with only slight Grenache character in the aroma. With light body and light to moderate acid, it is at best ordinary but has no technical faults.   (*)

Burgundy   A well-balanced wine of light to moderate body, tannin, and acid. Medium red in color with a pleasant, fruity, slightly woody aroma. While not great, this is a fairly good generic with a clean, fruity taste. May improve with a year or two of bottle age.   (**)

Hostess Burgundy   A very soft red wine with just a touch of sweetness. The light to moderate body and tannin and moderate acidity are fairly well balanced, and this wine may appeal to those who find many reds too astringent. Could use more fruit and flavor.   (*)

Gamay Beaujolais   Light red with a strawberry-redwood nose, this is a tart, woody wine of light body that does not have the pleasant freshness that is typical of this variety. Unbalanced and rough.   (BA)

Pinot Noir   A medium-red wine usually of some age that has a pleasant minty-berrylike aroma. With light to moderate body, acid, and tannin and soft flavors, it is not a great wine but is certainly as successful as many more expensive California Pinot Noirs.   (**)

Cabernet Ruby   Medium red with a slightly fruity-weedy aroma, this is an ordinary wine of light to medium body and moderate tannin and acid. The most recent sample tasted had a rather rough woody aftertaste and neutral flavors.   (*)

Cabernet Sauvignon   A wine of good varietal character with a minty-woody nose and light to moderate body, tannin, and acid. Though nonvintaged, this wine could generally use a couple of years more of bottle age to round out the flavors, which are good, though fairly simple.   (**)

Zinfandel   A fairly light, slightly woody-fruity wine with some varietal character. Tart and simple, though not unpleasant.   (*)

Chianti   A very light wine that fades rather quickly in the mouth. The most recent batch has some fruit and none of the flaws of prior bottlings.   (*)

Grignolino   Light red with a fruity-redwood aroma, light body, and noticeable tannin and acid. A bit unbalanced, with tart, slightly woody flavors.   (*)

Weibel Champagne Vineyards

Weibel is a fairly large winery currently producing about a million gallons annually of table, dessert, and sparkling wines. Presently located in Mission San Jose, the table-wine operations are gradually being transferred to a new plant in Mendocino, though sparkling wines will probably continue to be made at the Mission San Jose winery. Most of Weibel's grapes are now grown in the Mendocino region, so the move to Ukiah should not have any major impact on the style of Weibel's wines, although newer and more efficient equipment may of course lead to improvements in quality. The Ukiah winery won't be in full operation until 1975, but already many wines are being made there and a tasting room was opened in 1973.

Weibel's table wines are far from outstanding, but, with the exception of the Zinfandel and disappointing Pinot Chardonnays in 1968 and 1969, they are generally on a par with those of other large California wineries. The whites are on the light side and, while the flavors may be somewhat neutral, they are rarely unpleasant. The reds are often fairly tart, with some varietal character.

Two estate-bottled wines have recently supplemented the Weibel line, a Pinot Noir and a Pinot Chardonnay. These are made from grapes on the hundred acres surrounding the Mission San Jose winery and naturally command a higher price than the corresponding nonvintaged varietals. While the Pinot Noir in particular has been pleasant, the estate-bottled wines are often not really any better than the regular ones, and they are generally similar in style.

The Mission San Jose tasting room is surrounded by a very nice wine garden, and in fine weather it is quite a pleasant place to visit. All varieties except the estate-bottled wines may be sampled, and the hosts are generally quite friendly if not overly knowledgeable.

Sauterne   Fairly light in color with a vinous aroma, this is a slightly sweet wine of light body and acidity. Clean and not unpleasant, but with little character.   (*)

Chablis   A fairly dry, tart wine of little interest, though it is not unpleasant. Light to moderate in body, with a slightly rough aftertaste.   (*)

Pinot Chardonnay   A pleasant spicy-peachy aroma introduces this good, though not great, Chardonnay. Light to moderate in body and acid, it has good character and some depth.   (**)

Pinot Chardonnay (*estate-bottled*)   Since its introduction in 1967 this wine has not been terribly successful. The *1968* (BA) is a neutral wine of little Chardonnay character, light body and sharp taste. The *1969* has a slightly sulfurous aroma, which will dissipate, and slightly more flavor than the 1968. Dry, with light to moderate body and acidity, though without distinction.   (*)

Rhine Wine   Dry with light to moderate body and acid, this is an ordinary wine with a slightly rough finish. Pleasant, slightly flowery nose but low on flavor.   (*)

Johannisberg Riesling   Light to medium yellow with a fresh, fruity aroma, light to medium body and acid, and slight sweetness. While not complex, this is a very pleasant, agreeable wine with adequate fruit.   (**)

Grey Riesling   Generally a clean-tasting dry wine with some spiciness. Light yellow in color with light to moderate body and acid and a fairly fruity aroma.   (**)

Chenin Blanc   This is a medium-sweet wine with a fresh fruity aroma, but it seems a bit unbalanced and is quite simple. Light to moderate acid and body; not unpleasant but ordinary.   (*)

Green Hungarian   A medium-sweet wine with a light, slightly yeasty aroma, this is Weibel's best-selling varietal. Light to moderate in body with moderate acid, the wine is fruity but basically neutral in flavor. A pleasant wine that will probably be appreciated by those who like sweet wines with unusual names.   (**)

Vin Rosé   A medium-sweet wine with some Grenache character in aroma and taste; light to moderate in body and acid. Quite drinkable, but might become fatiguing after a glass or two.   (*)

Grenache Rosé   A dry rosé of light body and light to moderate acidity. Pleasant fruity aroma and ordinary taste.   (*)

Burgundy   Past bottlings have been unpleasantly sharp, but the most recent batch tasted had better balance, with light to moderate body, tannin, and acid. Ordinary flavors.   (*)

Pinot Noir   Weibel has done well with this grape in the past, producing a fairly distinctive wine with fruity-woody character that often needs a couple of years of bottle age. The most recent batch, however, was rather ordinary, with light to moderate body and tannin and moderate acidity. Not unpleasant, but simple.   (*)

Pinot Noir (*estate-bottled*)   Generally a bit fuller than the nonvintage Pinot Noir, though not always a better wine for the money. The *1966* (**) was a nice wine, with moderate body, tannin, and acid and fairly strong Pinot Noir character. *1967* was not as successful; lighter in style and a bit tart, it had some Pinot Noir distinctiveness but no complexity or potential.   (*)

Gamay Beaujolais   A very fruity wine that has a tendency to be unbalanced, with too much tannin and acid for the light body. Perhaps age will help, though for now the wine's fruit is lost and the aftertaste is a bit rough rather than clean and refreshing.   (*)

Claret   A fairly light wine with little tannin, a fruity aroma, and a simple smooth taste. Not unpleasant.   (*)

Cabernet Sauvignon　Light to medium red with a slightly fruity nose, this is a rather thin wine that is weak in Cabernet character. Light to moderate in body and tannin with moderate acidity, the taste is just a bit sharp, although the overall impression is not unpleasant.　(*)

Zinfandel　Medium red with an unpleasant musty, vegetable nose, this is a tart wine of little character and no potential. Slight grassy taste.　(BA)

Royalty　At its best this is a fairly deep, fruity wine whose soft character is imparted by just a touch of sweetness. Made from the Royalty grape, one of the few varieties with red pulp, the wine has dark color, moderate body, and quite low tannin. The most recent sample tasted did not have the deep fruit of previous bottlings; the taste was ordinary and lacked distinctiveness.　(*)

Summary List of Wines

The following lists are composites of the rankings already as-signed to the various wines in Part Two. They do not include some of the "specialty" wines, but we have attempted to list all of the major wine types produced by most California wineries.

While these summaries have been prepared to aid you in selecting a new wine, we cannot overemphasize the fact that they should not be overused. Many different kinds of wines may be found under the same varietal label or in the same group, and you should always refer to the detailed descriptions in Part Two before making a final choice.

Noticeable differences do exist among wines of the same type; however, it is very difficult to compare wines of different varieties, for there are many variables that prevent every "good" wine from being better than every "average" one. First, of course, is wine type: an "average" Chardonnay may well be more successful than a "good" Chablis, while a "very good" Burgundy may be no better than a "good" Cabernet. Price is also an important factor. You have a right to expect a $5 wine to be better than one that sells for $1.79; if they are pretty much the same, then the expensive one is likely to wind up with a lower rating.

Even though the majority of wines fall into the "average"

category, this certainly does not mean that they are all the same. Included in this group are wines that we liked, others that were pretty neutral, and some others that we didn't particularly care for. But our different reactions were due primarily to our own taste prejudices, not to any inherent differences in character or distinctiveness found in the wines. An "average" wine is simply one which, for its price and varietal reputation, is not disappointing when compared to the majority of similar California wines.

"Below average" is used to denote a wine with technical faults or, in many cases, a technically sound wine whose lack of varietal character and flavors (often while retaining a fancy price tag) was especially noticeable.

A wine that received a "good" has some distinction of flavor, varietal character, or economy of price that sets it apart from the typical wine of its variety. Included in this category are many pleasant wines that we would recommend purchasing or including in a wine cellar. Wines that received a "very good" or an "excellent" are, in our opinion, very fine wines whose quality is deserving of special recognition.

You may find a few surprises in the next few pages; we hope that some of them may guide you to "the" wine for your tastes. In any case, use the rankings as a beginning, not an end, in your exploration of the world of wine in California.

DRY SAUTERNE TYPES

(Including Semillon and Sauvignon Blanc)

***

Concannon Sauvignon Blanc Limited Bottling 1971
Robert Mondavi Fumé Blanc 1970
Robert Mondavi Fumé Blanc 1971
Spring Mountain Sauvignon Blanc 1967

**

Almadén Blanc Fumé
Beringer Fumé Blanc 1970
Concannon Dry Sauterne 1971
Concannon Sauvignon Blanc 1971
Inglenook Dry Semillon 1970
Korbel Dry Sauterne
Oakville Sauvignon Blanc Reserve 1971
Spring Mountain Sauvignon Blanc 1969
Wente Dry Semillon 1970
Wente Dry Semillon 1971
Wente Sauvignon Blanc 1971

*

Almadén Dry Semillon Sauterne
Almadén Sauvignon Blanc
Beaulieu Dry Sauternes 1971
Beringer Dry Sauterne
Charles Krug Dry Sauternes
Charles Krug Dry Semillon
Christian Brothers Dry Sauterne
Concannon Dry Sauterne 1970
Paul Masson Dry Sauterne

BA

Martini Dry Sauterne

SWEET SAUTERNE TYPES

(Including Semillon and Sauvignon Blanc)

**

Christian Brothers Sauvignon Blanc
Oakville Sauvignon Blanc
Wente Château Semillon 1969

*

Beaulieu Haut Sauternes 1969
Château Beaulieu 1970
Château Concannon 1971
Charles Krug Sauvignon Blanc
Christian Brothers Sweet Sauterne
Christian Brothers Haut Sauterne
San Martin Hostess Semillon
Weibel Sauterne
Wente Château Semillon 1970

BA

Cresta Blanca Sauterne

CHABLIS

***
Heitz

**
Beaulieu 1971
Beringer
Christian Brothers
Charles Krug
Mirassou 1970
Paul Masson
Souverain 1970
Windsor

*
Almadén
Buena Vista
Concannon
Cresta Blanca
Korbel
Martini
San Martin
Weibel
Wente

BA

Mirassou 1971
Sebastiani 1971

PINOT BLANC

***

Heitz McCrea Vineyard 1969
Mirassou White Burgundy 1971

**

Heitz Lyncrest Vineyard 1970
Heitz McCrea Vineyard 1970
Mirassou 1970
Wente 1970

*

Almadén
Paul Masson
Wente 1971

BA

Paul Masson Pinnacles Selection *Cuvée* 992

CHARDONNAY

****

Beaulieu 1970
Freemark Abbey 1969
Freemark Abbey 1970
Spring Mountain 1969

***

Beaulieu 1969
Charles Krug 1969
Charles Krug 1970
Heitz Lot 2-92-Z 1969
Heitz Lot Z-02 1970
Mayacamas 1970
Mirassou Harvest Selection 1971
Robert Mondavi 1969
Robert Mondavi 1970
Souverain 1970

**

Almadén
Buena Vista 1971
Chappellet 1970
Martini 1970
Mirassou Harvest Selection 1970
Souverain 1969
Spring Mountain 1970
Weibel
Wente 1970
Windsor

*

Beringer 1971
Christian Brothers
Heitz Lot UCV-91 1969
Inglenook 1970
Inglenook 1971
Martini 1971
Mayacamas 1969
Mirassou 1969
Paul Masson
San Martin
Sebastiani 1971
Weibel Estate-bottled 1969
Wente 1971

BA

Cresta Blanca
Paul Masson Pinnacles Selection *Cuvée* 951
Weibel Estate-bottled 1968

JOHANNISBERG (WHITE) RIESLING

***

Heitz 1970
Heitz 1971
Robert Mondavi 1971
Souverain 1970

**

Almadén
Beaulieu 1969
Beringer 1971
Charles Krug
Freemark Abbey Lots 91 and 92 1969
Freemark Abbey 1970
Inglenook 1971
Llords & Elwood *Cuvée* JR 5
Martini 1970
Sebastiani 1967
Weibel

*

Beaulieu 1970
Buena Vista 1971
Chappellet 1971
Christian Brothers
Llords & Elwood *Cuvée* JR 4
Martini 1971
Mirassou 1970
Mirassou 1971
Paul Masson
Paul Masson Pinnacles Selection *Cuvée* 972
Souverain 1971
Windsor

BA

Concannon 1971

GREY RIESLING

**

Beringer
Charles Krug
Weibel

*

Christian Brothers
Cresta Blanca
Inglenook 1969
Wente
Windsor

BA

Korbel

OTHER RIESLING-TYPE WINES

**

Beaulieu Riesling 1971
Christian Brothers Rhine
Mirassou Monterey Riesling 1971
Paul Masson Emerald Dry
Robert Mondavi Riesling 1971
Sebastiani Kleinberger Riesling 1969

*

Almadén Sylvaner
Christian Brothers Riesling
Charles Krug Sylvaner Riesling
Concannon Moselle 1971
Cresta Blanca Rhine
Inglenook Vintage Rhine 1970
Martini Rhine
Martini Riesling 1971
Martini Sylvaner 1969
Paul Masson Rhine Castle
Paul Masson Riesling
San Martin Hostess Emerald Riesling
Sebastiani Sylvaner 1969
Souverain Riesling 1971
Weibel Rhine Wine

BA

Inglenook Sylvaner Riesling 1969
Paul Masson Rhine
San Martin Rhine Wine
San Martin Sylvaner

GEWÜRZTRAMINER AND TRAMINER

***

Martini Gewürztraminer 1971
Mirassou Gewürztraminer Harvest Selection 1971

**

Almadén Gewürztraminer
Charles Krug Gewürztraminer
Martini Gewürztraminer 1970
Mirassou Gewürztraminer Harvest Selection 1970
Robert Mondavi Traminer 1970
Robert Mondavi Traminer 1971

*

Buena Vista Gewürztraminer 1971
Charles Krug Traminer
Inglenook Traminer 1971
Sebastiani Gewürztraminer 1971

BA

Buena Vista Gewürztraminer 1970
Buena Vista Gewürztraminer Cabinet 1971

CHENIN BLANC (WHITE PINOT)

****

Mirassou Chenin Blanc 1970

***

Robert Mondavi Chenin Blanc 1970
Robert Mondavi Chenin Blanc 1971

**

Beringer Chenin Blanc
Christian Brothers Chenin Blanc
Christian Brothers Pineau de la Loire
Charles Krug Chenin Blanc
Charles Krug White Pinot
Mayacamas Chenin Blanc 1971
Mirassou Chenin Blanc 1971
Oakville Chenin Blanc 1971
Wente Blanc de Blancs

*

Almadén Chenin Blanc
Chappellet Chenin Blanc 1970
Chappellet Chenin Blanc 1971
Chappellet Pritchard Hill Chenin Blanc 1971
Inglenook Chenin Blanc 1970
Korbel Chenin Blanc
Martini Dry Chenin Blanc 1970
Martini Dry Chenin Blanc 1971
Paul Masson Chenin Blanc
Sebastiani Chenin Blanc 1971
Pineau Souverain 1970
Weibel Chenin Blanc
Windsor Chenin Blanc

MISCELLANEOUS WHITES

***

Charles Krug Moscato di Canelli
Martini Folle Blanche 1971

**

Cresta Blanca French Colombard
Martini Folle Blanche 1970
Oakville House White Lot 71
San Martin Malvasia Bianca
Souverain Flora 1970
Souverain Green Hungarian 1970
Souverain Green Hungarian 1971
Weibel Green Hungarian

*

Christian Brothers Château La Salle
Concannon White Dinner Wine
Windsor French Colombard

BA

Buena Vista Green Hungarian 1971
Cresta Blanca Green Hungarian
Sebastiani Green Hungarian 1971

ROSÉS

***
Buena Vista Cabernet Rosé 1971
Oakville Gamay Rosé 1971
Robert Mondavi Gamay Rosé 1970

**
Beaulieu Beaurosé 1971
Christian Brothers Napa Rosé
Christian Brothers Vin Rosé
Charles Krug Vin Rosé
Concannon Vin Rosé
Concannon Zinfandel Rosé 1971
Llords & Elwood Rosé of Cabernet *Cuvée* R 6
Martini Gamay Rosé 1971
Mirassou Petite Rosé 1970
Robert Mondavi Gamay Rosé 1971
Sebastiani Vin Rosé 1971
Rosé Wente
Windsor Vin Rosé

*
Almadén Grenache Rosé
Almadén Mountain Nectar Vin Rosé
Beaulieu Beaurosé 1970
Beaulieu Grenache Rosé 1971
Beringer Vin Rosé
Buena Vista Zinfandel Rosé 1971
Cresta Blanca Grenache Rosé
Heitz Grignolino Rosé 1971
Inglenook Gamay Rosé 1971
Korbel Château Vin Rosé
Mirassou Petite Rosé 1971
Paul Masson Vin Rosé Sec
Paul Masson Pink
San Martin Grenache Rosé
Sebastiani Grenache Rosé
Weibel Vin Rosé
Weibel Grenache Rosé
Windsor Grenache Rosé

BA

Inglenook Vin Rosé
San Martin Vin Rosé

GENERIC REDS (BURGUNDY, CLARET, CHIANTI)

***

Beaulieu Burgundy Special Bottling 1968
Charles Krug Burgundy 1968
Mirassou Burgundy 1969
Sebastiani Burgundy 1967
Souverain Burgundy

**

Beaulieu Burgundy 1969
Beringer Burgundy
Christian Brothers Burgundy
Concannon Burgundy
Heitz Burgundy
Inglenook Vintage Burgundy 1970
Martini Burgundy
Mirassou Burgundy 1968
Oakville House Red
San Martin Burgundy
Sebastiani Burgundy n.v.
Wente Burgundy
Windsor Burgundy

*

Almadén Burgundy
Almadén Chianti
Buena Vista Burgundy 1967
Christian Brothers Claret
Charles Krug Burgundy 1967
Charles Krug Claret 1968
Concannon Red Dinner Wine
Cresta Blanca Burgundy
Korbel Burgundy

Paul Masson Burgundy
San Martin Hostess Burgundy
San Martin Chianti
Sebastiani Chianti 1970
Weibel Burgundy
Weibel Claret

GAMAY AND GAMAY BEAUJOLAIS

***

Christian Brothers Gamay Noir
Oakville Napa Gamay 1969
Robert Mondavi Gamay 1971
Sebastiani Gamay Beaujolais 1971

**

Beaulieu Gamay Beaujolais 1970
Beaulieu Gamay Beaujolais 1971
Charles Krug Gamay Beaujolais 1969
Inglenook Gamay 1969
Inglenook Gamay Beaujolais 1969
Mirassou Gamay Beaujolais 1970
Oakville Napa Gamay 1970
Paul Masson Gamay Beaujolais
Sebastiani Nouveau Gamay Beaujolais 1972

*

Almadén Gamay Beaujolais
Cresta Blanca Gamay Beaujolais
Mirassou Gamay Beaujolais 1969
Weibel Gamay Beaujolais
Wente Gamay Beaujolais 1970
Windsor Gamay

BA

San Martin Gamay Beaujolais
Wente Gamay Beaujolais 1969

PINOT NOIR

***

Beaulieu 1968
Freemark Abbey 1968
Llords & Elwood *Cuvée* PN 8
Mirassou Dedication Bottling
 1969

**

Buena Vista Cask 1968
Christian Brothers
Freemark Abbey 1969
Heitz n.v.
Llords & Elwood *Cuvée* PN 7
Paul Masson Pinnacles Selec-
 tion *Cuvée* 824
Robert Mondavi 1968
Robert Mondavi 1969
San Martin
Weibel Estate-bottled 1966

*

Beaulieu 1969
Charles Krug 1969
Heitz 1968
Inglenook 1968
Inglenook 1969
Martini 1969
Mirassou Harvest Selection
 1967
Paul Masson
Sebastiani 1967
Sebastiani n.v.
Weibel
Weibel Estate-bottled 1967

BA

Almadén
Beringer 1969
Korbel
Wente 1969

CABERNET SAUVIGNON

****

Beaulieu Private Reserve 1968
Charles Krug Vintage Selection
1966
Heitz 1966
Oakville Reserve 1968
Oakville 1970
Robert Mondavi 1968
Souverain 1968
Spring Mountain Lot H-68-69

***

Beaulieu 1968
Buena Vista
Concannon 1968
Chappellet 1968
Freemark Abbey 1968
Freemark Abbey 1969
Heitz Martha's Vineyard 1967
Inglenook 1966
Inglenook 1967
Inglenook Cask 1966
Llords & Elwood *Cuvée* CS 6
Mayacamas 1969
Mirassou   Harvest   Selection
1967
Mirassou   Harvest   Selection
1968
Oakville 1968
Robert Mondavi 1969
Sebastiani 1967
Spring Mountain 1970

**

Beaulieu 1969
Beaulieu Private Reserve 1967
Beringer 1969
Buena Vista Lachryma Montis
1967
Christian Brothers
Christian   Brothers   Brother
Timothy Selection, bottled
1967
Charles Krug 1967
Charles Krug 1968
Concannon 1967
Inglenook Cask 1967
Korbel
Martini 1967
Martini 1968
Mirassou 1968
Paul Masson
San Martin
Sebastiani Bin 32
Souverain 1967
Windsor

*

Almadén

Cresta Blanca

Llords & Elwood *Cuvée* CS 5

Mayacamas 1968

Paul Masson Pinnacles Selection *Cuvée* 843

Paul Masson Pinnacles Selection *Cuvée* 942

Sebastiani n.v.

Weibel

BA

Mirassou 1969

ZINFANDEL

***

Buena Vista Cask 160 1968
Martini 1968
Mirassou Harvest Selection 1967
Souverain 1970

**

Buena Vista 1968
Buena Vista 1969
Christian Brothers
Charles Krug 1969
Heitz Lot 63-69
Inglenook 1969
Martini 1969
Mirassou 1968
Mirassou Harvest Selection 1966
Oakville 1970
Oakville 1971
Sebastiani 1970

*

Beringer
Charles Krug 1968
Cresta Blanca
Inglenook 1968
Inglenook Vintage 1969
Mirassou 1969
San Martin
Windsor

BA

Almadén
Souverain 1969
Weibel
Wente 1968

MISCELLANEOUS REDS

****

Martini Barbera 1968

***

Freemark Abbey Petite Sirah 1971
Sebastiani Barbera 1967

**

Buena Vista Barbera Cask 149
Concannon Petite Sirah 1968
Concannon Petite Sirah 1969
Cresta Blanca Petite Sirah
Heitz Barbera
Heitz Grignolino
Heitz Ruby Cabernet
Inglenook Charbono 1968
Inglenook Charbono 1969
Inglenook Red Pinot 1967
Martini Barbera 1969
Mirassou Petite Sirah 1968
Sebastiani Barbera n.v.

*

Almadén Grenoir Original
Beringer Barenblut
Beringer Grignolino
Christian Brothers Pinot St. George
Cresta Blanca Barbera
Cresta Blanca Grignolino
Paul Masson Baroque
Paul Masson Rubion
San Martin Cabernet Ruby
San Martin Grignolino
Weibel Royalty
Wente Petite Sirah 1969
Wente Petite Sirah 1970
Windsor Petite Sirah

BA

Mirassou Petite Sirah 1969

PART THREE

A Sampling of Smaller Wineries

There are many wineries in California producing premium table wines that do not have the vast distribution or reputation of the larger wineries described in Part Two. In this section we will offer you a glimpse of several of these smaller wineries.

The limited distribution of these wineries is generally restricted to sales at the winery itself, through mail orders, or through a very few retail outlets. This is perhaps the most "touristic" part of the book, for the only way you will be able to taste most of the wines discussed in the next few pages is to stop by the winery or tasting room as you're driving through the area. For this reason, we have chosen to give only our general impressions of the winery as a whole, noting where appropriate the more interesting wines we have run across in our visits.

As the title of this section indicates, we have not attempted to include all the wineries in the state that produce varietal table wines. Very simply, we have included all those wineries which we had time to visit, whose wines were recommended to us by friends, or which happened to be near other wine-producing regions. Our list is not selective, for no winery was purposely excluded. If we did miss your favorite, please accept our apologies and write and let us in on your find.

If there is any moral to this section, it's that a winery's

size has little to do with the quality of its wines. Even within the small-winery category there are great differences in attitude and emphasis, ranging from a highly personal, rather exclusive dedication to the production of only a few premium varietals (Stony Hill, for example) to a more locally oriented business operation (Nervo or Bargetto, perhaps). A few very good wines may be found along with many more ordinary ones, but almost without exception these lesser-known wines compare favorably with most of the larger, better-advertised outfits. The next time you're out driving and stumble upon a new winery, do yourself a favor and stop by for a few minutes. There are no guarantees, but you just might be pleasantly surprised.

Small Wineries of
Napa County

Château Montelena Winery

Originally founded in 1882 as part of a nine-hundred-acre
estate in northern Calistoga, Château Montelena has had a
curious history that includes over forty years as a bonded
winery as well as a stint as a country castle, complete with
a man-made lake, oriental bridges, and a Chinese junk. While
the lake remains, the massive stone building has now returned
to its original use of producing fine wines.

Purchased by Mr. Lee Paschich and rebonded in 1968, the
winery is being completely renovated, and 100 acres surrounding the winery have been planted to Cabernet Sauvignon and
Zinfandel. The new Château Montelena's first commercial
crush was in 1972, and plans call for producing Chardonnay,
Johannisberg Riesling, and Gamay Rosé (with grapes
purchased from other growers), as well as Cabernet and Zinfandel. Under wine maker Mike Grgich, production is expected to reach 70,000 to 80,000 gallons by 1975 or 1976.
All wines will be finished in oak, and both the Johannisberg
and the Rosé will be in the dry style.

The two whites and Gamay Rosé should be released by the
end of 1973, and we welcome the Château Montelena part-

nership to the growing family of California wineries. At present, visits to the winery are by appointment only.

Cuvaison

Cuvaison began business in 1970 with the purchase of a small building on the Silverado Trail between Calistoga and St. Helena and a vineyard north of Calistoga planted to Napa Gamay, Pinot Noir, and French Colombard. Today the building houses a tasting room, which doubles as a bottling area whenever necessary, and a storage area for bottled wine and a few Limousin casks of Chardonnay and Cabernet Sauvignon. On a hill in back of the tasting/storage room, a concrete slab has been placed, and a crusher, press, and stainless steel temperature-controlled fermentors have been installed. In the fall of 1972 this was a busy place, for it housed not only the newly fermenting wines of Cuvaison, but also some tanks of Chardonnay and Sauvignon Blanc under the care of Spring Mountain and the first crushes of some brand new wineries, Dry Creek Vineyards' Sauvignon Blanc, and Zinfandel and Cabernet Sauvignon for the Napa-Bordeaux Wine Company.

Cuvaison's owner and wine maker is Tom Cottrell, and his goal is to capture fruit and freshness within his wines through a slow, cool fermentation process. All the wines are 100 percent varietals, with the selection varying somewhat from year to year depending on what grapes are available for purchase. The French Colombard from the vineyard is sold to other wineries, and since the emphasis at Cuvaison has been more on whites than on reds it has been the practice to trade the Pinot Noir grapes for Chardonnay grapes from another winery.

The *1970 Chardonnay* was on the light side, but did capture some fruitiness and good varietal flavors. The *1971* has promise of being a bigger wine, retains a fresh green-apple quality to the nose, and also has a slight sweetness to the bouquet imparted by the Limousin oak in which it was aged for several months. Fermented completely dry, this is a nice wine with good body, though it would have benefited from a touch more acidity.

After fermentation the other white varieties remain in stainless steel to preserve their freshness until bottling. A *1971 Grey Riesling* was a very fruity, lively wine that had a bit of the spicy flavor often seen in good wines of this variety. The *1971 Chenin Blanc* was a light, clean wine with a dry finish and pleasant, if not overwhelming, character. In 1972 a Chenin Blanc was again produced, but the winery could not obtain Grey Riesling grapes so a Sauvignon Blanc was produced instead.

Among the reds Cuvaison has produced two different Gamays, as well as a 1971 Cabernet Sauvignon. The *Gamay Rouge* of *1970* was bottled under a carbon dioxide blanket, and a considerable amount of gas was dissolved in the wine. The result was a dark purplish-red wine with good fruit and a strong fizz when poured into a glass. While it was likened by some to the *pétillance* often captured within a true French *Beaujolais de l'Année,* the bubbly finish was not one to be enjoyed by all. The *1971 Gamay,* labeled *Gamay Vivace* for its lightness and easy drinkability, was lighter in color and low in tannin. A very fresh, fruity wine meant to be consumed young.

Cuvaison is a very friendly place and a recommended stop for those who wish to compare wineries of all sizes and shapes in the Napa Valley. Their early wines show promise and we wish them continuing success.

Nichelini Vineyard

One thousand feet above the eastern floor of the Napa Valley lies a small, family-run winery owned and operated by Jim Nichelini. Open to visitors only on weekends, a selection of the nine Nichelini table wines (and a couple of dessert wines as well) is available for tasting. While your reception from the tasting terrace host may well be somewhat cool, questions are generally answered honestly if succinctly.

Nichelini wines are produced entirely from Nichelini's own vineyards. The reds are usually aged for three to five years in oak before being released, although the Burgundy at least has come out earlier than that. As with the larger California wineries, Nichelini is also feeling the pressures of impatient consumers.

The whites of Nichelini are generally clean, dry wines and include a *Sauvignon Vert,* which is rarely bottled as a varietal in California, a light, dry *Chenin Blanc,* and a *Chablis.* A *Vin Rosé* is produced primarily from Zinfandel; it is dry and has fairly deep color for a rosé, moderate body and acid, but is a bit harsh.

The reds are a little more distinctive. The *Burgundy* (from Zinfandel, Gamay, and Petite Sirah) has fairly good body and adequate tannin with a fruity aroma; it will age for a couple of years and is a good everyday wine. The *Zinfandel* is surprisingly light and rather tart, though it has a characteristic aroma. Completing the reds are a *Petite Sirah,* which is also tart though fuller-bodied and of better character than the Zinfandel, a *Gamay,* and a *Cabernet Sauvignon.*

Stony Hill Vineyard

Fred McCrea founded Stony Hill in 1951, years before most of the people now scampering about opening small wineries ever thought of planting vines. Over the years Stony Hill has gained one of the most respected reputations among California wineries, and each fall the small annual production of 4000 to 5000 gallons of wine must be rationed to those on the crowded mailing list.

The McCrea family home and the petite winery are located in the hills that border the west side of the Napa Valley and command a beautiful view of the valley below and the surrounding mountains. Thirty acres are planted in beautifully kept vines—Chardonnay, White Riesling, Gewürztraminer, and a small amount of Semillon that is not usually bottled under the Stony Hill label. In 1972 the last of a few old and tired Pinot Blanc vines were uprooted and replaced with Chardonnay. Inside the winery may be found rows of small to medium oak barrels that are used for both fermentation and aging.

The *Chardonnay* is usually a fine, well-balanced wine of good varietal character, often possessing a fresh applelike aroma when young. They are usually rather soft and seem meant to be drunk when fairly young, but they often have surprising staying power and acquire considerably more richness and intensity when aged five to six years.

The *Gewürztraminer* has usually been one of California's most distinctive wines of this variety, and the *1971* follows this style with a spicy aroma and good, crisp flavor well balanced with the good fruit acidity made possible by the relatively cool climate of the hills in which the vines are grown.

In 1970 *White Riesling* reappeared under the Stony Hill label; in prior years the grapes had been entirely sold to other wineries. The *1970* was a big, dry, distinctive wine, though one somewhat lacking in acidity, while the *1971* is fresher, has a very attractive aroma, a crisp, clean fruity finish, good balance, and a slight *pétillance*.

Wine lovers interested in visiting Stony Hill are requested to write ahead for an appointment.

Sutter Home Winery

Since the first edition of this book, the old redwood tank tasting room at Sutter Home has been replaced, and the winery itself has an air of life and activity that contrasts with its rather sleepy character of former years. Still a family-run operation, Sutter Home's distribution remains locally oriented, but at least a few of its wines may also be found in retail stores throughout California.

For a small winery, Sutter Home produces a fairly large number of varietals, which at present include five whites, five reds, and two rosés. The more unusual wines include a *Sauvignon Vert*, a medium-sweet *Mission Rosé*, made from the same grape variety originally planted by the early Spanish missionaries in California; and a *Moscato*. The latter is perhaps Sutter Home's most successful white: very fruity with a delightful Muscat nose, it is medium sweet and quite fresh and clean.

The growing interest in Sutter Home wines is in large part due to their Zinfandel, which now forms the bulk of their 25,000-gallon-a-year production. Since 1968, the Sutter Home Zinfandels have been produced from grapes of the Deaver and Ferrero vineyards in Amador County, where Zinfandel has long been a regional favorite. The *1968* and *1969 Zinfandels* (denominated "Deaver Vineyard" and released in two separate lots each year) were all fairly full, somewhat tannic wines of rich, spicy character, and they are prime examples of the truly premium qualities that can be found in the Zinfandel grape. The 1968s were probably the better balanced of the two years, but both should be aged for five to ten years before they will reach their peak. One wine from the 1971 vintage was released before the 1970 and was labeled *Petite Zinfandel* to distinguish it from its bigger and better predecessors. The Petite is, in fact, a pretty ordinary wine and has none of the depth or potential of the 1968, 1969, or, hopefully, 1970.

The *1970 Lot 1 Zinfandel* is even more tannic in its youth than were the 1968 and 1969. There is some fruit in the aroma, but the flavor is completely overcome by bitter astringency. At this point it is a matter of conjecture whether the wine will have enough depth of flavors to outlive the tannin.

The Trincheri family is very friendly, and all of the Sutter Home wines may generally be sampled at the tasting room. The winery is in the heart of the Napa Valley along Highway 29, and a visit here should provide a pleasant interlude among all the bigger, better-known wineries of the area.

Yverdon Vineyards

One of California's newest wineries is Yverdon, perched in a beautifully peaceful setting high atop Spring Mountain, with a commanding view of surrounding forests and Napa Valley below. The owner and wine master is Mr. Fred Aves, who was enticed into the world of wine by many trips to the European and California wine countries and by his experience as a home wine maker. He purchased some vineyards north of Calistoga in the mid-1960s, and in 1971 bonded the winery, naming it after the small Swiss village of Yverdon, near Neufchâtel, which was the birthplace of his grandmother.

The ninety acres of vines near Calistoga are planted in Cabernet Sauvignon, Gamay Beaujolais, Chenin Blanc, and

Johannisberg Riesling, and these are the varietals currently being produced. Twelve acres on the winery grounds were planted in 1972 to Gewürztraminer and Merlot; plans call for the latter to be eventually blended into the Cabernet Sauvignon. Fermentation is done in temperature-controlled stainless steel, and the whites and the Gamay are then aged here in 500-gallon casks of Yugoslavian oak that Mr. Aves feels do the perfect job of adding a hint of oak while preserving the fruitiness of the wine. Depending on the strength of the vintage, some Cabernet will also be held in the large oak, while others will be aged in sixty-gallon Nevers oak casks.

The first commercial bottling carrying the Yverdon label was the *1970 Johannisberg Riesling.* Since the winery was just receiving its equipment in 1971, this wine was actually made from Yverdon grapes by another Napa Valley winery. It is a good, fairly big Johannisberg in the Napa Valley style, and retains just a touch of sweetness for balance. The remaining 1971 wines were fermented by Mr. Aves himself, and the results are quite successful for a first commercial effort. The *Chenin Blanc* is light and fruity, with a clean, dry finish. It is lighter in style and without the richness of some of the most popular Chenin Blancs, but it is well made. Two barrels of *Gamay* were produced, and interestingly the wines acquired different styles. One is fairly light and fruity with a nose reminiscent of a French Beaujolais. It is low in tannin and was quite palatable after a year in the cask and should require little in the way of bottle age. The second cask is deeper in color and a bit fuller in body and tannin. Though still fruity, it will require a year or two in the bottle to round out. While the first will certainly be bottled under the Yverdon label, the fate of the second had not been decided at the time of this writing.

The *1971 Cabernet Sauvignon* shows good balance and Cabernet flavors, although it is on the light-bodied side. This probably reflects the fact that 1971 was a year when Cabernet did not ripen well in the Napa Valley and generally produced wines of a lighter style than usual. The wine has been kept in the larger oak casks so as not to overpower it with new oak flavors, and the marriage of grape and oak seems to be proceeding harmoniously.

Plans presently call for a tasting room and for some aging tunnels to be carved into the hillside, but it will be some time before the winery is complete and ready to accept visitors. Those of you who wish to keep current on the progress at Yverdon and the dates and outlets for future wines are advised to write to Mr. Aves at his St. Helena P.O. address. Present production is in the 10,000- to 15,000-gallon range, and it will probably be several years before sizable quantities of Yverdon wines are available, but if initial success is a sign of the quality of the future, the wait should be worthwhile.

Small Wineries of Sonoma County

Foppiano Wine Company

The Foppiano Winery is a reminder of the days when most Sonoma County wineries were small, family-run operations that aged their wines in large redwood tanks and sold them to a faithful clientele that regularly visited the winery, as well as in bulk to other wineries, where they were used primarily for blending purposes. The Foppiano family has owned the winery since 1896, and many practices have remained much the same, including the use of the large redwood tanks for aging vessels and the goal of achieving distinctive wood character in some of the reds. Of course, changes have occurred, such as the recent replanting of many of the vineyards.

The Russian River flows near the Healdsburg home of the winery, and the Russian River Valley appellation is now used on the label of some of the varieties. Estate bottlings of *Pinot Noir, Cabernet Sauvignon,* and *Petite Sirah* are offered. To date all three of these have had rather pronounced wood flavors and little varietal character. The 1970 Pinot Noir is perhaps the fullest of the varietals, but it does have a rather rough, astringent quality that may improve with some age. Two *Zinfandels* are offered, one with a cork finish and the other in a screw-top bottle. The latter is inexpensive and would serve as a good everyday dinner wine; indeed its flavor is more pleasant than the more expensive cork-finished bottling, which is rather dull and uninteresting.

A vintage *Burgundy* is also offered, usually after considerable aging in the wood. The *1964* was not bottled until it was about seven years old, the prolonged contact of wine with wood adding strength at the expense of softness and fruit. The resulting wine may best be termed a country wine with character, similar in style to many Sonoma County bottlings of years past.

Among the whites two *Chablis* are offered, one carrying the Russian River Valley label and the other denoted simply California. Both are really quite drinkable, though the former is a bit fresher and fruitier.

Foppiano wines are becoming more widely distributed, though the winery itself is the best source of the wines and a very interesting place to walk through. At the moment, no tasting is available.

Grand Cru Vineyards

Grand Cru is a small new winery whose first crush was in 1971. The winery itself is a small stone building that belonged to an old Sonoma County winery long since closed, and the only varietal currently produced is Zinfandel from the twenty-five acres of vines on the surrounding property. Most of these date from the early 1900s. Present production is about 3000 gallons a year, with plans eventually calling for around 10,000 gallons annually.

Three Zinfandels are produced—a red which receives its aging in fifty-gallon oak barrels, a rosé, and a white labeled Blanc de Noir. The *1971 Rosé* has a deep-pink, almost light-ruby color considerably darker than most California rosés. It is a dry wine of substance with a fruity aroma, good body and acid, and some astringency. It should remain at its peak through 1974, but it needs to be drunk with a meal, for otherwise its full flavors and slight tannin may seem somewhat awkward and heavy.

The *Zinfandel Blanc de Noir* is the pride of the winery, for the owners have joined the three other wineries in the state currently producing this unique wine in feeling that there is a future for white Zinfandels. The color of the 1971 is pale yellow, without the touch of deep gold or pink often found in the juice of black-skinned grapes, and the aroma is rather fresh. The flavor is clean and dry, if not terribly exciting, and it can probably be said that the Grand Cru is the best of the white Zinfandels we have tasted. The rather high price attached to the wine, however, seems beyond the amount that even rarity justifies, and we hope that as production increases prices will reach a more reasonable level.

Grand Cru is located just north of Sonoma in the little village of Glen Ellen, and is open on weekends and holidays to cordially receive visitors and offer them a taste of wine when available.

Hanzell Vineyards

Conceived by the late James D. Zellerbach as a replica of part of the famous Clos du Vougeot in Burgundy, the Hanzell winery was built in the 1950s and produced its first wine in 1956. After Mr. Zellerbach's death in 1963, the property was purchased by Mr. and Mrs. Douglas Day, who chose to continue the limited, exclusive nature of the operation. Only two varietals, a Pinot Noir and a Chardonnay, have been produced, and Mrs. Day has continued the policy of concentrating on these two since her husband's unfortunate death in 1970. Mr. Brad Webb, a well-respected Napa Valley enologist, serves as consultant with wine maker Kimball Giles.

In recent years Hanzell wines have become increasingly difficult to obtain, while their price certainly places them in the connoisseur's field. The wines are of course different from their Burgundian counterparts, but Hanzell remains European in its style and dedication to only two varieties. The *Chardonnay* has been the more successful of the two; always well above average for California, in the best years it will rank near the top. Recent vintages have all been fairly full-bodied, with well-balanced acidity and a pleasant oaky-spiciness present in both aroma and taste. The *1969* was fairly soft and drinkable though the flavors were quite complex, while the *1968* and *1970* were big wines of intense character which need three to five years of bottle age before they will reach their peak. All are fine, elegant wines that will last for several years.

The *Pinot Noir* while considered highly by many, has not often been that impressive to our tastes. *1967* is the most successful recent vintage, as its light to moderate body and moderate tannin and acid are well balanced and the flavors exhibit some complexity and more character than most California Pinot Noirs. Not rich, but distinctive and well made. The *1968* is fuller but at the same time disappointing. The flavors are somewhat clumsy and rough, and, while the wine will certainly benefit from several years of age, its present stage of development leaves it rather sluggish. It is possible that we just tasted it at an awkward moment, and its potential will have to remain an open question for a few more years.

Hanzell is not generally open to the public, but a visit may be arranged by first writing to Mrs. Day.

Kenwood Vineyards

About ten miles north of Sonoma, in the Valley of the Moon, is the small town of Kenwood. For many years the

Pagani Brothers Winery was a landmark, offering good-value
jug wine to local citizens and a devoted clientele that would
make the pilgrimage from the San Francisco Bay Area. Thousands of gallons of bulk wine were also produced each year
and sold to other wineries. In 1970 the winery was sold tó
the Lee family and renamed Kenwood Vineyards. Marty Lee
has become the resident family member and is helped by
relatives on weekends and of course at harvest time. The
atmosphere of the winery is one of genuine friendliness and,
judging by the wines that are currently maturing in oak cooperage, a fine future is in store for Kenwood. Inexpensive red
and white jug wines are still being made, and the steady
stream of cars to the tasting room every weekend seems to
indicate that the old Pagani clientele has remained loyal. The
Burgundy is a good buy at $1.50 a half gallon; it's a nice,
tart, fruity dinner wine. A *Reserve Burgundy* is also offered
at a slightly higher price, though we actually preferred the
regular.

Most of the cooperage acquired with the winery consisted
of redwood tanks typical of old Sonoma County vintners.
Under its new owners Kenwood Vineyards will be concentrating on premium varietals, and small cooperage in the form of
fifty-gallon American oak barrels is being acquired. Among
the first varietals produced was a *1970 Chenin Blanc,* a dry
wine with a nice flowery aroma and light, clean taste. The
1972 Chenin Blanc is fuller bodied and slightly less fruity
than the 1970, but has more complexity. The dry *1971 Grey
Riesling* shows a beautiful spicy-flowery nose unusual for this
variety and has a pleasant fresh taste. We tasted the *1970
Zinfandel* before it was transferred from a year in redwood
tanks to oak barrels for further aging. It already had good
color and Zinfandel aroma and is a fairly full-bodied, rich
wine which shows fine potential. It has continued to develop
well in the bottle and should reach its peak in 1976–78. The
1971 Zinfandel is lighter and fruitier, but is still a fine wine.
The *1970 Cabernet Sauvignon,* tasted at the same stage of

development, is a little lighter than the Zinfandel but exhibits good Cabernet character and flavors. A *Chardonnay* is also offered to fill out the line while other Kenwood wines mature, but this has been purchased from another California winery.

The grapes for Kenwood wines come from vineyards owned or leased by the winery and in the same immediate location, as well as from some vineyards in the Napa Valley. Plans call for replanting some of the acreage currently in older, rather ordinary vines, and the range of future Kenwood varietals will depend on which are deemed most suitable for planting in this area. The winery is certainly a nice place to visit and has promise of becoming a welcome addition to the California wine scene.

Nervo Winery

Despite losing part of its vineyard to a highway expansion program, the small Nervo Winery and tasting room remain on the east side of Highway 101 just south of Geyserville. On most days you can stop by and taste Nervo's sometimes rough but not unpleasant country wines, which presently include two whites and several reds.

Sauterne and *Chenin Blanc* form the white side of Nervo's line, and both are rather ordinary. Among the reds, the *Zinfandel* is still fairly full-bodied with good fruit, though the price has risen to the point where a fifth bottle now costs more than a half gallon did three years ago. Both a *Pinot St. George* and a very limited quantity of *Pinot Noir* have been available recently, along with the unique *Malvoise*. The latter is soft, mellow, and quite light in color and body, resembling a deep rosé as much as a light red; you might want to try it slightly chilled.

None of Nervo's wines can claim great distinction, and

paper cups and screw tops still dominate the tasting room. While Nervo has remained a very small operation producing average *vins de pays,* in this age of new money and expansion it is by no means certain that the winery will be able to continue in its present style.

Pedroncelli Winery

The Pedroncelli Winery is located just a few miles north of Geyserville, surrounded by a veritable sea of vineyards. Passing by here in late summer or early fall when the vines are brilliantly colored and heavily laden with fruit is a sight to inspire any wine lover. At the winery, John or Jim Pedroncelli will cheerfully offer for tasting any of their wines that are available.

Founded in 1927 by John Pedroncelli, Sr., today the winery has 135 acres of vineyards and produces about 150,000 gallons of wine a year. Most of their techniques are traditional; both the Cabernet Sauvignon and Pinot Noir, for example, are finished for a year in small oak barrels, the former in Nevers oak, the latter American.

Pedroncelli's whites are generally fairly light, and the more "common" *Chablis* and *Chenin Blanc* seem to be more successful than the more expensive varieties. The former is dry, clean, and quite pleasant; the *1971 Chenin Blanc* is medium sweet and a bit low in acidity, but has a very nice, melonlike aroma. The *1970 Chardonnay* is a very ordinary wine, again a bit lacking in fruitiness and acidity, while the *1970 Johannisberg Riesling* is disappointingly clumsy.

A *Zinfandel Rosé* is dry and a bit rough, though the most recent batch had a pleasant fruity nose. The red *Zinfandel* (*1969*) is one of Pedroncelli's best wines: light to moderate in body, acid, and tannin, it has good fruit and a fresh, berrylike aroma. Both *Pinot Noir* and *Cabernet Sauvignon* were fairly successful for Pedroncelli in *1968* and should improve for three to five years. Light to moderate in body with moderate tannin, both are honest wines of some character. Unfortunately, *1969* was not quite as good, and the wines are relatively light and less distinctive.

Pedroncelli wines remain about average for California, though the potential for improvement is clearly present. Their prices are quite competitive, and a visit might reward you with a wine that is just to your taste.

Russian River Vineyards

Set in a quiet hilly enclave just south of Forestville, Russian River Vineyards is a small, family-owned winery operated by Mr. Robert Lasdin. The limited range of wines available are all produced from vineyards owned by the winery, which include twelve acres each of Chardonnay and Cabernet Sauvignon, and some newly planted Zinfandel and Sauvignon Blanc. Production is small, presently around the 20,000-gallon mark, and all sales are either through direct mail orders or at the winery itself.

The varietals are often sold out soon after being released, and they include Chardonnay, Sauvignon Blanc, Gewürztraminer, Cabernet Sauvignon, and Zinfandel. The Pinot Noir is now utilized only in the *Burgundy* (which also includes Pinot St. George and Petite Sirah); this is a very smooth, fruity wine of some richness, with light to moderate body, tannin, and acid. The *1969 Zinfandel*, however, is rather rough and woody, though it does have a nice fruity-cocoa nose.

The winery began as a continuing hobby in 1958 and was bonded in 1964. After much experimentation, the whites are now fermented in stainless steel and the reds in large redwood tanks. Both are then aged in American oak barrels, the whites for twelve to eighteen months and the fuller Cabernet Sauvignon, for example, for three to five years; another several years of bottle age are often added before the wines are released.

Mr. Lasdin is evidently very concerned with the quality of his wines and, while they are on the expensive side, they should compare well with many better-known wineries. Mr. Lasdin is a very pleasant man, honest about his own wines and knowledgeable about California wines in general. Due to the small size of the winery, however, there is no tasting available, and visits must be limited to those with prior appointments. A mailing list has been established, should you wish to keep up on the activities of Russian River Vineyards.

Simi Winery

Near the town of Healdsburg, another fine name in Sonoma wine history is being revived. Simi was founded in 1876 as the Montepulciano Winery, but this was changed to the founder's family name when Montepulciano turned out to be too much of a tongue-twister for the customers. The winery reached its peak in the 1930s and 1940s and was providing special bottlings for many of California's most prestigious hotels. In recent years it became known for its low-priced, well-aged, and distinctive, if admittedly not always great, red table wines. In 1970 Mrs. Isabella Simi Haigh, daughter of one of Simi's founding brothers, sold the winery to Russ Green, a former president of Signal Oil Company who has been interested in vineyards since the late 1950s. He and a partner have acquired hundreds of acres of land in the nearby Alexander Valley, which is being planted in prime varietal grapes to supply Simi's future needs. At the present time, some Mendocino grapes are also being purchased.

Considerable energy and money have been plowed into the winery as evidenced by the beautiful new tasting room, the stainless steel fermentors, and row upon row of new sixty-gallon French oak casks. It will probably be 1974 before all the new Simi's red wines are ready for release, but the whites and rosés are already available. The vintage date is actually missing from several 1970 wines because of legal requirements, for the fermentation took place in borrowed space at a nearby winery. Among those wines available is a *Chardonnay* which shows a good nose and distinctive oakiness combined with rather full flavors. The *Johannisberg Riesling* has a lovely perfumed aroma and just a touch of sweetness, but perhaps tends to be just a bit heavy. The *1971 Gewürztraminer* is quite nice, with a characteristic spicy nose and soft, pleasant taste. A *Rosé of Cabernet* is also being produced.

One of the first tasks for Simi's new owners and wine maker was to sort through the hundreds of thousands of gallons of red wine aging in redwood tanks, blending and bottling the best under the new Simi label and selling the rest in bulk. The result is a *Cabernet Sauvignon, Pinot Noir, Carignane,* and *Burgundy* that retain some of the distinctiveness that has been Simi, but tend to be a little smoother, fruitier, and younger-tasting than former wines. The *Carignane* is a nice wine for what is considered an ordinary grape, and it has some aging potential. The price tag is a bit steep, though, especially when you consider that many neighboring wineries produce very drinkable Burgundies, which are often largely Carignane, at rather inexpensive prices. The *Pinot Noir* has a good vanilla nose, but it is a bit thin and shows signs of age. The style of the reds will probably change as Simi's 1971 vintage makes its appearance.

Trentadue Winery

While the Trentadue vineyards have been supplying grapes to Sonoma wineries for some time, it was not until 1969 that

Leo Trentadue crushed what was to be the first vintage of Trentadue Winery. All the grapes come from 130 acres of vineyards which surround the newly constructed winery south of Geyserville, and those grapes not used for wine under the Trentadue label are still sold to other producers. The vineyard includes plantings of Chenin Blanc, Semillon, French Colombard, and Sauvignon Vert among the whites, with Cabernet Sauvignon, Petite Sirah, Zinfandel, Napa Gamay, Carignane, and Early Burgundy comprising the reds.

A tasting room was opened in late 1972 and, although total production is still only 8000 gallons, the wines should become more accessible to the northern California visitor. Among those we have tasted, the *Gamay* is probably the most enjoyable. Fairly light-bodied and with light to moderate tannin, this very fruity wine is fresh, clean, and possesses good character and flavors. The whites all seemed to have slight problems, although these will hopefully be solved in the near future; the Semillon did exhibit good varietal character.

While many of the new wineries in California are managed and funded by relative newcomers to the wine industry, Leo Trentadue and his wife are continuing a way of life that has been theirs for many years. They are both open and very friendly, and you should enjoy a stop at the tasting room, which is set in the midst of the Trentadue vineyards.

Z-D Wines

Z-D Wines is the name of a new winery located near the village of Vineburg, just a few miles south of the city of Sonoma. The initials come from the names of the owners, Gino Zepponi and Norman C. de Leuze, two engineers who have had a penchant for wine making for several years. They began making wine commercially in 1969, and to date have produced some fine wines. The three whites are light-bodied, clean wines with excellent varietal character. The *White Riesling* is probably the best, with a nice fruity aroma, dry finish, and well-developed Riesling flavors. The *Gewürztraminer* has a lovely flowery-spicy aroma, but the taste is just a little on the light side without great richness or spiciness. The *Flora,* produced in limited amounts in 1971, is another well-made wine and has a nice aroma, once again a dry finish, and is a bit fuller in body than the other two. These wines were fermented in fifty-gallon American oak barrels and then aged in the wood for six to seven months before bottling. Despite the close contact with oak, the barrels have been refinished and most of the tannin removed so that little woodiness interferes with the wines' natural fruit.

Z-D's only red wine to date is a *Pinot Noir.* The *1969* vintage was blended with a small amount of Gamay Beaujolais grapes, while *1970* and *1971* were 100 percent varietals. This wine is fermented in redwood, and then aged in small American and Limousin oak for about two years. Light to moderate in body and tannin, the *1969* had good varietal character but could do with a bit more strength. The *1970 Pinot Noir* is fuller and richer than the 1969 and should have fine aging potential.

Z-D's grapes are purchased from an excellent vineyard in the Carneros region of Napa County which commands a 25 percent premium above the listed price for wine grapes, and the wines are on the expensive side. The back labels are extremely informative, with the date of harvest, sugar and acid content of the grapes, and bottling date all listed. Visitors are welcomed at Z-D, but since this is a small, family-run operation and the owners do not live on the winery premises, guests are requested to write or phone in advance.

Small Wineries of
Mendocino County

Fetzer Vineyards

The Fetzer family purchased the ranch on which their winery now stands in 1958 and soon began the task of replacing the old vines of Petite Sirah, Carignane, and Alicante Bouschet with premium varietals. The handsome new winery building was completed in the late 1960s and equipped with temperature-controlled stainless steel fermentors and sixty-gallon French oak barrels for aging purposes.

1968 was the first vintage for Fetzer, and has probably been their most successful to date. The *1968 Zinfandel* was a fine wine with good fruit and balance and did a lot to acquaint California wine drinkers with the new winery. The *1968 Cabernet Sauvignon* also showed good character, a nice varietal aroma, and the potential for aging into a very complex wine.

Subsequent vintages have been uneven and a little disappointing considering the winery's excellent start. The *1969 Zinfandel* was still a good wine, though lacking the depth and complexity of the 1968, while the fuller-bodied *1970* at this stage is rather rough and does not show the character that the 1968 exhibited in its youth.

The *1969 Cabernet Sauvignon* has a rather casky nose and does not exhibit much in the way of Cabernet character or flavors, while the *1970 Cabernet* is much better and returns toward the style of the 1968. Both the *1969* and *1970 Pinot Noirs* are fairly typical for this grape in California; they are not unpleasant wines, but ones without great complexity or distinction.

The *1971 Gamay Beaujolais* has a fruity, berrylike aroma, but little of this carries over into the flavor, which is rather simple and tart. A *Carmine Carignane* is also produced, one of the few varietal bottlings of Carignane in the state. While certainly not a great wine, for its moderate price it has been pleasant and the wine's tartness seems to balance spicy foods quite well.

Among the whites, the *Semillon* has shown fairly good varietal character. The *1971 Sauvignon Blanc* also manifests some distinctiveness, but it is marred somewhat by a slight harshness in the aroma and aftertaste.

Fetzer wines are available in selected retail outlets in California, and the current list can best be obtained by writing to the winery. Those of you in the area who would like to stop by the winery are requested to phone ahead to be sure that it is convenient for someone to show you around. Tasting is not generally available, but the tour through the winery is a very friendly and informative one.

Husch Vineyards

Founded only in 1971 by Gretchen and Tony Husch, the small winery and twenty acres of surrounding vineyards are located in Philo in the Anderson Valley, just west of Cloverdale. The vineyards were planted in the late 1960s, and the 1971 vintage wines were produced from either the Husches' own grapes or from vines of similar age from a neighboring vineyard.

Perhaps unfortunately for the future reputation of the winery, all four of their *1971* varietals were released at a young age in late 1972. Both the *Pinot Noir* and the *Cabernet Sauvignon* were thin and disappointing and possessed only minimal varietal character and too much tannin. While these faults are understandable in a wine produced from young vines, there is no excuse to release them so undeveloped and at prices over $5. The *Pinot Chardonnay* is a bit better, though again its oaky character is not balanced by either body or deep flavors. Not unpleasant, but light and lacking character. Husch's best wine is clearly the *Gewürztraminer,* which has a young, spicy aroma, light to moderate body and moderate acidity. The flavors are clean and exhibit good varietal character, though the dry aftertaste has a touch of the bitter aftertaste often found in Alsatian Gewürzes. Still, this is a well-made wine that should gain even more distinction as the vines mature.

If the other three varietals eventually follow the lead of the Gewürztraminer, Husch Vineyards may in time produce some good wines. For the present, however, the wines are overpriced, and the fact that they are apparently selling well reflects the unfortunate situation where any new, small winery can sell whatever it produces regardless of price or quality.

Parducci Wine Cellars

Parducci was one of the pioneers in the production of premium varietal wines in Mendocino County. The present winery, some three miles north of Ukiah, was founded in 1931 and for years the winery itself was virtually the sole source of the wines. In recent years distribution has expanded, and new vineyard areas are being developed to supply grapes for the expanding production.

Surrounding the winery are vineyards, some vines of which are twenty-five to thirty-five years old, planted in Pinot Noir, Cabernet Sauvignon, French Colombard, and Zinfandel. Recent plantings have been made in the Ukiah Valley to the south-east of the winery and in the Anderson Valley, near Philo, to the west of Cloverdale. Vineyards have also been acquired in the rich land alongside Highway 101 south of Ukiah, an area probably best for high-yielding grape varieties, and Parducci is also acquiring some of the first premium grapes grown in adjacent Lake County.

The Parducci reds are sometimes bottled unfined and unfiltered, and some bottlings are rather full wines that will throw a sediment with age. The *Petite Sirahs* of *1965* and *1967* and the *Zinfandels* of *1964* and *1966* were big rich wines of full flavors. There was evidently no 1968 Petite Sirah, and the *1969 Petite Sirah* is disappointing compared to its predecessors, being light and having a dull flavor. Many different bottlings of the *1969 Zinfandel* were probably produced, for the wine varied from being pleasant and fruity to dull and ordinary.

The *Pinot Noirs* are on the light and fruity side, with the *1969* being less successful than previous bottlings. It is marred by a lack of balance and some harshness that does not seem as if it will disappear completely with age. The *Cabernet Sauvignons,* including the *1968,* have generally been light and without deep character in the past. However, beginning with the 1969 vintage it appears that Parducci will be concentrating more on this varietal. Four individual wines have been released from this year—three from various vineyards in Mendocino County and one from Lake County.

Among the white wines the *French Colombard* and *Flora* have been the most successful, while the *Chablis, White Pinot,* and *Chenin Blanc* have generally been unexciting. The *Chardonnay* has tended to show some character and fairly nice flavors, but it has never been outstanding.

Occasionally the *French Colombard* can be made with a little residual sweetness and a slight effervescence. This was true of the *1968* and *1971,* and the result was a fresh, pleasant wine. In other years it has tended to be drier and heavier, though generally retaining more character than you would expect from this varietal. Parducci has been making the *Flora* for only a few years, but it shows promise. The *1970* is a fruity wine with a hint of sweetness and some spicy-earthy flavors.

The wines of Parducci range from well made and exciting to dull and uninteresting. The winery appears to be in a transition phase, with new vineyards coming into bearing and some varietals being added while others are discontinued. Past performance has certainly been promising enough to merit following the winery's progress closely, and one nice way to do this is by periodic visits to the winery and its adjacent tasting room.

Small Wineries of the San Francisco Bay Area

Within an hour's drive of San Francisco and still within the confines of the Bay Area may be found four small wineries offering premium wines to the public. They range from long-established operations to recently opened extensions of the proprietor's hobby, and each of them provides a selection of interesting wines. In addition to the wineries described in the following pages, Windsor Vineyards maintains its tasting room in picturesque Tiburon, across the bay from San Francisco. Here all the wines of Windsor-Tiburon may be sampled in the setting of a charming Victorian house.

Davis Bynum

The Bynum winery, tasting room, and primary retail outlet are presently located in a small roadside building in the East Bay community of Albany, right next door to Berkeley. Here most of the wines are available for sampling, and you are certain to meet with a very friendly and informative reception.

Established only in 1965, the wines of Davis Bynum have already won many friends in the San Francisco and, more recently, Los Angeles areas. The grapes come from twenty-five acres north of Rutherford owned by Bynum as well as from other growers, primarily in the Napa Valley. About half the wine is currently purchased in bulk from other producers and then finished and aged in the Albany cellar. Plans now call for a winery to be built in 1973–74 at the site of the Napa Valley vineyard, and production will then increase to a maximum of 20,000 to 25,000 gallons from its present level of 8000 gallons annually.

The white wines of Davis Bynum include *Colombard* and *Green Hungarian,* both of which are fairly ordinary and reflect the lack of character in the grape varieties rather than any wine-making failings. Bynum is also one of the few wineries to produce a varietal *Flora,* which has generally been a fairly fresh, well-made wine with some hints of spiciness. A pleasant *Petite Sirah Rosé* has also been introduced recently. The *1972* is a dry, slightly *pétillant* wine with well-balanced fruity flavors and good character.

The Bynum reds are more consistent than the whites, with fairly good varietal character and good balance between wine and wood. All the reds are aged in oak, many of them in seventy-gallon French cognac barrels, for an average time of two to two and a half years. Among those due to be released in late 1973 are the *1971 Charbono,* which has light to moderate body, acid, and tannin with good fruit and a slight spicy character, and the *1971 Petite Sirah.* The latter is similar in style to the Charbono, though it is a bit fuller and more tannic at present. Most of the red wine production is in Zinfandel, and the regular *Zinfandel* has been consistently a good buy in the "reasonably priced" category. A *Reserve Zinfandel* is also offered, and its moderate body and tannin and good Zinfandel flavors generally require a few years to blend harmoniously.

Two less expensive wines, denominated *Barefoot Bynum,* are available, and they often are among the most attractive buys in the half-gallon class. The *Chablis* is quite fresh and pleasant, perhaps reflecting the Traminer grapes present in the wine, the bulk of which is Golden Chasselas. The *Burgundy,* produced from approximately 50 percent Early Burgundy, 25 percent Zinfandel, and 25 percent press wine, is a clean, very drinkable red.

On the whole, Davis Bynum's wines go a long way toward meeting his goal of producing the best possible everyday wine and honest varietals, and there seems to be a real concern in maintaining prices at a reasonable level. In keeping with this, the unusual (for California) practice of offering wine "futures" has been developed for those who are willing to buy at least two cases of wine while it is still in the barrel, although unfortunately this is limited by the tax and license laws of some states. What better way is there to get in on the ground floor of the California wine scene?

Gemello Winery

Nestled in the middle of the sprawling San Francisco Peninsula alongside busy El Camino Real, once the principal highway from San Francisco to San Jose, is a small winery owned by the Gemello family since 1934. Until recently the winery had undergone few changes in tradition over the past twenty or thirty years and continued to operate in the old Italian style, concentrating on long-term aging of red wines in large redwood cooperage. Recently some new small French oak barrels have been introduced for the aging of selected wines, with quite successful results. Grapes come primarily from the Santa Clara and Morgan Hill areas, although some, such as the Gamay, come from Napa. From time to time some wines are purchased in bulk from other producers and then blended and aged by Gemello.

For a small winery, Gemello produces a surprisingly full line of wines. The reds have consistently been the most interesting, while the whites are rather ordinary wines on the rough and alcoholic side. The Johannisberg Riesling offered in the late

1960s was the most pleasant, but the latest bottling of this variety purchased at the winery was oxidized.

Among the reds, though, many fine wines may be found. The *Ruby Cabernet* has consistently been impressive, showing good balance and richness and smooth, well-aged character. It is certainly an excellent buy and among the best wines of this varietal that we've found. The *1968 Cabernet Sauvignon* has a nice green-olive aroma and dark color and is developing richness in flavor, although the high tannin and good acid indicate that it has a long future ahead of it. The *nonvintage* Cabernet Sauvignon has varied over the years, often being quite good, but the latest blend does not have the depth nor potential of the 1968. The *Petite Sirah* is a new addition to the Gemello list and is a fairly young wine of good character and fruit that should develop well. The *Pinot Noir* is a bit woody, while the *Gamay* is a nice wine with some fruit and more body than the typical California Gamay.

The current *Zinfandels* have been aged in small French oak and are considerably improved over the Zinfandel offered several years ago. Though not vintaged on the label, those carrying the "35th Anniversary Selection" notation are from the 1968 harvest. Selections aged in both Nevers and Limousin oak were bottled, and the wines both display good fruit and balance and have the potential of developing excellent character and complexity by the late 1970s.

The winery is open to visitors on weekdays for an informal tour, although there is no tasting. The primary retail outlet for Gemello wines is a liquor and wine store adjacent to the winery just off El Camino Real, which has always been a friendly place to talk about Gemello or California wines in general.

Nepenthe Cellars

The title of smallest winery may well belong to George Burtness' Nepenthe Cellars, which was founded in the garage of Mr. Burtness' Portola Valley home in 1967. Production at the present time is very limited—about 1000 gallons annually —but future plans call for expanding to larger quarters and planting more vines, hopefully in the Portola Valley area. Presently grapes for Nepenthe wines come from an acre of vines which gently slope down from the back of the house, about five acres in the Vine Hill district of the Santa Cruz Mountains, and from grapes bought in the Hecker Pass area near Gilroy. The white varieties are purchased from the Ruby Hill vineyards in Livermore.

Despite its small size, a number of different varietals have been offered under the Vines of Nepenthe label. The wines are neither fined nor filtered, and all spend at least some time in French oak barrels. In general, the red varieties are more successful than the whites, though the *1971 Riesling* is a good, clean, dry wine and the *1972* tasted in barrel also shows good promise. A pleasant, tart *Petite Sirah Rosé* has also been produced.

There is quite a bit of variation among the red varieties, though on the whole they exhibit good varietal character. The *Zinfandels* are good, with the *1971* from the Hecker Pass area showing excellent fruit which promises good future development when it is bottled. The *1968* and *1971 Cabernet Sauvignons* from the Santa Cruz Mountains have a distinct minty character, though the latter will probably not be bottled until late 1973 or early 1974. Both need seven to ten years' bottle age to smooth out the rather rough tannin. A red *1969 Grenache* is surprisingly full-bodied, though it still retains good fruit, while the *1969 Petite Sirah* is typically big, spicy, young, and a little bitter now. A small amount of 1971 *Pinot Noir* will be available, though because of legal technicalities it may end up being bottled as a nonvintaged wine. This is a fairly full, well-balanced wine with complex aromas and flavors that certainly compares very favorably with most other California Pinot Noirs.

While to our tastes many of Nepenthe's wines would be better balanced with a little less wood, all evidence care and dedication to the art of wine making. There are understandably no tours or tasting available, but those wishing further information about the winery or wines are encouraged to write to Mr. Burtness. The wines are available at the winery and in limited quantities at a few wine shops in the San Francisco Bay Area.

Woodside Vineyards

Nestled in the rather unlikely setting of a residential peninsula community, Woodside Vineyards was founded in 1963 by Robert Groetzinger and Robert Mullen and their wives and was bonded a year later. Today the winery is owned by Robert and Polly Mullen, the Groetzingers having moved to Europe, and they continue to make the fresh, delightful wines that have characterized the Woodside label.

Still primarily a hobby, Woodside's production has increased only slightly over the past few years to its present total of 1100 gallons annually. A total of five acres of vines are scattered throughout the community and planted in Cabernet Sauvignon, Pinot Noir, Chardonnay, and Chenin Blanc. The yield of the young vines is still small, and at present some Chardonnay and Pinot Noir is purchased from the Carneros region of Napa to supplement the local grapes. The Mullens hope that as their own vines mature the yield will increase sufficiently to supply the entire needs of the winery.

One of the smallest wineries of the state, the building is actually a cellar beneath the family carport and measures in at twenty-four by twenty-four feet. Harvest time is a community tradition, with friends and neighbors joining in with the work and festivity of the season.

Although a veritable midget compared to the giants of the California industry, Woodside produces wines easily capable of competing with other California vintners in the premium retail market. The *1971 Chenin Blanc* continues in the style of previous vintages as a light, crisp wine with a very fruity flavor. The *1970 Chardonnay* is a bit fuller in body, though still relatively light compared to other California Chardonnays, and it has very good color and excellent acid balance.

Woodside's *Cabernet Sauvignon* is bottled under the famous La Questa label, since the grapes are from vines located on the old La Questa Vineyard property that was first cultivated in 1883. We have tried several vintages of the Cabernet and found it to be a fruity wine with light to medium body and very fine, herbaceous Cabernet character in the aroma and flavor. The *1968* continues this style and shows good Cabernet flavors; the aroma develops into a nice green-olive character upon breathing. Although relatively light-bodied compared to some of the big Cabernets of other wineries, the wine will improve with bottle age and acquire depth and roundness of flavors.

The best source of Woodside wines is the winery itself, although a small amount is occasionally available at one of the local shops. Those of you who would like to meet the Mullens may write or phone to request an appointment to "tour" the one-room winery and may be assured of a very friendly and informative visit.

Small Wineries of the Santa Cruz Mountains

Bargetto Winery

Located just a few miles from the beaches of Santa Cruz in the small town of Soquel, Bargetto is a family-run winery that was founded in 1933. Production has gradually increased to around 125,000 gallons annually, but most of the grapes for Bargetto wines continue to come from vineyards in the Santa Cruz area. Many of these are owned by the Bargettos themselves, while others are owned by local growers who have supplied the winery for years.

Bargetto produces a complete line of table, dessert, and fruit wines, and the table wines include both the premium Bargetto label and the less expensive Santa Cruz Cellars brand. The latter is primarily press wine, though some varietal wine may be added to the seven generic blends produced.

The Bargetto whites are generally pleasant, and recently have tended more toward the lesser-known varieties than to the more famous *Chardonnays* or *Johannisberg Rieslings*. These latter, when available, usually evidence good varietal character. Among those wines tasted recently, the *Chablis* is a pleasant, clean wine with fairly fresh flavors, and an interesting *Haut Sauterne,* produced from Semillon and Muscat grapes, is less sweet than most similarly labeled wines. The

Muscat grapes are grown in Modesto, in the Central Valley, and are used to produce a very flowery, medium-sweet *Moscato Amabile* that is not cloying and finishes well, and also a recently introduced *Dry Muscat*. Actually off-dry, it unfortunately does not seem to capture the freshness and fruit of the sweeter Moscato.

Most of the red wine production is in *Zinfandel*. A *nonvintaged* blend of 1969–70 is very fruity, with moderate body, acid, and tannin, and it should develop fairly well. The *1969 Cask 27* is lighter than the above, but it is well balanced and has good characteristic berry flavors. No 1970 Zinfandel will be produced, since most of this vintage went towards the *Claret* and *Burgundy* blends. The former is perhaps the more pleasant; fairly light, it contains 75 percent Zinfandel and 25 percent Ruby Cabernet grapes. The Burgundy is 80 percent Zinfandel and 20 percent Carignane, and while it is a bit fuller, it is ordinary.

Among the other reds, the *Barbera* is clearly the leader. *1968* produced a deep, fairly full wine that will probably not peak until the late 1970s. Dark red in color, it has a rich, minty aroma, and moderate body, acid, and tannin. The most disappointing wine is the *1968 Ruby Cabernet,* which is fairly big but rather rough and overpriced.

A new tasting room overlooking a small creek is now open at Bargetto, and your reception there should be very friendly. Most varieties may be sampled, and your hosts are both knowledgeable and personable. The best source for the wines remains at the winery itself, and most are well made and bear investigating.

David Bruce

Dr. David Bruce is a dermatologist who began making wines as a hobby in the 1950s and in 1964 founded the winery that bears his name. Located in a beautiful setting in the foothills of the Santa Cruz Mountains, the Bruce family home is adjacent to thirty acres of vines planted in Chardonnay, White Riesling, Pinot Noir, and Cabernet Sauvignon. An additional supply of Zinfandel and Grenache grapes is obtained from growers in the Hecker Pass region east of Gilroy.

David Bruce wines are certainly distinctive, with both whites and reds tending to be big and alcoholic. The best ones have considerable intensity and character, while the less successful are simply overpriced. Most bottlings fall within the $4 to $8 range, although the *1969 Chardonnay* was offered at $22 a bottle because Dr. Bruce considered it superior to a Montrachet priced at that amount.

1971 was the first vintage for the *White Riesling,* and the wine is big and dry, with about 15 percent alcohol. A bit rough in the finish and without the fruitiness that usually characterizes this varietal, it is still an interesting wine. The *1969 Grenache* was made as if it were a white wine, except for contact with the skins for about twenty-four hours. The resulting wine is like a big rosé, with medium-pink color, a dry finish, and lots of Grenache character and fruit both in the aroma and flavor. Part of this vintage was kept back for additional aging in new Limousin oak barrels and released as a special cask bottling.

The *1969 Zinfandel* was produced from very ripe, late-harvested grapes. Most of the wine was aged in Limousin oak, with small batches also having spent some time in Nevers and American oak. This is a big, intense, fruity wine with very high alcohol, good tannin, and a rich, complex flavor. It is probably one of the most successful David Bruce wines of recent years, and it should continue to improve for five to ten years in the bottle. A *White Zinfandel* has also been produced in several different vintages since 1964. The wine is produced in the style of a white, hence the name, although the actual color is tinged with orange or pink depending on how long the skins remained in contact with the juice. As with other wines of this type, we have yet to be very impressed and can't help feeling they might have been better fermented out as red wines.

The wines of David Bruce are available by direct mail order and at a few selected retail outlets, a current list of which may be obtained by writing to the winery. Those of you who would like to visit Dr. Bruce are requested to write ahead for an appointment.

Martin Ray

From a mountainside in the Santa Clara Valley just above Saratoga come the most expensive wines produced in California, those of Martin Ray. Wine maker under the Paul Masson label until he sold the name in 1943, Martin Ray has developed an exclusive and high-priced operation and grows only Pinot Noir, Cabernet Sauvignon, Chardonnay, and White Riesling grapes (although none of the Riesling wines are presently available).

The original Martin Ray plantings were gradually extended until the twenty-five-acre Martin Ray Domaine consisted of five vineyards under separate ownership, but all farmed by the Rays. Recent legal activity has resulted in the Domaine's being split: the winery and two vineyards are now controlled by Mr. Ray's son, Peter Martin Ray, who is continuing to make wine under the Martin Ray label, as he has since 1958. The other three parcels are in the hands of former shareholders and are now unconnected with Martin Ray.

While the rampant egotism of Martin Ray's literature has kept pace with the price of the wines themselves (which may reach $50 a bottle), Martin, Eleanor, and Peter Ray are themselves very hospitable, friendly people. The wines are 100 percent varietals and all do possess a certain distinctive Martin Ray character. Yet just because a wine is full-bodied and different doesn't necessarily make it a great, or even a good, wine. "Character" must be pleasing, not merely distinctive.

The *Chardonnay* is the star of the Martin Ray cellar, and those we have tasted are certainly the fullest, most intensely flavored California whites we have encountered. Deep gold in color, forceful, and chewy, they exhibit strong wood character which reflects the one to two years spent in Limousin oak barrels. Some of the richness, though, comes at the expense of the high fruit acidity needed to balance such a big wine.

None of the reservations we felt upon tasting the Chardonnays extend to the *Pinot Noir,* although many novice or even intermediate wine drinkers may find its rather heavy, overwhelming flavor and aroma unpleasant. Both the *1963* and *1964* should be opened an hour or so before serving; they are full, rich wines with complex, earthy character and deep fruit, quite different from the light Pinot Noirs generally found in California. Of the two, the 1964 is a bit fuller and better balanced.

We have tasted four Martin Ray *Cabernet Sauvignons:* the *1964* was terrible, with an unpleasant burned aroma and taste; the *1968* has a strong green-olive character that, while it is certainly distinctive, we found only marginally less distracting than the 1964; the *1953,* tasted in 1970 and described in the first edition of this book, can only be termed an enigma in view of its apparent age yet closed-in, youthful taste; and finally the *1966* is a big, gutsy wine that we greatly enjoyed and would rank among California's best. Again, character and distinctiveness are present in abundance, but there seem to be wide variations from year to year.

Many of Martin Ray's wines, particularly the Chardonnay, offer unique tasting experiences, though we must repeat that the experience might not always be one you would like to repeat. Only with a fairly extensive wine-drinking background can one appreciate the intensity and complexity of Martin Ray, and even then . . . But in any case, the prices attached to the Ray wines are absurd; while it may be a valid method of restricting demand when a wine is first released, no wine is worth $50 a bottle, or probably even $20.

The Mt. Eden winery is not open to the public, although you may write well in advance and request an appointment. The wines have a very limited distribution, and inquiries along these lines should be directed to the winery.

Novitiate of Los Gatos

The Jesuit Fathers and Brothers at the Novitiate of Los Gatos have been producing wine since 1888, the great majority of which has always been dedicated to sacramental use. In response to the increased demand for premium wines and to continue to provide revenue to support the activities of the Novitiate, approximately one third of the winery's output is now offered commercially. Eventual plans call for the commercial wines to comprise just over half of the total production, with the traditional sacramental wines remaining as a large minority.

Much of the equipment at the winery has been bought from other wineries or created by the brothers themselves, and expansion is continuing. Together, the ensemble affords a complete and modern operation. All grapes for Novitiate wines come from the brothers' own vineyards, most of which surround the winery. Only free-run juice is used, while the press wine is distilled to provide the base spirits for Novitiate's many dessert wines.

A fairly complete line of table wines is offered, including six whites, a rosé, and three reds. In addition, their *Johannisberg Riesling* and *Pinot Noir* will be restored to the list as soon as newly planted vines come into bearing.

Novitiate's whites are generally sound, not unpleasant wines of about average character, and include a *Dry Sauterne, Chablis, Pinot Blanc,* medium-dry *Chenin Blanc,* and fairly sweet *Château Novitiate*. The newest wine is a very nice *Dry Malvasia*, which is fairly soft, fruity, and off-dry, with the delightful orange-blossom aroma characteristic of the grape.

Although none of the Novitiate wines are vintaged, the reds are usually about five years old when released. The *Burgundy* has light to moderate body, tannin, and acid; it is a pleasant wine of some character that has a fresh Zinfandel-like aroma. Both a *Ruby Cabernet* and a *Cabernet Sauvignon* are produced. The former is light and pleasant enough, while the latter is a well-balanced wine of light to moderate body, tannin, and acid, although it is a bit woody and slightly rough.

One of Novitiate's most successful wines remains its *Grenache Rosé*, which has a characteristically fresh, fruity aroma, light to moderate body, and good acidity. It is medium dry and quite pleasant.

Now that distribution is improving, wines from the Novitiate should be more easily obtainable and will probably compare favorably with many of the better-known labels. A new tasting room is now open Monday through Saturday, and tours are scheduled on Tuesday and Friday afternoons. Certainly the beautiful setting in the hills above Los Gatos and the friendly, if slightly commercial, reception awaiting you should make a visit to Novitiate very enjoyable.

Ridge Vineyards

Located 2300 feet above sea level on the Monte Bello Ridge of the Santa Cruz Mountains, Ridge Vineyards was founded in 1962 and since that time has continued to grow both in reputation and production. The original ramshackle wooden winery is now used only for storage and tastings, while the remodeled Montebello winery a mile farther up the road houses the wine-making facilities and barrel-aging room.

David Bennion, one of the original founders of the winery,

served as wine maker through the 1968 vintage. Today he continues to supervise care of the vineyards and day-to-day business operations, while Paul Draper is very capably filling the role of wine maker. The vineyards surrounding the winery supply Cabernet Sauvignon, a small amount of Chardonnay, and some Zinfandel. Other Zinfandel grapes are purchased from different areas in the state, while the white varieties come from plantings owned by Ridge in the Santa Cruz Mountains.

The red wines of Ridge are known for their sturdiness and intensity, and they are made in a very traditional way, without fining or filtering. Although the winery is not old enough to have wines that have proved they will withstand the test of time, many of the young reds do exhibit great potential. In the past few vintages, perhaps reflecting a difference in wine-making goals, the wines have shown more elegance and balance when young, while still retaining fine depth. Still, they are not for everyone, and you have to have a strong palate to chew through the tannin of a young Ridge red.

The *Cabernet Sauvignons* have consistently shown good varietal character. The *1963* is lighter in style than subsequent vintages, while the *1965* and *1968* are huge wines with great depth and tannin. Both are a long way from their peak, and if their fruit outlives the tannin they may be great. The *1970* is another tremendously big wine with a fine future. The *1971 Montebello* has a nice green-olive aroma and shows good balance. It is lighter than preceding years and should mature in less time (late 1970s). Three nonvintage blends have also been offered, though they are less distinctive than the vintaged wines.

About 60 percent of their annual production is in Zinfandel, and Ridge has probably contributed more than any other winery to this variety's rise in prestige. Wines from individual vineyards are bottled separately, and, while the result is often a confusing array of labels, a comparative tasting of several Ridge Zinfandels can be a very interesting experience.

Ridge produces some of the biggest *Zinfandels* in the state, and such wines as the *1969 Montebello* may well require two decades of bottle age. The *1970 Late Harvest* from Occidental, in Sonoma County, is another very substantial wine with deep fruit, high alcohol (16.5 percent), and a trace of residual sweetness. It will age well, although its ripeness imparts a roundness that will make it quite drinkable in a few years.

The best *1971* Zinfandels are from *Mendocino* and *Occidental*. The former has deep color, a vanilla nose, good tannin and fruit, while the latter is another late-harvest wine with big body, high alcohol, and an intense prunelike nose. Both appear to have excellent potential. 1971 also continues a line of successful *Geyserville* Zinfandels, including a fruity *1971 Primeur Zinfandel* which was released after only a few months in wood and is meant for early consumption.

Ridge's search for Zinfandel has also extended to Lodi, in the northern San Joaquin Valley. Some of these have been good for wines from such a warm area, although generally they lack the intensity and fruit of the North Coast wines. The *1971 Lodi* is rather ordinary, with light-red color and an undistinguished aroma and flavor.

In 1970 Ridge became one of the few wineries in the state to bottle a *White Zinfandel*. Like others we have tried, the wine is not particularly exciting, and the flavor is rather heavy and cumbersome.

In some vintages a *Zinfandel Essence* has also been produced from extremely ripe grapes, often with some *Botrytis* present, and it has a deep-red color and a rich, sweet, portlike finish.

Two new varietals for Ridge are *Gamay* and *Petite Sirah*, both of which were quite successful in *1971*. A *Pinot Noir* of the same vintage, however, was rather light in flavors and character.

The white wines of Ridge comprise but a small amount of the total production, and they have not achieved the distinction and complexity of the reds. For the most part they are alcoholic and awkward, although their full body and strong flavors may appeal to some wine drinkers.

Ridge wines are available in a few retail outlets, and periodic tastings at the winery are announced through a mailing list. Those wishing to visit the winery are requested to write or phone ahead for an appointment.

Small Wineries of
South Santa Clara County

Bertero Winery

Bertero is in many ways a typical small California country winery, with large redwood casks being the predominant cooperage and the friendly owners happy to offer you samples of their wine while talking of the current vintage or of the future of the California wine industry. Bertero is located in the Hecker Pass region and is a pleasant change from some of the overtly commercial tasting rooms that lie clustered along nearby Highway 101. The Berteros have been making wine for years and selling most of it in bulk to other wineries, but in 1965 they began offering some wines under their own label.

In the past Bertero has produced several fine wines, particularly the *Barbera* and *Pinot Noir,* that were well worth the long drive out into the countryside to buy them. The recent wines we have tasted seem to have slipped a bit, however, and have not retained their former balance and flavors. The *Pinot Noir* remains a palatable, fruity wine that is rather nice, but the remaining reds have had a pronounced redwood bouquet and flavor and a tartness that borders on sharpness. These include a *Cabernet Sauvignon, Barbera, Grignolino, Zinfandel,* and *Burgundy.* The whites include a *Sauterne* that is dry and without significant flavors and a new dry *Chenin*

Blanc that has a very nice, pineapplelike aroma and good fruit, but some harshness in the aftertaste.

Certainly the past successes of Bertero provide reason to expect improvement, and the winery merits revisiting. Hopefully the current style is but a temporary lapse and some nice *vins de pays* will come from Bertero in the future.

Bonesio Winery

Another friendly reception awaits you as you approach the rather ramshackle museum of curios that doubles as the Bonesio tasting room on the Watsonville Road west of Gilroy. All varieties may be leisurely sampled, and the atmosphere is definitely informal. Bonesio wines are bottled under the *Uvas* label, the Spanish word for grape and the local name for the valley in which the winery is situated.

A full line of wines is available, including table, sparkling, dessert, and fruit wines. The sparkling wines are of the bulk process variety, made by San Martin and bottled with plastic closures.

Among the table wines, the whites are generally light and soft, with the regionally popular *Malvasia Bianca* probably heading the list. Off-dry, it is light-bodied and has the nice orange-blossom character typical of the grape. The reds include several unusual varieties: A *Malvasia Nera* is a very light red wine with only slight tannin and a slightly sweet flavor reminiscent of the Malvasia Bianca. An exception to the general rule regarding reds, it is probably best served chilled. Bonesio also produces a red *Grenache,* which is again quite light and more like a full-bodied rosé than a red. It may also be served chilled, which reinforces its roselike character. A third oddity is the *Mataro,* a Zinfandellike wine from the Spanish Mataro grape. Light to moderate in body, it is a fairly soft wine with a fresh, fruity nose.

The more familiar wines include an average *Burgundy* with slight raisin character, a pleasant, though fairly light, *Cabernet Sauvignon,* and a somewhat disappointing *Pinot Noir.*

Bonesio also has a few vintage wines available which usually average five or six years old. These wines (Cabernet Sauvignon, Pinot Noir, Grignolino, and Zinfandel) generally display complex, well-aged character and seem worth their extra price. The *1966 Pinot Noir* and *1964 Grignolino* show considerable age already, reflecting the light style of most of Bonesio's wines, and should probably be drunk in the near future.

In general, Bonesio's wines are light, soft, and of adequate though not overwhelming character. At best, this may result in a delicate, elegant wine; at worst, the wine may be rather bland but will rarely be unpleasant. Since prices have remained fairly reasonable, you might enjoy becoming acquainted with the Uvas label.

Los Altos Vineyards

It was with some trepidation that we returned to Los Altos after thoroughly unpleasant previous visits, but thankfully our fears were ill founded this time. While the emphasis is still on the commercial side, the first words you hear upon entering the tasting room are likely to be, "Would you like to taste some wine?" The accent is now on youth, with an appropriately hirsute host and some natural foods for sale, and the atmosphere is certainly less oppressive than previously.

Unfortunately, tasting samples are still served sparingly in cone-shaped sherry glasses, so it is difficult for you to adequately judge the wines from just a visit to the tasting room. The whites tend to be bland and inoffensive, though they generally lack any great varietal character. The reds have a bit more to them, and the soft, fairly smooth *Burgundy* might be the best buy of the group. The *Zinfandel* and *Barbera* will both benefit from another year or two of bottle age and are not unpleasant wines of average character. The *Gamay Beaujolais* is a very light, rather nondescript wine; the *Pinot Noir* is similar, but heavier and with a bit more tannin.

In addition to the usual line of varietal and generic table wines, the specialties of the house include Ambrosia, Mead, mint, and coffee wines, and a wide selection of fruit and dessert wines. Sales are made through the tasting rooms in Gilroy, California, and Chicago, Illinois.

Pedrizetti Winery

The Pedrizetti Winery lies amid orchards and vineyards to the east of U.S. Highway 101 in the rather sleepy Santa Clara Valley town of Morgan Hill. Though the winery itself is closed to visitors, a relatively new Pedrizetti Family Wine Shop and Tasting Room is now located in a tourist-trap collection of stores in Morgan Hill called the Gallery. A sign in the tasting room requests that you "please do not abuse our hospitality. Three tastes are sufficient," but all varieties are generally available for sampling, and if it isn't too busy the three-taste limit may be overlooked. The sherry glasses formerly employed for tasting have been replaced, and though the wineglasses now used are an improvement they are still quite small and it is sometimes difficult to adequately judge the sample offered.

A full line of table, dessert, and sparkling wines are available, with yearly production in the 100,000-gallon range. Some wines are estate-bottled from Green Hungarian, Grenache, Barbera, and Zinfandel grapes, while others, including Gamay Beaujolais and Cabernet Sauvignon, are made from grapes purchased in Sonoma County. A *Pinot*

Noir and *Chardonnay* have recently been discontinued due to scarcity and high prices of the grapes.

Pedrizetti wines are generally sound and without technical flaws though without great distinction. Among the whites the *Green Hungarian* is probably the most successful, though its slightly low acidity does not back up the promise of a pleasant, minty aroma. The *Chablis* and *Chenin Blanc* are simple, the latter slightly sweet, but the *1969 Pinot Blanc* is disappointing and quite overpriced. An off-dry *Grenache Rosé* has a nice, fruity nose but is rather thin in flavor.

Like many Santa Clara Valley wineries, Pedrizetti's best red wine is its *Barbera,* which is generally released when it is around six years old. The *1966* had a rich, complex nose, though its moderate body and tannin need a few more years to smooth out. The *Gamay Beaujolais* is also nice, with light to moderate body and tannin and good fruit. The *1969 Cabernet Sauvignon* is fairly light-bodied, and its average Cabernet character needs another couple of years to develop. Both the *Zinfandel* and *Burgundy* (primarily from Carignane and Petite Sirah) are simple and a bit rough, with rather heavy, raisinlike aromas.

The winery's only retail outlet is the tasting room itself, so you are encouraged to taste before you buy. Weekends might be a bit crowded, as the Gallery is a frequent stop for tour buses.

Thomas Kruse Winery

One of California's newest wineries, Thomas Kruse is nestled between Bertero, Bonesio, and a commercial cactus patch in the Hecker Pass region of the southern Santa Clara Valley. It is essentially a one-man operation, with Tom Kruse in charge of everything from recoopering barrels to grafting vines to fermenting and finishing the final product. Most of his grapes come from vineyards in the Hecker Pass area, and future plans call for some acres surrounding the winery as well.

1971 was the first commercial crush for Tom Kruse, and it has been introduced by a white Sauvignon Vert and a whole range of rosés: Grenache, Zinfandel, Grignolino, Carignane, Grand Noir, and Cabernet Sauvignon. The *Sauvignon Vert* is a clean, dry wine which is fairly distinctive for this grape variety. All the rosés are dry; the *Grignolino* is fairly light and tart with a pleasant fresh taste, while the *Cabernet Sauvignon Rosé* is a bit fuller and does have some Cabernet character. While most of the reds are still aging in fifty-gallon oak barrels, a fairly pleasant though still young *Burgundy* (from Alicante Bouschet and Grenache grapes) has already been released.

Production is very limited at the moment, and no firm decisions have been made as to what varietals will eventually become "regular" members of the Thomas Kruse family of wines. Certainly the rosés are considered experiments at this stage, and it is doubtful that all will be continued. Methods are traditional, including fermentation in fifty-gallon oak barrels and the complete renovation of the existing winery building rather than constructing a new one.

The wines can currently be purchased only at the winery, and limited tasting is generally available. The first vintage thus far seems very encouraging, and we wish Mr. Kruse continuing success.

Small Wineries of
Monterey County

Chalone Vineyard

Vineyards have been planted in the Pinnacles Mountains east of Soledad since the early 1900s, but it was not until the mid-1960s that Dick Graff began producing wines from the small winery in the shadow of Mount Chalone. There are presently 30 acres of the veteran vines still in production, and plans call for planting about 10 additional acres per year, primarily in Chardonnay and Pinot Noir, until the total acreage reaches 100.

To date there has been no Pinot Noir offered commercially, but already Chalone's Chenin Blanc, Pinot Blanc, and Chardonnay rank among the finest California whites. The vinification methods are traditional, and all Chalone wines are fermented and aged in sixty-gallon French oak barrels. The distinctive, oily character of the oak is present in all the wines; the Chardonnay is aged for approximately a year in new Limousin barrels, the Chenin Blanc and Pinot Blanc in once-used barrels for six to eight months. Mr. Graff also feels that the soil in the Chalone vineyards imparts a recognizable *goût de terroir,* or earthy character, to his wines.

While we felt that the woody character of the 1969 *Chenin Blanc* was a bit overpowering, the 1970 is a well-balanced, spicy wine that successfully combines the richness of oak with the fruitiness of the Chenin Blanc grape. Although dry, the intense fruit leaves the impression of a slight sweetness in the flavor. The 1969 *Pinot Blanc* is the biggest wine of this variety that we have tasted, and its full, spicy flavors are much richer than many California Chardonnays. The 1970 is similar, and both will benefit from a couple of years of bottle age. The 1969 *Chardonnay* is again a full, dry, oaky wine similar in style to many of the finest French white Burgundies. Well balanced and with excellent varietal character, this wine will also improve with bottle age and should be at its peak in 1973–75.

For those who like full, intensely flavored white wines, Chalone may well be the best that California has to offer. They are excellent wines of their type, and their bigness does not come at the expense of sacrificing fruitiness or elegance. Unfortunately, Chalone wines are presently in very short supply, though they should become more available as the new vineyards come into bearing. The winery is not equipped to handle visitors, but inquiries about Chalone wines should be addressed to Mr. Graff. The first two vintages of Chalone have certainly been impressive, and we hope that the future is as successful.

Small Wineries of San Luis Obispo and Santa Barbara Counties

Wine growing dates back more than a century in San Luis Obispo County, and today several small wineries are carrying on this heritage. The prime varietal grown here has been Zinfandel, although in recent years small plantings of other premium grapes have taken place.

In neighboring Santa Barbara County the planting fervor is even greater, and since 1960 two thousand acres of Cabernet Sauvignon, Chardonnay, Gewürztraminer, Pinot Noir, White Riesling, and Merlot have been planted. The major areas being planted are along the Sisquoc and Santa Ynez Rivers, and the initial success of the vines indicates that this may become an important new California wine-growing region.

Pesenti Winery

The first Pesenti vineyards were planted in 1923, and the winery, located on Vineyard Drive just three miles west of Templeton, was bonded in 1934. Some new vines have been added, and today the vineyards comprise nearly 100 acres. The Pesentis also buy grapes from neighboring fields and offer a full line of dry, sweet, sparkling, fruit, and dessert wines.

Several large signs along the highway direct you to the winery and tasting room where all the wines may be sampled, both from the less expensive Private Stock line and the higher-priced Premium Stock label. While there seems to be no reluctance to pour any wine requested, the samples are often quite small and the glasses leave a bit to be desired considering the evident attempt to attract visitors.

The only varietals bottled are a Golden Muscat, Zinfandel, Zinfandel Rosé, and Cabernet, but a wide selection of generics is available, including several sweet reds. The Private Stock *Zinfandel* is blended with Carignane and produces a rather simple, fairly light, but not unpleasant wine that would be fine for everyday drinking. The Premium Stock *Zinfandel* has a higher complement of Zinfandel grapes and offers a deeper, slightly raisinlike character for its higher price (which, at least in the fifth size, seems excessive). The *Ruby Cabernet,* labeled simply Cabernet, is a pleasant wine with light to moderate body and tannin and fair fruit.

Pesenti's thirty table wines would take most of the afternoon to taste, but the reception is friendly and it's a pleasant stop if you're in the area.

Rotta Winery

Founded in 1856 and owned by the Rotta family since 1907, the Rotta Winery is the oldest of the three wineries presently clustered a few miles west of Templeton in San Luis Obispo County. Its production is limited to a few varieties and the redwood tank–tasting room and the simple old-fashioned style of the winery itself is in marked contrast to many more modern California wineries, both large and small.

The grapes for Rotta wines come from the Rotta's own vineyards, which are planted primarily to the regional favorite of Zinfandel. While a couple of Muscats as well as the usual

Chablis and Burgundy are produced, the bulk of the winery's production is made up of four variations of Zinfandel: "old," regular, medium, and sweet. Aged in 7000-gallon redwood tanks, the *Old Zinfandel* is seventeen years old at the time of bottling, while the regular is thirteen. The regular *Zinfandel* is rather harsh and tastes of the redwood in which it is aged; its light to moderate body and tannin leave it a rough country wine. The *Old Zinfandel* is a bit smoother and more interesting, but also possesses the redwood flavor of the regular.

The wines are bottled in screw tops even in the fifth size, and all may be tasted at the winery. While plastic cups serve as tasting glasses, the samples are generous and the atmosphere friendly.

Santa Barbara Winery

With the goal of reviving Santa Barbara's wine-making heritage, Pierre Lafond crushed the new Santa Barbara Winery's first grapes in 1965. Grapes were purchased from local growers in Santa Barbara and San Luis Obispo counties, and Mr. Lafond hopes to retain a distinctive regional character in his wines. Eventual production will be in the 75,000- to 100,000-gallon range, and the winery is currently planting vines of its own.

Because of the limited availability and high prices of grapes, Santa Barbara Winery produced no table wine in 1971, 1972, or 1973, concentrating instead on their very successful fruit wines which are sold under the Solvang label. Forty acres of grapes on the Santa Ynez River north of Santa Barbara have recently been planted, primarily in Chenin Blanc and Zinfandel, and it is hoped that these and other vineyards in the area will enable the winery to recommence the production of table wines in 1974. A new winery, exclusively for table wines, is also planned for the Santa Ynez Valley.

Although the true direction the winery will take cannot be determined until the 1974 vintage is available, we have tasted a few Santa Barbara wines that may be indicative of future trends. One of the most successful whites was the *1970 Johannisberg Riesling,* a fresh, medium-dry wine that retained good acidity and Riesling character. As with other wineries in the Santa Barbara-San Luis Obispo region, the *Zinfandel* is perhaps the most important red variety. Santa Barbara's *Lot #1* (two thirds 1966, one third 1967) was a fairly substantial wine with distinct redwood character; while it had good fruit and character, it was also a bit rough and unbalanced. The *1968* and *1969* vintages were quite a bit lighter than the Lot #1, and both possessed a very distinctive strawberrylike nose. Fresh and fruity, both are pleasant, though the 1968 seems to have more zest and complexity than 1969. A very light-bodied *1968 Cabernet Sauvignon* was also produced, which had a pungent green-olive character in both nose and flavor.

The winery is presently located in beautiful downtown Santa Barbara, and a tasting room and small shop are attached to it. All varieties available may be sampled, though small sherry glasses make this difficult. Santa Barbara wines are also available through a number of retail outlets in Southern California, but it will be 1975 before the table wines begin to reappear in commercial quantities.

York Mountain Winery

Set in the eastern slopes of the Santa Lucia Mountains, York Mountain Winery is just seven miles as the crow flies from the Pacific Ocean. And while its location on quiet, winding York Mountain Road (just off California Highway 46) is a bit below the summit of York Mountain, its 1500-foot elevation makes it one of the few true "mountain" vineyards in California. Originally founded in 1875 and bought by Andrew York in 1882, the winery remained in the hands of the York family until 1970, when, after a few years of relative inactivity, it was purchased by Max Goldman. Mr. Goldman, who has been active in the wine industry in both California and New York for over thirty years, intends to preserve the York Mountain name while completely renovating both the winery and vineyards.

Currently planted primarily in Zinfandel, future plans call for gradually uprooting the old vines and replacing them with Chardonnay, Chenin Blanc, and French Colombard in the whites, and Cabernet Sauvignon, Pinot Noir, and Zinfandel in the reds. To provide the grapes for an eventual production in the neighborhood of 75,000 to 100,000 gallons, approximately ninety acres of vines will be planted.

Wines currently available under the York Mountain label have been primarily bought in bulk and bottled for York Mountain by other California wineries. 1972 will be Mr. Goldman's first crush, and his wines will become available in the mid-1970s. Until that time, there has been a conscious effort to offer wines that are similar in style to those that will eventually be produced from the replanted York Mountain vineyards.

York Mountain wines are currently for sale only at the winery, and both an informal tour and tasting are available. Certainly we are looking forward to the revival of this historic winery, and we wish Mr. Goldman every success.

Small Wineries of
the Sierra Foothills

Thoughts of the rolling hills that lead up to the majestic Sierra Nevada Mountains usually bring forth images of Gold Rush days and small mining towns rather than vineyards, but actually the first vines were planted here only shortly after the excitement of the gold fields had subsided. Today several hundred acres of vines remain in Amador and Placer Counties, and smaller lots may be found in neighboring Calaveras and El Dorado. The majority of vineyards are Zinfandel, although some Mission and other common varieties may be found, as well as a few new plantings of Cabernet Sauvignon and other premium grapes.

The Sierra foothills are certainly a scenic place to visit, and the added attraction of a glass of wine at a local winery makes them even more interesting. Several Napa Valley vintners have recently purchased grapes from Amador County vineyards, and this should serve to further increase the recognition of this region as a wine-growing area.

Butler Winery

Butler is a small new winery located in Sonora, California in the foothills of the Sierra Nevada. The back labels of Butler's bottles speak of wine making as an art rather than a process and disdain the use of modern sterilant chemicals or other than natural fermentation and clarification. While it sounds good on paper, the results we have tasted to date have been rather disastrous. The *Carignane* possessed very light color and a hazy suspension of yeast cells; the *Zinfandel* finished last in a tasting behind two homemade bottlings; and the *Alicante Bouschet,* while the most interesting of the three, had a dark-red color, considerable tannin, and clumsy, ill-balanced flavors.

We certainly enjoy seeing small wineries prosper and would wish the same to Butler, but there must obviously be considerable improvement in the state of the art practiced here before we would encourage anyone to try the Butler wines.

D'Agostini Winery

Set in the beautiful Sierra foothills that comprise the California Gold Rush Country, D'Agostini was founded in 1856 by Adam Uhlinger, a farsighted vintner who correctly surmised that vineyards would outlive the gold mines. One of the oldest California wineries, it acquired its present name when it was purchased by Enrico D'Agostini in 1911 and has remained in the family ever since. His four sons have been operating the winery since his death in 1956.

All D'Agostini wines are finished in oak after some time in redwood, and most are produced from the D'Agostinis' own 130 acres of vineyards, which still include a few of the original Zinfandel vines planted in 1856. Production is about 250,000 gallons a year, most of it being sold locally to both individuals and restaurants.

Only five wines are currently produced, and there are no plans for expansion of the list. In a demonstration of honesty and good sense too often absent in California, the D'Agostinis have decided to concentrate only on those varieties with which they feel most comfortable and which have been most successful for them. The *Sauterne* is primarily Golden Chasselas and, while possessing no great character, it is smooth, drinkable, and dry. A *Dry Muscat* is actually off-dry, with a light, fresh character enhanced by the typically fruity aroma of the Muscat Canelli grape. An average *Claret* is produced primarily from press wines of Zinfandel, Carignane, and Grenache grapes.

D'Agostini's two most successful wines are probably the Burgundy Reserve and the Zinfandel. The *Burgundy Reserve,* from Carignane grapes, is aged approximately four years before bottling and is a good, inexpensive wine, relatively fruity and smooth. The *Zinfandel* is a 100 percent varietal and is the only variety finished with a cork rather than a screw top. Though a bit rough, it has good Zinfandel character and will benefit from a couple of years more in the bottle. Light to moderate in body, acidity, and tannin, it is a good example of the wine for which Amador County is most noted.

Tasting (unfortunately from cone-shaped sherry glasses) and an informal tour of part of the original 1856 winery are available; you can even view some barrels made on the property from native oak in the nineteenth century. Your reception should be quite friendly, and the thirty-mile drive from Placerville is a very enjoyable one.

Lodi District

The Lodi District is located in the northern end of the fertile San Joaquin Valley. With almost 50,000 acres of vines, this is one of the most heavily planted vineyard regions in the world. It is also the home of the Flame Tokay grape, a prolific vine, used for both table grape and wine use, that will grow taller than a man's head and turn brilliant colors in the fall. The warm climate, rich soil, and use of irrigation assures production of large quantities of grapes that have traditionally been used in the production of jug wines, ports, sherries, and for the distillation into brandy.

Recently, however, plantings have concentrated more on varietals that will make better table wines, including Barbera, Petite Sirah, and Zinfandel among the reds; Chenin Blanc and Colombard among the whites; and the Ruby Cabernet, Emerald Riesling, and Gold developed specially at Davis for growing in warm areas.

Several wineries from the Lodi District are now producing table wines worthy of recognition, and many other vintners from throughout the state are using Lodi grapes, particularly Zinfandel, in their wines. Although most of the wineries in this region are a far cry from the small country winery discussed elsewhere in this section, the total percentage of their production devoted to varietal table wines remains fairly small and their distribution rather limited.

EAST-SIDE WINERY is a fairly large grower-owned co-operative that markets wines under the Royal Host label. The *Ruby Cabernet* has good body, a green-weedy aroma that suggests the Cabernet Sauvignon parentage of the vine, and a fair amount of tannin that will smooth out with age. Also produced are a slightly sweet, not unpleasant *Chenin Blanc* and a medium-sweet *Gold* that is very soft and has a nice floral-muscat aroma. Visitors are welcome at East Side and may taste all the wines at the tasting room adjacent to the winery.

A few miles away from the home of Royal Host is the BARENGO CELLARS, which is also open to visitors. Barengo has produced some nice wines, most notably a *Burgundy* that is an adequate everyday table wine and a *Ruby Cabernet* that tends to be lighter and fruitier than the Royal Host, but will also age fairly well.

Though certainly not up to the quality of the finest wines of the North Coast Counties, the varietal wines of the Lodi region probably deserve more recognition than they usually receive. In these days of skyrocketing wine costs they offer lower-priced alternatives of some rather palatable table wines.

Considerably south of Lodi near the town of Madera is another Central Valley winery that also deserves recognition for its table wines. FICKLIN VINEYARDS is most famous for its port, but it does produce a small quantity of reasonably priced *Emerald Riesling* and *Ruby Cabernet*. The former is a pleasant wine that compares favorably with many Riesling types from coastal vineyards, while the most recent sample we tried of the Ruby Cabernet was somewhat unbalanced and not as good as prior bottlings. Because of their limited supply, the wines are best available at the winery.

PART FOUR

Sparkling Wines

Although the first sparkling wines were not made until the late seventeenth century, today they are the most delightful, festive, and well-known family in the wine world. Legend has it that a blind old French monk named Dom Pérignon, who was cellar master of a Benedictine Abbey, discovered the process of making Champagne, and he has since been immortalized in numerous statues in the French Champagne capitals of Reims and Epernay. His name even graces the label of one of the finest and most expensive French Champagnes, produced by Moët et Chandon. But while Dom Pérignon may have been one of the first to use corks, which could trap the bubbles created during secondary fermentation within the bottle, it was probably not until well after the monk's lifetime that the scientific process of making sparkling wines became well known.

All fine French Champagnes are still produced by the original *méthode champénoise* of bottle fermentation, although this is a time-consuming process involving considerable hand labor and patience. The harvest and primary fermentation of Champagne grapes follows the same pattern as for still white wines. While almost any wine grapes can be used to make sparkling wines, one desirable attribute is a relatively high fruit acidity, which will give the wine a fresh tartness and help to preserve it during its years of aging during and after the second fermentation. The northern location and chalky soil of the Champagne district are well suited to produce just this style of wine.

In spring the still wines are clarified and then blended together under the direction of the wine master to create the particular Champagne *cuvée,* or blend, he desires. Most Champagnes are nonvintaged, so wine from a previous harvest may also be added. Even vintaged French Champagnes need be only 80 percent of the designated year. A carefully measured amount of yeast and cane sugar, the *tirage,* is then added to the *cuvée,* and the wine is bottled in heavy glass to begin its secondary fermentation and aging. This second fermentation may take many months, as the yeast slowly changes the sugar into alcohol and carbon dioxide. Because the amount of sugar used is small, there is only a slight increase in the alcohol content, but this time the bubbles of gas are trapped within the closed bottle, producing the natural sparkle that is Champagne.

French Champagne gains much of its character from remaining in contact with the yeast sediment in the bottle long after the completion of the secondary fermentation. French law requires that wine labeled Champagne be aged in the bottle for at least nine months after the addition of the *tirage,* and most premium Champagne houses age the wine for two to four years before removing the yeast sediment. The slow decomposition of the yeast cells induces complex chemical changes that add much to the richness and flavor of the finished product.

When aging "on the yeast" has been completed, the bottles are taken from the horizontal position in which they have been resting to an A-frame rack called a *pupitre.* During the ensuing weeks or months a winery worker makes the rounds of thousands of bottles of Champagne several times a week, shaking each bottle and gradually changing its position to a vertical one. This process is known as *remuage,* or riddling, and its purpose is to remove the cached yeast sediment from the side of the bottle and to send it down into the neck, where it can be more easily removed. The wine is now ready to be disgorged.

The bottles are carried into the disgorging room in an upside-down position, and the sediment in the neck is often quickly frozen in a very cold brine solution. The disgorger then takes the bottle and, in one smooth motion, turns it upright, pries off the temporary closure, and aims the bottle into an empty cask. The pressure of the dissolved carbon dioxide expels the sediment and a small amount of wine, leaving behind the clear Champagne. The bottle is then quickly placed on a bottling machine, where the lost wine will be replaced and the dosage of additional sugar dissolved in either wine or brandy may be added to give the desired sweetness to the finished wine. As the bottle continues along the line, the permanent finishing cork is inserted, a protective wire hood added, and the bottle is ready for market after labeling and a few months' rest to recover from the shock of disgorging.

Both France and California produce sparkling wines in varying degrees of sweetness; the different types may not be determined until the final *dosage,* although some vintners use different *cuvées* for each level of sweetness. Champagne to which no *dosage* has been added is called "Natur" or "Natural." Extremely dry to the point of being unpleasant to many palates, it is produced only in limited quantities and its appreciation is generally restricted to true Champagne devotees. "Brut" Champagne is made by the addition of up to 1½ percent sugar and is thus a bit softer, although its taste remains quite dry and allows enjoyment of the full Champagne flavor. "Extra Dry" sparkling wines are actually noticeably sweet, with 1.5 to 3 percent sugar; "Sec" and "Demi-Sec" may go as high as 4.5 or 6 percent, respectively. "Doux," the sweetest Champagne appellation, may contain as much as 10 percent residual sugar. When Champagne was becoming world-famous in the years before World War I, sweet wines were very popular, but today Brut and Extra Dry are the two most important styles, and very little Doux is still produced.

Fine sparkling wines in California are also produced through fermentation in the bottle, and those that follow the traditional French process outlined above will be labeled "naturally fermented in this bottle." A few labor-saving devices have been introduced: Korbel, for example, has patented an automatic riddling device, and some wineries use mechanical disgorging machines. The main requirement is that the wine undergo its secondary fermentation in the bottle in which it is sold (whose maximum size is one gallon).

A variation in the bottle-fermentation process known as the "transfer method" has come into widespread use in California since the 1950s, and sparkling wines made from this method are labeled "naturally fermented in *the* bottle" rather than "naturally fermented in *this* bottle." While the wine is still fermented and aged in individual bottles, instead of riddling and disgorging, the contents of each bottle are transferred under pressure (to retain the sparkle) to a large holding tank. Here the yeast sediment is filtered out and the *dosage* added, and the clarified wine is then rebottled in washed and sterilized bottles. Proponents of the transfer claim that it is more efficient, saving both time and handling, and also that the final blending-*dosage* in the holding tanks ensures a more consistent final product. Traditionalists argue that the extra handling and filtering, no matter how carefully controlled, will detract from the wine's quality. While the controversy will probably continue for years, many large producers have adopted the more economic transfer method. The most important factor is that in both the traditional and transfer methods the wine is fermented and aged in individual bottles, in contact with the yeast. While it is interesting to note which wineries use which process, certainly there is no reason to assume that all sparkling wines fermented in "this" bottle are superior to those fermented in "the" bottle.

A quite different process is utilized in California to produce less expensive sparkling wines. Developed in 1910 by a Frenchman, Eugene Charmat, this "Charmat process," or "bulk process," involves the utilization of large (usually 500- to 1500-gallon) tanks for the secondary fermentation. The tank acts as a giant bottle, trapping the carbon-dioxide bubbles in the wine. Fermentation takes only a couple of weeks by this method; the wine is then cold-stabilized, filtered, adjusted for the proper sugar content, and bottled under pressure. The whole process from base wine to bottling rarely takes longer than several weeks; the traditional method usually takes years. Without the prolonged secondary fermentation and intimate contact of wine with yeast during aging, bulk-process sparkling wines cannot hope to capture the character and complexity of flavors of the bottle-fermented variety. However, some quite pleasant wines can be produced in this manner, and they are much easier on the pocketbook.

Sparkling wines of both the bottle-fermented and bulk varieties are much more expensive than comparable still wines. Much of this cost can be traced to the additional handling that making a sparkling wine entails; even the bulk process necessitates expensive equipment that is not needed for producing still wines. But much of the premium placed on sparkling wines results from the unreasonable taxes that are levied on all sparkling and crackling wines just because they contain bubbles. The federal tax per gallon of still wine is $.17; the tax on sparkling wine is $3.40 per gallon! California adds another $.30 to sparkling wine and $.01 to still wine. Little wonder that even the cheapest Champagne will cost $2 a bottle, since $.74 must go to the government.

Sparkling pink or red wines can be made from any of the processes described above, though of course the base wine will have to be different. They are often quite sweet, falling into the Extra Dry or Sec categories. Some sparkling pink wines are produced by mixing white Champagnes and red

Sparkling Burgundy types, though these will often be inferior to those produced from a still rosé wine.

No discussion of sparkling wines would be complete without some comment on the multitude of Cold Ducks, Cold Turkeys, and other fowls that have recently invaded the sparkling wine market. For a while it seemed that every bird but the lowly chicken was going to have a wine named after it! In any case, the inspiration for Cold Duck is said to have come from Germany, where for a number of years various blends of still and sparkling wines have been popular. The slang term for this brew was *Kaltes Endes,* or cold "ends" (leftovers), but this soon developed into *Kalte Ente,* or Cold Duck. In the mid-1960s a Midwestern winery produced the first American Cold Duck, and the idea took off like its namesake on the first day of the hunting season. The resulting wine and its many offspring are generally deep-pink blends of white Champagne and Sparkling Burgundy. Most are made by the bulk process, and they are usually quite sweet; often Concord wine is added for sweetness and fruit, both in the East and in California. While Cold Duck has pleased millions of people, we only hope that news of its existence has been sheltered from poor Dom Pérignon.

In 1972 the Ducks began to lose altitude and, although they remain quite popular in some areas, their astounding popularity is clearly decreasing. Much of this decrease is due to the trend toward lighter, special natural wines, often called "mod" or "pop" wines. These wines are generally lightly carbonated to just below the legal limit of sparkling wines (about seven pounds per square inch), and they often contain fruit flavors. Despite their slight *pétillance,* they remain legally classified as still wines.

Sparkling wines can be produced from virtually any grape variety, and the less expensive ones often are. French Champagnes are produced primarily from the noble Chardonnay and the Pinot Noir, and many *cuvées* contain as much as two thirds of the black Pinot Noir grape. Since virtually all French Champagne is white, only by carefully crushing and immediately removing the pigment-laden skins can the yellow or golden color of the Champagne be maintained. The Pinot Noir contributes greatly to the strength, character, and richness of many French Champagnes. A few Champagnes, lighter and more delicate in flavor, are produced entirely from white grapes; these will be labeled "Blanc de Blancs."

The delightful, usually sweet, Asti Spumante of Italy is made from Moscato di Canelli grapes, while sparkling German Sekt is often a blend of Riesling and Sylvaner. In the eastern United States large quantities of native American *Vitis labrusca* varieties are used, including Catawba and Delaware, and many Eastern sparkling wines are quite pleasant, without the excessive "foxy" character that generally characterizes *labrusca* table wines.

In California dozens of grape varieties are employed in sparkling-wine production, though the most important white varieties are probably French Colombard, Folle Blanche, Chenin Blanc, and Pinot Blanc. The first two generally have fairly high acidity; the Chenin Blanc is valued for its fruitiness; and the Pinot Blanc is a good substitute for the expensive Chardonnay. Some premium wineries do use a substantial amount of Chardonnay in their Champagnes, though it is certainly not a part of the average California *cuvée*. Other white grapes used include Semillon, the Riesling varieties, Ugni Blanc, and, unfortunately, Thompson Seedless. California also produces Champagnes labeled Blanc de Blancs, but these can legally be produced from any white grapes, not just Chardonnay.

It is very difficult to make a white Champagne from black grapes in California, so only rarely will a variety such as Pinot Noir be used in white California Champagnes. Among the most common grapes used to produce sparkling pink and red wines are the Zinfandel, Gamay (Beaujolais), Ruby Cabernet, and Grignolino.

Since California Champagnes are produced almost exclusively from white grapes, they tend to be light and fruity in character, without the mustiness or intensity of many French Champagnes. The French products also have a heavier yeast character, though many California Champagnes do possess a less pronounced, fresher yeastiness that is quite pleasant. The most common Champagne grapes in California do not have distinctive varietal character, and the goal of the California Champagne master is often to produce a clean, fruity wine with perhaps just a touch of yeast and good effervescence.

The finest California sparkling wines, made primarily from Chardonnay and Pinot Blanc, may retain considerable varietal character in addition to the distinctive flavors imparted by the Champagne-making process itself. A few of the less commonly used but distinctive varietals, like Semillon or White Riesling, also create different nuances in the final *cuvée* and offer the consumer a fairly wide range of styles from which to choose.

The bulk-process sparkling wines of California are relatively consistent in quality control, and most people not well acquainted with wine in general or Champagne in particular will probably find them much more palatable than their drier premium cousins. The best of these inexpensive wines are quite fruity and pleasant, and our only caution is that they are generally quite sweet (often 3 to 4 percent sugar). While less "interesting" than the bottle-fermented Champagnes, they are just the thing when merriment and drinking are more in order than tasting. It is difficult to believe that those who serve very expensive California or French Champagnes at large receptions are not more interested in the impression they create than in how their guests actually enjoy the wines. The next time you serve Champagne, mask the bottle first: you'll get a much more honest response, and you just might be surprised.

It has long been said that Champagne can be served anytime during a meal, but for our tastes a still wine remains preferable with the main course, while sparkling wines come into their own either before or after. Certainly a Brut or Natural Champagne is a splendid and elegant aperitif, far superior to a cocktail. A bottle of Extra Dry, Sec, or pink, on the other hand, will lend itself well to dessert, where the drier varieties would clash unpleasantly with cake or sweet fruit. But one of the best times to break out a festive bottle of bubbly is on some impromptu occasion—a late weekend morning, a sunny summer afternoon—and turn a beautiful day into a memorable one.

Sparkling wines should be well chilled to conserve their sparkle and to enhance their refreshing character, and the bubbles help to release flavor and aroma even when the wine is quite cold. The traditional shallow sherbet-style glass is now wisely being replaced by the taller, more slender tulip- or flute-shaped glasses, which accentuate the rising bubbles as they concentrate the aroma of the wine.

Since most of a Champagne's development occurs during its aging on the yeast sediment, the wine is generally ready to drink soon after disgorging and does not need further bottle age. While the best sparkling wines may improve with several years in the bottle, they also run the risk of losing some of their sparkle or, like other white wines, of oxidizing. The finest Champagnes, however, will remain in excellent condition for up to ten years when properly cared for. As with all corked wines, they should be stored either upside down or on their sides to keep the cork moist.

Tasting sparkling wines is similar to tasting still wines, though obviously the effervescence present creates an added dimension. The escaping carbon-dioxide bubbles bring the aroma and bouquet of the wine to your nose, and thus swirling the wine is not absolutely necessary for full enjoyment of sparkling wines; indeed, overenthusiastic swirling will only hasten the destruction of the bubbles that were so carefully put there in the first place. While the yeast character present in many of the better Champagnes sometimes makes varietal character more difficult to detect, wines from highly distinctive grapes like Chardonnay, White Riesling, or Muscat should have characteristic aromas. Of course, most sparkling wines are blends and thus will generally not present an identifiable varietal nose.

The bubbles and, in the vast majority of wines, the sweetness present in the *cuvée* make judging sparkling wines difficult. However, you will soon discover that wines of good character and fruit do stand out on your palate, while more neutral wines often leave you simply with an impression of bubbles. Of particular importance is the acid balance of a Champagne, which keeps it fresh tasting and balances the sugar. And is the sweetness being used properly to create a different style, or does it merely cover up defects in the wine?

Finally, the bubbles themselves. Do they last through the whole bottle or glass? It is often said that the smaller the bubbles, the better the Champagne, but while smaller bubbles may indicate a slower secondary fermentation, they do not in themselves change the taste or overall character of the wine. A good bottle of sparkling wine should retain its effervescence for at least an hour after opening.

One word of caution: sparkling wines often attain a pressure of sixty pounds per square inch or more, and care should be exercised in opening them. Always point the bottle away from people, including yourself, as the cork may fly off as soon as the wire hood is removed. Remove the cork with a gradual twisting motion so that it stays in your hand rather than prying it open and loosing a potentially dangerous missile among your guests.

In the following pages we have tried to describe many of the sparkling wines available from California vintners. While we have mentioned all the major producers, both those in the bottle-fermented category and the less expensive bulk-process varieties, we have not attempted to include every label in California. In fact, despite the multiplicity of labels on retail shelves and in wineries, there are little more than a dozen producing Champagne cellars in California.

In the bulk-process category, private labels are available to both stores and wineries from several large vintners. While the names are different, the wine may well be exactly the same.

For bottle-fermented Champagnes the situation is much the same. While many wineries feel obligated to offer sparkling wines as part of their line, they have neither the equipment nor the expertise to make them themselves. They may either supply a sparkling-wine producer with the base wine from which to make a Champagne or simply buy the finished sparkling wines and sell them under their own label. In fact, few premium wineries (with the exception of the big three of Almadén, Paul Masson, and Christian Brothers) make their own Champagne; the great majority of it is produced by Hanns Kornell, Weibel, and San Martin.

Unfortunately, the fact that the Champagne or Sparkling Burgundy or Cold Duck was not actually produced by the winery under whose label it is sold is not immediately ascertainable. As detailed in the section on How to Interpret a California Wine Label, the widespread use of fictitious names allows a winery to disguise the name of the actual producer. The best guide, though even it is imperfect, is to look at *where* the wine was produced. Particularly if you know that the vintner named on the label does not actually have a winery in the designated city, odds are that sparkling wines produced in St. Helena are made by Hanns Kornell; those from Fremont or Mission San Jose will probably be from Weibel; and you can guess who makes Champagne in San Martin.

We feel the above practices are misleading, but they are very common and perfectly legal. Certainly the wine inside the bottle can be good, even excellent, despite the fact that it was not made by the winery selling it. If the base wines are different, wines made by the same sparkling-wine producer can be quite different in character and thus offer the consumer a wider choice. But if a winery does not produce Champagne, yet still feels it needs to have one to sell, at least it can be honest enough to apprise the consumer of that fact.

The most common reason given for all this subterfuge is that it is the base wine which is important and there is thus no need to indicate who made the wine into Champagne. First, this does the Champagne producer a great disservice by relegating him to the status of mechanic. Secondly, it implicitly recognizes that if the consumer knew that someone else was making the Champagne, he might not buy it.

All the wines have been ranked in accord with the system we established for still wines in Part Two, ranging from Excellent (****) to Below Average. A summary list arranged by wine type will be found at the end of this section, though we would again like to urge you to be guided by the full descriptions of the wines.

Almadén Vineyards

All Almadén sparkling wines are bottle-fermented, though they are produced both under the Almadén and Le Domaine labels. The former are produced from premium varietals such as Pinot Blanc or Chardonnay and spend approximately three years on the yeast before being disgorged. Le Domaine has the distinction of being the lowest-priced bottle-fermented Champagne available; its base wine is described as a "generic blend" and it will probably be left in contact with the yeast for one and a half to two years.

Despite the fact that Almadén's sparkling wines are doubtless the object of a good degree of attention, they are amazingly inconsistent. While even the best cannot be called great or even highly distinctive, the Blanc de Blancs and Extra Dry are fairly nice. The rest of the line certainly has room for improvement.

Blanc de Blancs *Cuvées 1967* and *1968* are typically soft, off-dry wines of light to moderate body and acid that are a bit lacking in the character one would expect from a wine that is supposed to be made entirely from Chardonnay. The aroma is pleasant and fruity and the wine is well made, but it could use a bit more depth and complexity. (**)

Brut Light to medium yellow with a slightly sulfurous, vinous aroma and a slightly sweet taste. Light-bodied with adequate acid but rather thin, unpleasant flavors masked somewhat by the sweetness. (BA)

Extra Dry Much better than the Brut, with a dry, slightly yeasty nose and light to moderate body and acid. Medium sweet, simple, but with a clean, pleasant finish. (**)

Rosé Champagne A fairly pleasant, easy to drink sparkling wine, though one without distinction. Light to medium orange in color, with a slight pinkish cast. The aroma is fresh and fruity, with fairly good fruit in the flavor. Medium sweet, with light to medium body and acidity. (*)

Pink Champagne Quite similar to the Rosé Champagne, except for one bottle which had a heavy, slightly unpleasant aroma. Otherwise with medium orange-pink color, medium sweetness, light to medium body and acidity. Some fruit, but little character. (*)

Sparkling Burgundy A dull, unpleasant wine marred by a strong sulfurous aroma and rather bitter taste. (BA)

Le Domaine Brut Less expensive than the Almadén Brut but also disappointing, with a slightly sweet, yeasty taste and bitter aftertaste. Aroma is rather grassy and the flavors are dull. (BA)

Le Domaine Extra Dry A medium sweet, simple wine that

for its price is probably as good as some "premium" Champagnes. Light in body and acid, with a slightly yeasty-grassy aroma.   (*)

Le Domaine Cold Duck   Quite sweet, with a bubble gum-cherry syrup aroma and flavor. Slightly bitter aftertaste.   (*)

Beaulieu Vineyard

One of the few relatively small wineries that actually produces its own Champagnes, Beaulieu has been making a limited amount of bottle-fermented Champagne for some time. The one exception to the string of self-produced sparkling wines was 1967, when the Champagnes were made by Hanns Kornell from Beaulieu's base wine while the new Champagne facility was being constructed at BV. All are individually disgorged and finished with the traditional multilayered cork and wire hood.

The Beaulieu Champagnes are generally a bit older and richer than many other premium California Champagnes, and their deep fruitiness approaches the complexity that one associates most often with the Champagnes of France.

Private Reserve Brut   Generally very similar to the regular Brut, though just a bit drier and with a more pronounced yeasty character. The *1966* is fairly full and well balanced, with more austere, less fruity flavors than the regular and a rich gold color. Well made and complex, with good staying power.   (***)

Brut   Both *1966* and *1967* are deep, rich, fruity wines of moderate body and acid and complex, chalky-peachy flavors. The aroma is fruity and yeasty, while the finish is off-dry. Past vintages have also been quite successful, and the Beaulieu Bruts make up in depth and complexity what they may lack in elegance or finesse. (***)

Extra Dry Champagne The *1966* has light- to medium-yellow color with a very pleasant full apple-yeasty nose. With good sparkle and complex flavors, it is light to medium in body and acidity. Slightly sweet with fine balance and no sign of fatigue or old age. (***)

Beringer Bros.

Presently made by Hanns Kornell ("Beringer Champagne Cellars, St. Helena") from Beringer base wine, all the Beringer Champagnes are fermented in "this" bottle by the traditional method of disgorging.

Brut A fairly ordinary wine of light to moderate body and acid and simple, slightly yeasty flavors. Some bottles had traces of sulfur, though it was not so strong as to be highly objectionable. Primarily from Chenin Blanc grapes. (*)

Pink Champagne Medium orange-pink in color with a heavy, fruity aroma. Slightly sweet, with light to medium body and acidity and good sparkle. Not unpleasant, but without much character. (*)

Sparkling Burgundy Medium red, with a fruity-woody aroma and taste. Undistinguished with light to moderate body and acid and a slightly bitter aftertaste. Off-dry. (*)

Christian Brothers

The Christian Brothers are one of the largest Champagne producers in California, and all their sparkling wines are made by the Charmat bulk process in stainless steel tanks of approximately 1000 gallons. The secondary fermentation takes two to three weeks, and the finished Champagnes are then filtered twice and bottle aged for six to twelve months before being released. The wines are probably the most expensive bulk-process Champagnes generally available, though they usually fall a dollar or two below the premium bottle-fermented varieties. Particularly when this extra dollar of savings is taken into account, the Christian Brothers compare very favorably with other California Champagnes, both bulk and bottle-fermented. While they cannot be termed outstanding, the base wines, which differ for each wine, are obviously well selected, and most of the various sparkling wines produced are consistently above average.

Brut   A pleasant wine from Chenin Blanc, French Colombard, and Pinot Blanc grapes, off-dry, with a very nice pearlike aroma and fruity taste. Light and fresh rather than complex, but well balanced and as good as many bottle-fermented varieties. (**)

Extra Dry   Medium sweet with a fairly fruity aroma, this is a simple wine that again comes off well in higher-priced company. Light to moderate in body and acidity, the prime taste is sweetness, but some fruit is also present. From Semillon, Ugni Blanc, and French Colombard. (*)

Champagne Rosé   A pleasant, fruity wine of Gamay, Ruby Cabernet, and Grignolino grapes. Medium-pink color with a fruity aroma, light to medium acid and body. Slightly sweet. (**)

Sparkling Burgundy Made from a well-aged *cuvée* of Napa Gamay, Early Burgundy, and Zinfandel grapes, this leaves the impression of a red wine with bubbles rather than a well-integrated Champagne. One of the few dry sparkling reds, it has light to moderate body and acid and some tannin. The aroma is light and slightly fruity. (*)

Extra Cold Duck A simple, fairly fruity wine with a slightly rough aftertaste but without the cloying sweetness often present in Cold Ducks. Not unpleasant. (*)

Concannon Vineyard

Concannon's champagnes are available only at the winery. They are bottle-fermented in the traditional *méthode champénoise* and are produced and bottled by Hanns Kornell under the "Concannon Champagne Bottling Cellars, St. Helena" label.

Brut A not unpleasant, slightly yeasty, wine of light to moderate body and acid and slightly alcoholic character. Dry, though lacking distinction. (*)

Extra Dry Champagne Light to medium yellow in color with a light, fruity nose. Off-dry (approximately 1 percent sugar), with good balance between light to medium body and acid. Some yeast complexity present, though this is not a deep wine. (*)

Cresta Blanca Winery

Though the production is relatively limited, Cresta Blanca has long made its own Champagnes and considers them an integral part of their line. The varieties are bottle-fermented, and the transfer method is employed for disgorging, which usually comes after six to nine months on the yeast. The same *cuvée* is used for both Brut and Extra Dry, the only difference being the amount of *dosage* added. In keeping with the somewhat scattered existence of the present Cresta Blanca Winery, the Champagnes are actually produced in the Central Valley from grapes brought in from the cooler North Coast Counties region, primarily Mendocino.

Brut A well-balanced wine from Semillon, French Colombard, Pinot Blanc, and Sauvignon Blanc grapes with a slight yeastiness in both aroma and taste and fairly pleasant flavors. Off-dry with good effervescence. Not overly distinguished, but well made.   (**)

Extra Dry Light yellow with a fairly yeasty nose and fresh, pleasant taste. Good fruit, light to moderate body, and moderate acid, with medium-sweet finish.   (**)

Pink Champagne A simple, ordinary sparkling wine of very pale-pink color and a faint, slightly yeasty nose. Medium sweet, with light to medium body and acidity.   (*)

Franzia Brothers

Franzia is the third of the major bulk-process Champagne producers, and it will be familiar to many as the Champagne served to all passengers on Western Airlines flights. Western uses nearly 300,000 gallons of the bubbly a year, which is still only 10 percent of Franzia's production. For the price the wines are certainly not unpleasant, though they are perhaps not quite as successful as the best of Gallo or LeJon.

Extra Dry   Light yellow with a rather heavy, sweet aroma and a cooked-fruit taste. Not at all unpleasant, but quite ordinary. Medium sweet (about 3 percent sugar), with light to moderate body and acidity.   (*)
Cold Duck   Though not at all distinguished, this is a well-made wine of light to moderate body and acid with a fairly fruity aroma and taste. Made from California grapes, it does not have the sweet grape-jam character of some of the American Cold Ducks.   (**)

Gallo Vineyards

In overall drinkability and pleasantness of taste the bulk-process Gallo sparkling wines compare very favorably with many of the higher-priced bottle-fermented California Champagnes. They do tend to be sweeter and have a different character than the more expensive labels, but the bubbles and fruity flavors keep the sugar from being cloying. In addition to the Gallo brand, the even less expensive André wines are also available. While André Cold Duck is probably one of the most popular of the $2 sparkling wines, the Gallos are usually fresher and fruitier and often worth the extra few cents they cost.

Extra Dry A fresh, fruity wine that is more pleasant than many of its higher-priced competitors. Medium sweet with light to moderate body and acid and a fruity-taffy aroma. While not up to the best of the "premium" Extra Drys, its price makes this one of the best buys for those who prefer a Champagne with some sweetness. (***)

Pink Champagne A medium-sweet wine with a pleasant, sweet strawberry aroma and taste. The light to moderate body and acid are well balanced, and while the flavors are simple they retain good fruit and freshness. (**)

Cold Duck A fruity, sweet, grape-jam wine that is rather heavy and cloying and certainly not as good as the other Gallo sparkling wines. (*)

Hanns Kornell Champagne Cellars

Although Hanns Kornell recently celebrated the twentieth anniversary of the founding of his Champagne Cellars, his products are just now becoming as well known as those of many other California wineries. Production is in the neighborhood of 50,000 gallons annually, though Kornell is also responsible for making much of the Champagne that is sold under the labels of other well-known California wineries. In some cases he puts the sparkle into a base wine supplied by the named winery, while in others a winery will simply buy Champagne from Kornell's existing stock.

Hanns Kornell received his training in Champagne making through his family's involvement in the wine industry in Germany, from where he came to the United States in 1940. His first job in California was as Champagne master for the historic Fountaingrove Winery in Santa Rosa, but it was not until 1952 that he was able to rent a small winery in Sonoma and to found the Hanns Kornell Champagne Cellars. In 1958 he moved to his present location in the old Larkmead Winery four miles north of St. Helena.

Kornell does offer a very small amount of table wine, but the overwhelming interest in the Champagne Cellars is naturally in the production of sparkling wines. All the wines are made in the traditional French method and individually disgorged by hand after spending a minimum of three years in contact with the yeast. Kornell makes none of his own base wine, preferring to purchase the wines each year from other producers. His Champagnes contain large proportions of Riesling and Semillon grapes, which are fairly unusual in California Champagne making, and some Pinot Noir is used in the production of the Sparkling Burgundy. The *dosage* is dissolved in brandy and is generally lower than that added by most other California producers: the Sehr Trocken has no *dosage,* the Brut contains about .5 percent residual sugar, and the Extra Dry is around 1 percent.

The Brut and Extra Dry rank among the most successful California Champagnes, and the recently released Sehr Trocken shows promise of becoming an interesting wine, particularly if future *cuvées* attain a better balance between fruit and yeast. Unfortunately the rest of the Kornell line is not as good, and we found the Sec and Muscadelle de Bordelais particularly disappointing. This should not detract from the quality of the better wines, however, and certainly some of California's most consistently fine Champagnes can be found under the Hanns Kornell label.

The winery is open to visitors for an informative tour that ends with the tasting of a glass of Champagne.

Sehr Trocken (bottled 1964, disgorged 1972) This is the first bottling of this extremely dry Champagne made primarily from Riesling grape varieties. The aroma is pleasant, with a chalky-yeasty character, though the fairly strong yeasty flavor and slightly bitter aftertaste may not be to everyone's taste. Well made, with moderate body and acidity, but a bit too austere and lacking in fruit. (**)

Brut A well-made, fairly tart wine of light to moderate body and moderate acid made primarily from Riesling grape varieties. One of the few truly dry Bruts, with good effervescence and a good balance of fruit and yeast in taste and aroma. Consistently one of California's better Champagnes. (***)

Extra Dry Quite similar to the Brut, with explosive bubbles and fruity-yeasty character. With fairly good flavors and a slightly bitter aftertaste, it is an off-dry wine that is actually drier than some California Bruts. (**)

Sec Very disappointing, with a sulfurous aroma, thin flavors, and an unpleasantly bitter aftertaste. Slightly sweet and devoid of character. (BA)

Muscadelle de Bordelais Light to medium yellow with a slightly sharp Muscat nose, this is a light, tart to slightly sweet wine. While pleasant, it is a bit weak in flavor and lacking in fruit, and should be considered to fall into the "extra dry" category rather than the sweet dessert group. (*)

Pink-Rosé Medium orange in color with a slightly woody-fruity aroma. Slightly sweet, with light to medium body and acidity. Some roughness in the aftertaste. (*)

Sparkling Burgundy Undistinguished though not unpleasant, this is a medium-sweet wine with slightly fruity, slightly woody flavors. Medium red in color with a vinous aroma. (*)

Heitz Wine Cellars

Heitz sparkling wines are made by Hanns Kornell under the Heitz Champagne Bottling Cellars, St. Helena, label. While it is not clear whether or not Heitz actually supplies the base wine for the Champagnes, all are bottle-fermented. They are sold only at the winery.

Brut   Light to medium yellow in color with a pleasant, flowery aroma and light to moderate body and acid. Well made with slightly yeasty flavors, but simple and nothing out of the ordinary.   (*)

Extra Dry   Light to medium yellow in color and somewhat lacking in aroma. Off-dry (about 1.25 percent sugar), with a good sparkle, and not particularly rich or fruity in flavor. Slight yeast character is present.   (*)

Sparkling Burgundy   Medium red with a raisiny-woody aroma and flavor. Slightly sweet, light to moderate in body and acid, and simple. Could use more fruit.   (*)

Inglenook Vineyards

The only Champagne offered under the Inglenook label is a vintaged, bottle-fermented Brut. Its premium price tag seems dictated by the name Inglenook rather than the distinction of the wine.

Brut   1969 produced a dry wine with a slightly bitter aftertaste and some yeast character in flavor and aroma. Light
to moderate body and acid, light yellow in color, and
ordinary.   (*)

Korbel Winery

The Korbel Winery was known for its sparkling wines long
before it entered the table wine field in the 1960s. Its Champagnes remain the winery's major interest, and the Korbel
name continues to be identified primarily with sparkling wines.
All the Korbel Champagnes are bottle-fermented and individually disgorged, the latter accomplished with the aid of a
patented automatic riddling rack and a disgorging machine
that is an integral part of the final bottling line. The base
wine is generally aged for two to four years before beginning
its life as Champagne, and the grapes used include Pinot
Blanc, French Colombard, and Chenin Blanc.

While Korbel Champagnes have enjoyed the reputation of
representing the best in California sparkling wines for many
years, our tastings have shown that in many cases this honor
is undeserved. None of the wines were unpleasant, but most
are rather simple and undistinguished and rank about average
when compared to the products of California's other premium
sparkling-wine producers.

Natural   A dry, clean wine of light to moderate body and
acid with a pleasant, slightly yeasty taste. The flavors are
fairly soft, and the wine does not have the austerity often
associated with Natural Champagnes. Aroma is good, with
both fruity and yeasty characteristics.   (**)

Brut   Light to medium yellow with a fairly yeasty aroma and
rather simple flavors. Well balanced and with good effer-

vescence, but lacking the depth or elegance that has been associated with Korbel in the past. Needs a bit more fruit and character. (*)

Extra Dry A wine of explosive bubbles that is somewhat lacking in depth and flavor. Slightly sweet, with light to moderate body and acid. (*)

Sec A pleasant, medium-sweet wine with a fairly nice, fruity aroma. Light to moderate in body and acid with lots of bubbles, but a bit thin in flavor. (*)

Rosé-Pink Champagne Medium pink in color with a candy-sweet aroma and noticeably large bubbles. Medium sweet, with light to medium body and acidity. The sweetness over-powers otherwise weak flavors. (BA)

Rouge Much drier than other Sparkling Burgundies, with light to moderate body and acid and a touch of tannic bitterness. Spicy aroma but simple flavors and little distinc-tion, though the bottle is quite attractive. (*)

Cold Duck One of the drier Cold Ducks, though still fairly sweet. The grape-jam aroma clearly reflects the Concord grapes present, and the taste is not unpleasant. (*)

Llords & Elwood Winery

Llords & Elwood selects the base wine for their one Cham-pagne and sends this to another winery in the San Jose area, where the champenization takes place. The wine is fermented in the bottle and disgorged by the transfer method.

Superb Extra Dry Cuvée Pale yellow in color with a rich vanilla-yeast bouquet, good sparkle, and fine balance. Slightly sweet, with about 1.25 percent sugar, and with good fruit and body. A very pleasant wine. (***)

Louis M. Martini

Martini's only sparkling wine is produced in very limited quantities and is generally available only at the winery itself, but it is such a unique wine that we felt it should be included here. While its instability makes it difficult to transport long distances without great care, it remains quite an enjoyable experience that provides an additional reward for the wine aficionado who makes the trip to Napa instead of just buying wines at his neighborhood wine shop.

Moscato Amabile Medium yellow in color with a fresh, fruity Muscat nose, this is one of California's most delightful dessert wines. Lightly sparkling and quite sweet, it is bottled in a Champagne bottle but finished with a normal table wine cork. With good acidity to balance the sweetness, its relatively low alcohol content necessitates that it be kept chilled at all times.   (***)

Mirassou Vineyards

Mirassou's sparkling wines have acquired a well-deserved reputation. They are dry, elegant wines of well-balanced character and, even though we cannot claim to include Sparkling Burgundies among our favorite wines, the Sparkling Gamay Beaujolais follows in the successful Mirassou tradition. The whites are produced from Pinot Blanc, Chenin Blanc, and

French Colombard grapes, and they spend approximately two and a half years in contact with the yeast before disgorging. All are fermented in the traditional *méthode champénoise.*

Au Naturel 1968 was perhaps a bit richer than the 1969, though the latter continues the tradition of very fine Mirassou Champagnes. The *1969* has a light, slightly fruity aroma, light to moderate body, and moderate acid. Very dry; the flavors are elegant and austere rather than rich or fruity, but the wine remains round and well-balanced with good character. No *dosage* is added. (***)

Brut The *1969* is very light in color but otherwise a wine of very good character and interest. The aroma is complex, with fruity-cocoa undertones which carry over into the taste. Similar to the *1968*, it is well balanced, with light to moderate body and acid, good fruit, and explosive bubbles. Off-dry. (****)

Sparkling Gamay Beaujolais Introduced as a varietal in *1969*, this wine looks very pretty in the glass with its brilliant medium red color. Quite fruity in the nose, with fairly dry finish, medium acidity, and good flavors. Surprisingly full-bodied for a sparkling wine. Very good character and distinction. (***)

Paul Masson Vineyards

Masson is one of the top three premium Champagne producers in terms of gallonage, and its sparkling wines are considered the most prestigious items in the large Masson line of wines. It is the Paul Masson Champagne Cellars in Saratoga that are open to visitors, and Masson Champagnes have long been a part of California celebrations. Only one premium label is offered, and no wines are made for other members of the industry. All are bottle-fermented, and Masson was one of the first wineries in California to begin using the transfer method of disgorging on a large scale.

Paul Masson Champagnes are generally aged in contact with the yeast for about two years, and this aging plus the style of the base wine results in a distinctively dry, yeasty character. The *dosage* is lower than that of most other vintners, leaving a wine that is clean and austere rather than fresh or fruity.

Blanc de Pinot   Produced from Pinot Blanc, Pinot Chardonnay, and a small amount of Pinot Noir grapes, this is the top of the Masson line and is aged on the yeast for four years instead of the usual two. It is a quite dry wine of light to moderate body and moderate acid with good yeasty flavors and a slightly bitter aftertaste. The aroma is pleasant, with both fruit and yeast overtones. Clearly a well-made wine, but one that could use a bit more fruit and complexity and will appeal primarily to those who like dry, austere Champagnes.   (**)

Brut   A dry, fairly tart wine with a fresh, slightly chalky taste. The aroma is both fruity and yeasty and the overall impression is of a rather austere, flinty wine that is nevertheless quite pleasant.   (**)

Extra Dry Champagne   Light yellow, with a grassy-yeasty nose. A good wine with fairly good body and rather dry finish for this type (approximately 1 percent sugar). Could use a bit more fruit.   (**)

Pink Champagne   A well-balanced medium-sweet wine with freshness and fruit. Light pink in color, with a slight yeasty-strawberry nose, light to medium body and medium acidity. A pleasant wine.   (**)

Crackling Rosé   The most recent sample tasted was not as pleasant as some bottles we had enjoyed some time ago, as it was marred by a vegetable character in both aroma and taste. Otherwise, it is a soft, medium-sweet wine of good sparkle and a brilliant medium-pink color.   (*)

Sparkling Burgundy   A slightly sweet, light- to medium-red wine rendered unpleasant by a sulfurous aroma and rather bitter aftertaste. Light to moderate body and acid.   (BA)

Very Cold Duck   Made from California grapes without the *labrusca* added by some producers, in the past this has been a fairly pleasant, not overly sweet wine. The most recent bottling, however, is clearly faulted, with a skunky-sulfurous nose and heavy, sweet taste.   (BA)

San Martin Winery

San Martin bottles about 100,000 gallons of sparkling wines a year under one of its own labels and also is active in preparing Champagnes for other wineries or under various private labels. Two major brands are offered, San Martin and the less expensive Maison Martineau, both of which are bottle-fermented and disgorged by the transfer process. Both cork and plastic closures are used, and the absence of much yeast character in the Champagnes probably indicates that the wines spend a relatively short time in contact with the yeast before disgorging.

While San Martin's sparkling Malvasia is one of the best wines of its type available from California vintners, the rest of their Champagnes are sweet, unbalanced, and very disappointing. While the simple grapiness of a few varieties may appeal to the novice wine drinker, the products of many of the less expensive bulk producers are more pleasant and only half the price of the bottle-fermented wines of San Martin.

Brut Slightly sweet, with light to moderate body and acid and little character. The bubbles are rather low, and the simple, sweet style is disappointing for what purports to be a premium bottle-fermented Champagne. (BA)

Extra Dry Quite a sweet wine with a rough, harsh taste and aftertaste that unfortunately does not match the fairly pleasant, fruity aroma. Body and acidity are both fairly light. (BA)

Gran Spumante Malvasia The only one of San Martin's sparkling wines made by the Charmat process. Pale gold in color with a fresh, flowery nose, this might be the winery's best sparkling wine. Medium sweet with good fruit, it is a bit heavy but retains a pleasant, grapey taste. (**)

Pink Champagne Light orange-pink in color with a displeasing chemical aroma. A medium-sweet sparkling wine of little character. (BA)

Champagne Rouge A heavy, harsh wine that tastes like concentrated grape juice. Medium sweet. The aroma is pleasant, but this does not overcome the cloying, clumsy flavors. (BA)

Cold Duck Not an unpleasant wine of light body and acid, but simple. Medium sweet with a light, fruity aroma and taste. (*)

Maison Martineau We tasted only the *Extra Dry* and found it much in the style of the regular line. There is a slight bitterness in the aftertaste, but otherwise this is an ordinary, medium-sweet sparkling wine devoid of any character, good or bad. (*)

Schramsberg Vineyards

The story of the Schramsberg winery, nestled in the slopes of Mount Diamond near Calistoga on the west side of the Napa Valley, began in 1862 when it was founded by Jacob Schram. Premium vines were planted and extensive aging tunnels dug into the hillside, and by the late 1800s the Schramsberg label had acquired an international reputation for fine wines. The winery was immortalized in Robert Louis Stevenson's *Silverado Squatters,* and in 1957 it was declared a historical landmark by the state of California.

Five decades of idleness followed Schram's death in 1905, interrupted only for a brief period in 1951–60. Then in 1965 the Schramsberg winery and its three-story Victorian house were purchased by Mr. and Mrs. Jack Davies, who immediately began restoring both house and winery to their former greatness. The vineyards are being replanted in Chardonnay and Pinot Noir, and by the early 1970s it is hoped that all the wine will be made only from grapes on the original Schram property. Although in the nineteenth century Schramsberg was known only for still wines, today the winery produces only Champagnes, anticipating a maximum production of 10,000 to 20,000 gallons.

While Mr. Davies was not a wine maker by profession, the results he has thus far achieved with the Champagnes of Schramsberg are truly remarkable. From our first bottle of the then nonvintaged Schramsberg Blanc de Blancs, which we enjoyed one summer's afternoon with friends on the shores of Crater Lake, we have been very impressed by the balance and complexity that seem to characterize Jack Davies' wines. While a couple of vintages have been disappointing, on the whole the wines have exhibited consistently high quality and deserve most, if not all, of the praise which has been directed their way.

The Champagnes are produced in the traditional bottle-fermented, hand-disgorged method, although standard modern improvements like low-temperature fermentation are employed as well. The grapes are harvested quite early to preserve their fruit acidity, and most of the base wine is kept away from any contact with wood. After the secondary fermentation is initiated the wine spends two to three years on the yeast and an additional three to nine months of bottle aging after disgorging. The regular Blanc de Blancs is made from Chardonnay and Pinot Blanc, while the unique Blanc de Noir is made using the classic French Champagne proportions of Pinot Noir and Chardonnay.

While there is no tasting available at the winery, those who would like to spend what is sure to be a very enjoyable visit with Mr. Davies are requested to write or phone ahead for an appointment.

Blanc de Noir   At its best this can be one of the fullest and most flavorful California Champagnes, reflecting its high percentage of Pinot Noir grapes. The *1967* (****) was very successful, exhibiting a fine balance of body, fruit, and flavors, but in comparison the *1968* is a bit disappointing. Its light to moderate body and moderate acid are well balanced and the flavors are pleasant, but it lacks the depth and character of the 1967. Dry, it has a pleasant, apple-like aroma and slightly dull color.   (**)

Blanc de Blancs Reserve Cuvée   Generally has a higher proportion of Chardonnay and is aged longer than the regular Blanc de Blancs. The *1967* (***) was a fine, well-balanced wine, and the *1968* is even better. Its complex, chalky-yeasty flavors are set off well by good fruit and acidity, while the aroma is both fresh and intense. Truly a fine wine.   (****)

Blanc de Blancs Light to medium yellow in color with a very good, fruity-chalky aroma, the *1969* (****) is one of the best of Schramsberg's recent vintages. It is an elegant, well-balanced wine of good fruit and complex flavors that should last for several years. The *1970* is again very dry and has a pleasant apple-yeasty aroma. A clean-tasting wine of moderate body and acidity, though it does not capture the depth of flavors and complexity of prior vintages. (***)

Cuvée de Gamay Made entirely from Napa Gamay grapes, at its best this can be a delightful, fresh, fruity wine. The *1970* has a nice salmon color and a very pleasant, pear-like aroma, but the slightly bitter taste is disappointing. Dry, it has light body and light to moderate acid and could use more fruit. Still, this wine exhibits much more character than most California Pink Champagnes. (**)

United Vintners

The United Vintners-Italian Swiss Colony sparkling wines are sold primarily under the LeJon label. While the LeJon Champagnes cannot be said to possess any particular distinctiveness, they are generally sound, honest wines that are worth the price they carry and may in fact stand up well in competition with some of the more expensive brands. All LeJon Champagnes are made by the Charmat bulk process and closed with plastic corks. They are on the sweet side, and evidence the grapey flavors that characterize the better bulk-process Champagnes.

An even less expensive line is available from United Vintners under the Jacques Bonet label.

LeJon Blanc de Blancs   Not as pleasant as the less expensive regular LeJon, with the main taste difference being less sweetness. The aroma is rather heavy, and the acidity is on the low side and does not leave the fresh taste of the regular. Slightly yeasty flavors.   (*)

LeJon Extra Dry Champagne   Medium yellow with a soft, fruity aroma, this is a medium-sweet wine of fair fruit and a pleasant aftertaste. Little depth, but a good wine for the money; a bit lighter and less sweet than Gallo.   (**)

LeJon Pink Champagne   Bright pink in color with a fairly fresh, fruity aroma. The flavors though are a bit heavy and rough. Medium sweet, with light to moderate body and acid.   (*)

LeJon Cold Duck   The freshly fermented grape character of this wine is fairly pleasant, as is the fruity-citrus aroma. Sweet and simple, but as good as many of the more expensive varieties.   (**)

Weibel Champagne Vineyards

Approximately 10 percent of Weibel's million-gallon production consists of sparkling wines, and in the past Weibel has also been a large supplier of private-label Champagnes for wineries, restaurants, and retail liquor stores. All the Champagnes are bottle-fermented and disgorged by the transfer method. None has very noticeable yeast character, as disgorging generally takes place about six months after the secondary fermentation begins. The premium line of sparkling wines is made from grapes which include Pinot Blanc, Chardonnay, and Riesling varieties, while the "crackling" wines are produced from lesser varieties such as French Colombard and Sauvignon Blanc. The sparkle in the crackling is not noticeably less than in the premium line, though the less expensive crackling varieties may spend only three months in contact with the yeast.

In general, the Weibel Champagnes do not exhibit the complexity or character that one expects in a premium sparkling wine, though the sweet fruitiness that characterizes most of the wines is more successful in the Muscat and the Pink.

Champagne Chardonnay Brut A pleasant wine with a fruity, pineapple aroma, and a slight sweetness in the taste that seems inappropriate in a premium Brut. Light to moderate in body with moderate acidity and soft, fruity flavors. Rather simple but fairly fresh. (**)

Brut A slightly sweet wine of light to moderate body and acid with a freshly fermented pearlike aroma. While not unpleasant, the taste is more like sparkling grape juice than Champagne and has little yeasty or chalky character. (*)

Extra Dry Quite a sweet wine with light to moderate body and acid. Both aroma and taste are fruity, but sweetness predominates and becomes a bit cloying after a while. (*)

Sec Perhaps a bit less sweet than the Extra Dry, this is a heavy, unpleasant wine characterized by a cooked fruit aroma and taste. (BA)

Moscato Spumante A fresh medium-sweet wine that captures the pronounced flowery character of the Muscat grape. Light to moderate in body and acid with good sparkle and clean aftertaste. (**)

Pink Champagne A medium-sweet, pleasant sparkling wine, a little heavy in the finish but still with fairly good fruit. Light to medium pink-orange in color, a fruity nose, and flavorful aftertaste. (**)

Sparkling Burgundy Dark red with a rather heavy, raisin-caramel aroma and light to moderate body and acid. Slightly sweet with good effervescence, but the flavors are a bit dull. (*)

Crackling Blanc de Blancs Again quite sweet, with a citrus-taffy aroma and very simple flavors. Similar in style to many bulk-fermented wines, though not unpleasant. (*)

Crackling Rosé Light pink in color with a fruity aroma, light to medium body and acidity. Medium sweet, with some softness and fruit for a relatively inexpensive sparkling wine, though certainly without significant character or complexity. (*)

Crackling Duck A fairly well-balanced wine with a strawberry-jam aroma and slightly heavy, sweet flavors. Smooth and drinkable, but rather cloying. (*)

Windsor Vineyards–Sonoma Vineyards

In the past, Windsor Champagnes have been made by other wineries, but recently the production of sparkling wine has begun in a facility near the winery in Windsor. The first wine is a Brut, made primarily from Chardonnay grapes, in the traditional *méthode champénoise*.

Brut Cuvée 102 Fairly light in color with a spicy-basil aroma, light to moderate body, and moderate acid. Off-dry and a bit alcoholic, but with good fruit and some character. Certainly a good wine, though not outstanding. (**)

Summary List of Sparkling Wines

NATURAL AND BRUT CHAMPAGNES

****

Mirassou Brut 1968
Mirassou Brut 1969
Schramsberg Blanc de Noir 1967
Schramsberg Blanc de Blancs Reserve *Cuvée* 1968
Schramsberg Blanc de Blancs 1969

***

Beaulieu Private Reserve Brut 1966
Beaulieu Brut 1966
Beaulieu Brut 1967
Hanns Kornell Brut
Mirassou Au Naturel 1968
Mirassou Au Naturel 1969
Schramsberg Blanc de Blancs Reserve *Cuvée* 1967
Schramsberg Blanc de Blancs 1970

**

Almadén Blanc de Blancs *Cuvée* 1967
Almadén Blanc de Blancs *Cuvée* 1968

Christian Brothers Brut
Cresta Blanca Brut
Hanns Kornell Sehr Trocken (disgorged 1972)
Korbel Natural
Paul Masson Blanc de Pinot
Paul Masson Brut
Schramsberg Blanc de Noir 1968
Weibel Champagne Chardonnay Brut
Windsor Brut *Cuvée* 102

*

Beringer Brut
Concannon Brut
Heitz Brut
Inglenook Brut 1969
Korbel Brut
Weibel Brut

BA

Almadén Brut
Le Domaine Brut
San Martin Brut

EXTRA DRY AND SEC CHAMPAGNES

***

Beaulieu Extra Dry 1966
Gallo Extra Dry
Llords & Elwood Extra Dry

**

Almadén Extra Dry
Cresta Blanca Extra Dry
Hanns Kornell Extra Dry
LeJon Extra Dry
Paul Masson Extra Dry

*

Christian Brothers Extra Dry
Concannon Extra Dry
Franzia Extra Dry
Heitz Extra Dry
Korbel Extra Dry
Korbel Sec
Le Domaine Extra Dry
LeJon Blanc de Blancs
Maison Martineau Extra Dry
Weibel Crackling Blanc de Blancs
Weibel Extra Dry

BA

Hanns Kornell Sec
San Martin Extra Dry
Weibel Sec

SPARKLING MUSCATS

***

Louis Martini Moscato Amabile

**

San Martin Gran Spumante Malvasia
Weibel Moscato Spumante

*

Hanns Kornell Muscadelle de Bordelais

PINK CHAMPAGNES

**

Christian Brothers Champagne Rosé
Gallo Pink
Paul Masson Pink
Schramsberg *Cuvée* de Gamay 1970
Weibel Pink

*

Almadén Pink
Almadén Rosé
Beringer Pink
Cresta Blanca Pink
Hanns Kornel Pink-Rosé
LeJon Pink
Paul Masson Crackling Rosé
Weibel Crackling Rosé

BA

Korbel Rosé-Pink
San Martin Pink

RED CHAMPAGNES AND COLD DUCKS

***
Mirassou Sparkling Gamay Beaujolais 1969

**
Franzia Cold Duck
LeJon Cold Duck

*

Beringer Sparkling Burgundy
Christian Brothers Extra Cold Duck
Christian Brothers Sparkling Burgundy
Gallo Cold Duck
Hanns Kornell Sparkling Burgundy
Heitz Sparkling Burgundy
Korbel Cold Duck
Korbel Rouge
Le Domaine Cold Duck
San Martin Cold Duck
Weibel Crackling Duck
Weibel Sparkling Burgundy

BA

Almadén Sparkling Burgundy
Paul Masson Very Cold Duck
Paul Masson Sparkling Burgundy
San Martin Rouge

PART FIVE

Jug-a-lug

Virtually every one of the world's great wine countries produces much more inexpensive, ordinary wine than premium varietals or château bottlings. In many European and South American countries, wine is the national beverage and a natural accompaniment to both the noon and evening meal. Something that is this much a part of daily life is understandably treated quite casually, just as most Americans give little thought to milk or coffee. We will never forget sitting in a cafe in the marketplace of Paris in the wee hours of the morning savoring our *gratinée* and watching four truck drivers at the table next to ours fortifying themselves for the long trip home with a plate of liver and onions and a liter of wine apiece. The carafes and barrels of reds and whites from which these liters came are easily as indispensable to the workingmen, farmers, and cafe owners as the great vintages are to the *haute bourgeoisie* of Bordeaux.

California is no exception to the rule, and here, too, the vast majority of table wine is produced and bottled in large quantities. While much of this American *vin ordinaire* does find its way to the dinner table, it is more likely in our society to become a part of parties and picnics and punches—times when premium wines would be not only too expensive but where they would be sure to get lost in the shuffle of food and drink. Paper-cup or straight-from-the-jug guzzling is as much a part of the scene as spareribs dripping with barbecue sauce or the all-American hamburger.

We have used the terms *vin ordinaire* and "jug wine" interchangeably to designate the primarily generic wines produced in large quantities and sold at relatively low prices. The wine industry often uses the term "standard" to identify these wines, as opposed to "premium" for the more expensive varieties. The usual containers for these wines are screwtopped half-gallon or gallon jugs, although many producers do offer the wines in fifth-size bottles also. Regardless of the size or shape of the individual container, however, all are filled with the same wine.

Both California and European *vins ordinaires* should be distinguished from regional wines, or *vins de pays*. Among the latter you may find some charming, quite distinctive wines, but these are much more akin to the smaller California wineries discussed earlier than to the mass producers of the Midi in France or California's Central Valley.

Jug wines are relatively inexpensive because they are produced in quantity and are made from grape varieties chosen for their high yield and moderate price tag. Here in California, for example, many Central Valley varieties produce ten to twelve tons per acre and sell for $50 to $100 per ton, compared to the one- to two-ton yield and $800 to $1000 price of a Chardonnay or Cabernet Sauvignon grown on a cool coastal hillside. Harvesting, crushing, fermenting, and aging are all done with little fanfare and without the individual care and patience that a premium wine demands. Indeed, the entire process from vine to vat to bottle may take but a few weeks. The results of all this run from the pleasant and inoffensive to a brew you wouldn't give to your cat, though in all fairness most California jug wines are fairly palatable.

In California jug wine is produced wherever vineyards are found, although the majority comes from those areas where the warm climate and rich soil are best suited for high-yielding grape varieties. California's San Joaquin Valley is heavily planted in vines, and the flat areas of northern Sonoma and southern Mendocino Counties also supply grapes for a large quantity of jug wine.

Grape varieties from the North Coastal Counties that often end up in jug wines include Carignane, Alicante Bouschet, Durif, and a fair amount of Zinfandel among the reds and French Colombard and Sauvignon Vert among the whites. Many small wineries and grower-owned cooperatives produce wines from these grapes, and then sell them in bulk to the large producers, for these wines have a higher natural acidity than those from the Central Valley and are thus desirable for blending purposes.

Press wines are sometimes added to the secondary lines of some premium wineries, as well as being sold in bulk to the large producers of the Central Valley. The quality varies tremendously, depending primarily on how much pressure is applied to the pulp. The greater the pressure, the higher the yield of wine, but also the more likely that undesirable flavors will be released from the crushed seeds and skins.

In the Central Valley, from San Joaquin County in the north to Kern County in the south, are thousands of acres of jug wine grapes which include Carignane, Grenache, French Colombard, and Golden Chasselas (or Palomino). In the northern end of the valley large plantings of Zinfandel are also present. Tremendous plantings of Thompson Seedless (about 250,000 acres) may be found in the southern part of the valley. While much of this is for table grape and raisin use, a too-large percentage of this very ordinary, neutral grape is still used in wine production. Indeed, in 1971 more than half of the total number of grapes crushed in California were Thompson Seedless. Some of this was used for distillation into brandy, but much of it found its way into sparkling- and still-wine production. The standard joke in the wine industry is about someone else's wine being a 100 percent varietal—100 percent Thompson Seedless may not be far from the truth in some cases.

This situation is gradually being remedied, although the tremendous demand for wine, the extent of existing plantings, and the time that it takes new vines to fully mature all indicate that large amounts of table and raisin grape varieties will continue to be crushed for wine making for many years to come. Some large producers, most notably Gallo, have been encouraging the planting of better grapes by offering guaranteed minimum incomes to those growers who will replace existing vines with more suitable varieties.

Up and down the Central Valley large new plantings of vines may be found. Some of these include grapes specially developed by the University of California at Davis for planting in warm areas, like the Ruby Cabernet and Emerald Riesling. The high-acid Barbera and French Colombard are two current favorites, and the hope is that even in this warm climate they will continue to produce quality wine of adequate acid content. In 1972 more Barbera was planted in California than any other grape variety, and virtually this entire amount was concentrated in the San Joaquin Valley. There are now 12,000 acres of young Barbera vines and over 10,000 acres of immature French Colombard grapes in the Valley. Chenin Blanc and Semillon are two additional premium varietals being tried in this warm climate, and two grapes noted for their highly colored juice, the Rubired and Royalty, are also being widely planted. These new plantings will have considerable effect on the quality of the *vin ordinaire* from the Central Valley in the next few decades, although it is unlikely that they will equal the quality of wine produced from the same grapes in the cooler coastal areas.

East of Los Angeles, in the Cucamonga district of San Bernardino County, several producers continue to make wine in an area that, before the onslaught of real estate developers and tract houses, was an important wine-growing region. The principal varieties planted here include Grenache, Golden

Chasselas, Zinfandel, and the largest remaining plantings of the Mission grape in the state.

No matter what the method or grape-growing region, the technical standards of California's bulk-wine producers remain as high as those followed for varietals. Temperature-controlled fermentors, huge stainless steel and glass-lined storage tanks, and modern filtration systems all play their part in ensuring that the final product will be pure. By the way, despite persistent rumors to the contrary, all California wine, even the cheapest, is natural, not synthetic, wine. While Italy had its oxblood-and-water scandal a few years ago, you may rest assured that, questions of character or interest aside, the liquid in your glass is exactly what it purports to be. California wines, on the other hand, are generally marked by a consistency that renders the undrinkable bottle very rare— though this also negates almost any possibility of an unusually pleasant surprise.

Given the existing technical expertise and almost limitless vineyard possibilities in the Central Valley and elsewhere in California, it is not surprising that bulk-wine production has become a willing ward of big business. Automation and hydraulic pumping systems have made it possible for a single company to produce millions of gallons of wine a year—and to expand along the way. Blending the products of both their own and independent vineyards with wine purchased in bulk from producers in the North Coastal Counties, E. & J. Gallo and United Vintners (owner of Italian Swiss Colony and others) together turn out more wine than all other California wineries combined. Along with such familiar names as Guild and Franzia, these companies are responsible for the vast majority of California wines on the market today. It is these wines that enter the everyday life of millions of thirsty consumers.

The typical California *vin ordinaire* is intended to be just that—an ordinary, drinkable wine with no claim to greatness or distinction. While mass production is certainly an economic windfall, it tends to result in wines with assembly-line character: one alcohol content, one degree of sweetness, and three different colors to break the monotony. Lacking the complexity and ever-changing nuances of premium wines, most bulk wines satiate rather than stimulate the palate, often becoming quite dull and lifeless by the end of a meal. But, as the saying goes, you get what you pay for; it's no real criticism to say that bulk wines aren't as interesting as premium wines costing two or three times as much—something would be wrong if they were. So, given the millions of gallons and hundreds of brands available, where do we start?

While the following observations are specific, they are certainly not intended to present an all-inclusive picture of inexpensive wines. The best we can hope to offer is a representative sample of the largest and best-known producers, and even there we will only be talking about those wines which somehow stood out from the rest in one way or another. We have concentrated on those wines that we think are familiar to most Americans, both among the purely jug-wine producers and among the *vin ordinaire* lines of several premium producers. A few premium wineries, like Christian Brothers and Paul Masson, simply bottle some of their regular line of generic wines in jugs. In these cases they have been discussed along with the premium wines in Part Two.

The two most well known names in the jug-wine business are E. & J. GALLO and ITALIAN SWISS COLONY. Gallo is one of the largest family-owned businesses in the United States, while Italian Swiss Colony is now part of the Heublein Corporation. Their prices and wine types are virtually identical, and they compete in every major American market. The home Gallo Winery is located in Modesto in the Central Valley, while Italian Swiss Colony is at Asti in Sonoma County. Both wineries, however, buy grapes and wine from the North Coast County areas as well as the Central Valley.

Among the wines, Gallo's *Chablis Blanc* is light, fresh, and flowery with an off-dry finish. It is one of the most successful of California's inexpensive whites. The Italian Swiss *Chablis* is drier, with a duller aroma and flavor. The Gallo *Rhinegarten* is medium sweet with considerable sparkle and soda-pop flavors, while the Italian Swiss *Rhineskeller* has similar sweetness, but no bubbles, and is fresher-tasting.

Both wineries produce a *Pink Chablis* and a *Vin Rosé*. The former tends to be a medium-sweet wine with some *pétillance,* with the Gallo being perhaps the more lively of the two. The Italian Swiss rosé is varietally labeled as a *Grenache* and has the flowery aroma of this grape. It is slightly sweet and, though simple, is fairly well made. The Gallo Vin Rosé has deep-pink color and a flowery aroma not unlike the Italian Swiss. It, too, is pleasant, and probably also contains a large proportion of Grenache grapes.

The Italian Swiss *Burgundy* has a musty aroma and dry taste. Okay for an inexpensive red, it could use a cleaner finish. The Gallo *Burgundy* is off-dry and more cloying than the Italian Swiss. Gallo also bottles a *Hearty Burgundy* that is sweeter and higher in alcohol than the regular Burgundy. It is a smooth wine, and one that our tastings have shown is enjoyed by beginning wine drinkers, but the sweetness is definitely noticeable and may bother those who prefer a cleaner, drier finish. The Gallo *Paisano* is a little lighter and less sweet than the Hearty Burgundy, yet it retains some fruit and is one of the better inexpensive California reds.

Both wineries produce *Chiantis* which are off-dry and similar in style, with the Gallo being slightly fuller and smoother. Both are slightly sweeter than the regular Burgundies. Italian Swiss also produces a *Tipo Chianti,* which comes packaged in straw-covered *fiaschi.* This is a dry wine, with more character than the regular Chianti and slight astringency.

The Italian Swiss Colony *Zinfandel* is one of the least expensive varietal bottlings in California, yet recent improvements in this wine make it a very good value for the money.

Dry, with some astringency, fairly good body, and fruity Zinfandel flavors, it is a very pleasant everyday wine.

The RED MOUNTAIN label is owned by Gallo and is one
of the least expensive lines of wine on the market. Because
of its price and the fact that this is one of the few wines that
are not harmed by the addition of large quantities of hard
liquor, it has become a familiar scene at fraternity parties.
The *Rosé* and *Pink Chablis* both have sweetness, though the
latter is sweeter and has a slight *pétillance*. Both are rather
sluggish and less fresh than the Gallo and Italian Swiss rosés.
The *Burgundy* has a heavy raisined aroma and a sweet taste
and is not very good.

The GUILD WINE COMPANY, California's third largest
producer, is actually a huge cooperative composed of more
than five hundred grape growers from throughout California.
It includes five separate wineries, four of which are located
in the Central Valley near the cities of Lodi and Fresno, while
the fifth is just north of Ukiah in Mendocino County. Wine
is produced at all five locations and then sent in bulk to Lodi
for blending, finishing, and bottling. Well over thirty table
wines are produced under four different labels, and Guild is
also a major producer of dessert and sparkling wines and
brandy.

The three major Guild labels are Famiglia Cribari, Vino da
Tavola, and Winemasters. Similarly priced, the main difference
among the three lines is sweetness. Famiglia Cribari is the
sweetest—or most mellow, if you prefer—of the three, and offers
a full line of generic wines in addition to the simple red, white,
and rosé. Cribari wines are generally pleasant, light, and un-
pretentious, and their mellowness makes them easily palatable
at picnics and suppers for people not used to drinking wine.

The Vino da Tavola wines with their red checkered label
have become sort of a trademark with Guild. The *Red* is particularly well known, and according to the company was America's first mellow red table wine. It is off-dry, has a slightly

minty aroma, and rather average character. The Vino da Tavola *White* is a simple wine with rather dull flavors.

The *Winemasters* label (the name was purchased, incidentally, from the Bargetto Winery in Santa Cruz) provides a full line of generic wines as well as a varietal Zinfandel. The wines are generally pleasant, if not overly distinguished, and, although tending to be the driest of the Guild labels, some retain noticeable sweetness.

FRANZIA, whose winery is located at Ripon in the northern San Joaquin Valley, is the fourth largest California producer and offers a complete line of inexpensive wines. Included in these are a *Chablis Blanc,* which is a fairly dry, though rather ordinary white with a slightly flowery aroma and a *Burgundy* that has a casky-vegetably nose, dry finish, and not particularly pleasing flavors. Two varietals are also offered, a fruity, slightly sweet and *pétillant Grenache Rosé* that is fairly nice for its inexpensive price tag, and a *Zinfandel* that is dry, with a ripe fruity aroma and rather unbalanced flavors.

The major winery in Southern California's Cucamonga district is BROOKSIDE. Recently Brookside merged with Mills Winery, whose home base is near Sacramento, and now Brookside-Mills tasting rooms may be found up and down the state. Many wines are offered under the Brookside, Mills, Assumption Abbey, and Vaché labels. The jug wines are rather light in flavor, but have the advantage of being relatively inexpensive and of being available for tasting at all the retail outlets.

Several of the larger premium wineries also offer lines of *vin ordinaire,* or jug wines, either under their own or subsidiary labels. They are consistently priced somewhat higher than the wines of the large producers we have just discussed, and are likely to contain higher percentages of North Coast County grapes. They may also contain varying amounts of press wine, as well as some valley-grape wine. Often they are a little more distinctive than their lesser-priced cousins, but it is difficult to generalize and in some instances they are actually less palatable and not worth the extra money.

The Charles Krug Winery produces inexpensive wines under two different labels, and in so doing follows many of the practices used, to one degree or another, by most other premium wineries that bottle jug wines. The MONDAVI VINE-YARD line is priced above the average California *vin ordinaire* and is produced from grapes originating in Napa County. Generally speaking, these are lesser grapes than those that go into Krug's premium wines, although small quantities of some premium grapes may be used to add a little more character. A White Burgundy (Chablis), Rhine Wine, Chianti, and Burgundy are available and, with the exception of the Rhine, all are rather successful everyday wines. The *Chablis* is dry, light, and has some freshness, the *Burgundy* has a fruity aroma and rather light body for a red, while the *Chianti* is fuller and fruitier and rather drinkable. The *Rhine* is off-dry and slightly heavy and has little character.

Krug's other label, CK, is priced just below the Mondavi Vineyard line. Seventy-five percent of the CK wine comes from the North Coast Counties, much of it in the form of lightly pressured press wine; the remainder comes primarily from the Central Valley. These have been among California's more successful jug wines, although their price has crept up in the past few years. The *Chablis* is light and tart, with a dry, rather clean finish, and the *Burgundy* has a fruity aroma and a light, pleasing taste. The *Zinfandel* has some character, although the Italian Swiss Zinfandel is probably as good yet is less expensive. In the past the *Barberone* has been one of the most successful CK wines, but the last bottle we tried was rather woody and rough.

LOUIS MARTINI is well known for his jugs of Mountain White and Red, and these rank among the best of California's *vins ordinaires*. The *White* has a tart fresh aroma and a dry, fairly fruity flavor, while the *Mountain Red* has a slightly woody aroma and is fairly tart, and light. The *Mountain Vin*

Rosé is the least successful of the three and is a dry, rather ordinary wine distinguished from less expensive rosés primarily by its lack of sweetness.

SAMUELE SEBASTIANI also produces three "Mountain" wines, a Burgundy, Chablis, and Rosé. The *Burgundy* is another good, inexpensive wine, being rather light and soft with good fruit. The *Chablis* and *Rosé* are less distinguished, dry wines with neutral flavors.

BERINGER BROS. also produces a large quantity of "Mountain" wines, using both Napa Valley and Central Valley grapes. In contrast to Martini and Sebastiani, the most successful Beringer wine is probably the *Vin Rosé*. It has bright-pink color, is fairly dry, and has more body and flavor than most jug rosés. The *Mountain White Chablis* is off-dry and, though easy to drink, has little distinction. The *Mountain Red Burgundy* is quite soft in flavor, but has an overfiltered taste leaving it quite dull in the mouth.

Recently INGLENOOK has entered the *vin ordinaire* business with its line of *Navalle* wines. These are actually produced at the United Vintners winery in Asti rather than at Inglenook's historic St. Helena winery, and contain grapes from several California wine regions. The *Burgundy* is probably the most successful with light to moderate body, tannin, and acid and good, though slightly rough flavors. The *Claret* is lighter and the *Chablis,* and *Rhine* are similar except for the slight sweetness in the latter. The *Rosé* is fairly dry, with about average quality for its price range.

ALMADÉN offers a well-distributed line of jug wines, but unfortunately they are prime examples of the *caveat* that higher price is not a guarantee of better quality. Among the whites the *Mountain White Chablis* is probably the best and freshest, though is still a rather listless wine. The current *Mountain White Sauterne* has a sulfurous aroma and a dry, heavy, not particularly pleasing flavor. The *Mountain Rhine* is simply sweet and sugary. With the reds, the *Mountain Burgundy* is light and ordinary, while the *Mountain Claret* is lighter yet and captures some sulfurous tones in the aroma. Certainly better California jug wines are available at a lower price.

This certainly does not exhaust the list of bulk wines on your grocery store shelves, but we hope we have given you an idea of what to expect. Particularly in the East, many private labels appear in limited geographical areas, and most California wineries are reluctant to discuss them in any detail. Often the lowest echelon of California wine is represented by these brands, so we hope that you will not take them as representative of California wine in general. And if you do happen to find a good one, let us know. As for those wineries well known to you which we may have omitted, please accept our apologies and believe that they were left out not by design but by necessity.

Several conclusions may be drawn from the above observations which in themselves provide a convenient summary of the state of California jug wines.

1. The generic names given to theoretically different types of bulk wine are, for the most part, meaningless. Even within one winery's family of wines, the slight differences that may exist are inconsistent. Among the whites, there is some tendency for Rhine-type wines to be a little sweeter, but Chablis and Sauternes are indistinguishable. Clarets are generally light, but the range of Burgundies is so vast that it includes every possibility from very light and dry to medium and mellow. Nowhere did we find a wine that we could term "full" or "robust."

2. While it is possible to compare the jug wines of one vintner with those of another, the distinctions are less meaningful than when comparing premium varietals. The various wines are often quite similar in style, and differences are in drinkability rather than in character or distinctiveness.

3. The major difference between jug wines produced by premium wineries and those from wineries specializing in mass production is that the former are almost universally less sweet than the latter. In enough cases to be noted, the bulk wines of premium wineries do show more definition and distinction,

but this does not mean that they are more "drinkable"—the true test of an everyday wine—than those of the larger producers.

4. The preceding paragraph leads more or less directly to the conclusion that you don't necessarily get what you pay for. If you are willing to accept at least some minimal amount of sweetness in a table—or barbecue or picnic—wine, your best bet is to start with the cheapest and work your way up until you find something to your taste. The wines we have singled out as more pleasant than the masses come from all price ranges, so there's no reason to assume that the most expensive Burgundy or Sauterne is the best.

5. Finally, all California jug wines or *vins ordinaires* are, indeed, ordinary. Generally distinguishable from even premium generics, they are made to be drunk, not tasted. While some are certainly worth investigating as everyday wines, you should not enter the half-gallon arena looking for a wine with any degree of complexity or finesse or you will be certain to be disappointed.

Jug wines must be accepted for what they are. The fact that they are not as interesting from a tasting point of view as more expensive premium wines should certainly be no criticism, for they fulfill a completely different function. Their prices are right for everyday drinking and, after you've done some preliminary wading through, you just might discover a pleasant everyday wine that will fit into your life as easily as coffee, water, or milk. When the French say, "A day without wine is like a day without sunshine," they don't mean that the sun has to be a perfect ball of red fire. In most cases, a little warmth will do.

PART SIX

Conclusion

In trying to conclude this edition we are faced with the nearly impossible task of describing an instant of time in what has become one of the most rapidly expanding and changing industries in America. As wine sales and production soar and new wineries spring up by the score throughout the state, it would be misleading to try to talk about California wines in a fixed or static context.

Yet certain general trends are identifiable, and many of the observations we made three years ago remain true. The golden era of the 1960s has continued into the early 1970s, as California vintners can still sell nearly everything they produce, regardless of quality or price. Even more often than before, the premium varietals of some wineries are sold out for several months each year, and many wineries and wine shops have begun to ration the more popular varietals like Cabernet Sauvignon. While this rationing does ensure that the wines will be available for a longer period of time, the strong demand created often results in prices that border on the ridiculous. In addition, the very limited production of some of the smaller wineries has led to considerable publicity, not all of it deserved, for "great" California wines that are simply not available to the average consumer.

The constant praise received by California wines in earlier

years is gradually being balanced by a more realistic approach which is critical as well as laudatory. While some of the recently published magazines remain dependent on wine advertisers and thus must find it difficult to be overly critical of certain segments of the industry, at least the idea of ranking or comparing California wines is no longer regarded as an anathema. Unfortunately, the Wine Institute, the primary publicity arm of the California wine industry, has generally continued its blunderstrong approach to consumer "education." While it has done a needed job of exposing the public to the quality and availability of domestic wines, the 1972 chairman of the board of the Wine Institute still proclaims that anyone who favors imports over American wine is a wine snob. Such chauvinism is as out of place in the wine world as it is in the political arena, and its defensive tone does a disservice both to the knowledgeable consumer and to many wineries. No one would deny that California is capable of producing some very fine wines—nor should anyone claim that every California wine is a great one.

And while more information is generally available today about wine and wine-making practices, some wine advertising practices continue to insult the consumer. You can still hear references in tasting rooms to the "Chablis" grape that makes the inexpensive generic of the same name and to the fact that a rosé can be made from any "pink" grape. One winery insists that "reputation is more important than profit" at the same time that its production is doubling and tripling due in large part to the introduction of a less expensive line of wines made at another winery!

In any overview of the history of the world's wine-producing regions, the first experiments with different grape varieties and blending techniques have always culminated in specialization —the perfect matching of grape, soil, and climate. California's wine history is much shorter than Europe's, yet with modern techniques and the invaluable research of the University of California at Davis we have already come a long way in the experimentation stage. Yet the trend in California's commercial wineries has not been to specialize, to produce fewer and better wines; instead they have continued to expand their wine lists with more regard for the commercial appeal of the grape name than for its success in the vineyards.

While the above "diversification" should theoretically give the consumer a wider selection, its result is often the opposite; grown under similar conditions and processed exactly the same, the grapes tend to average out and produce a whole host of undistinctive wines. No one complains because all Bordeaux wines are produced from only a few different grapes, for these have proven to be the most successful for the area. Varying microclimates, soil, and vinification methods then combine to yield a range of wines—lighter or heavier, more or less fruity, soft, or tannic—that offers the consumer a choice without sacrificing the basic union of grape to region. If each winery in California's four or five premium-wine-producing areas concentrated on a few grape varieties, the result would almost certainly be a higher and more consistent quality standard with little real decrease in the selection of wines available to the consumer.

Many of the newly established smaller wineries have found that specialization is the key to their survival, and often these wineries will offer only three or four varietals. While in some cases these choices are dictated by enological considerations, in others the decision to concentrate on the top varietals is solely an economic decision based on the price for which the wine can be sold.

In his search for the best in California wines, the consumer has all too often relied on price alone as an indication of quality. In the past few years price has been supplemented by varietal name and size of the winery, the belief in many quarters being that a Cabernet Sauvignon must be great and that a new small winery must make better wine than an older larger one. One new winery, for example, released a Cabernet that was just over one year old for $5.50 a bottle, and you can be assured that the meager supply was soon exhausted. As long as demand for the "name" varietals continues to far outstrip supply, it is unlikely that there will be any change in the present pricing policies. Of course, in all fairness to the California vintner, it must be pointed out that prices for famous French and German wines have risen at least as much as those of their California counterparts, if not more.

Since in the current situation price does not generally vary with quality, there is little financial incentive to make better wine. As long as every Chardonnay can sell for a premium price, why not make an ordinary wine blended with less expensive grapes that will return a much easier profit? While we do not mean to imply that California vintners are concerned only, or even primarily, with profits, some wineries may be tempted to take advantage of the ridiculously low legal requirement that only 51 percent of a varietal wine need be made from the named grape. While many changes in federal regulations have been sought by the industry in recent years, there has as yet been no move to raise the varietal minimum to a more reasonable 75 or even 65 percent level.

If a winery feels the need to blend more extensively, there is no reason for it to bottle a varietally labeled wine. Paul Masson has been one of the more successful users of proprietary names, and its Emerald Dry, Rubion, and Baroque are more honest and certainly as commercially acceptable as a 51 percent Chardonnay or Johannisberg Riesling.

The vintaging laws have recently been amended so that now a vintaged wine need be only 95 percent from the year stated. This is a reasonable change, and hopefully it will encourage more vintners to vintage-date their wines. Some wineries insist that blending from various years achieves the consistency that the consumer wants, but this is just not always the case. We have noticed in particular that a newly introduced wine is often more interesting and better aged when first released than in subsequent blends, yet there is nothing to notify the consumer of the possibility of such a change until he opens the bottle and finds it not quite as pleasant as he remembered. We cannot help but feel that the real reasons for nonvintaging often do not revolve around the "fact" that there is little difference from year to year, but rather reflect easier bookkeeping requirements and a desire to avoid tumbling sales should a particular year gain the reputation of being a bad one.

In a search for some form of distinction other than price, many California wineries enter the competition at the Los Angeles County and, until recently, state fairs. While basically an excellent idea, the myriad categories and prizes of these judgings are as laughable as the Academy Awards. In 1972, for example, 60 percent of the entrants were awarded prizes—hardly a stiff competition. In addition, there is no requirement that the wines presented actually be commercially available. Many of the varieties sent for judging are in fact small lots specially selected for the fair and thus not at all representative of the wine generally sold by the winery. As a result of all this, half the tasting rooms in California are plastered with ribbons and awards of every description; other wineries probably have them stored in warehouses. One former wine judge told us that once the judges were asked to evaluate and rank forty-seven different red wines in one afternoon. Since the task was obviously impossible, they decided to award the gold medal to the first wine to attract one of the many fruit flies buzzing around! True or not, this story brings out the realities of the situation. This is no reflection on the judges themselves; it's just that with so many ribbons and categories—plus the fact that many of the wineries don't even bother to enter—it's almost impossible to place any real meaning on these awards.

A new form of wine judgings is reflected in the many newsletters and magazines now available that purport to rank the various wines in the state. In general these tastings do have more significance than the county fair medals, and several are indeed quite well done. But the system can be abused; no one we have spoken to believes that one can competently rank over thirty wines in numerical sequence at one sitting, yet the news media have unfortunately widely publicized such tastings and used their results to establish the "best" wine in California. Many consumers, armed only with a name from a newspaper or magazine article, then stampede their local stores, rapidly buying out a wine that for snob appeal or lack of knowledge is often consumed long before it has reached its prime.

In spite of the criticisms we have voiced of overblending, overproduction, and overdiversification, we must recognize the fact that the technical standards of the California wine industry are probably the highest in the world. While stainless steel and centrifuges may be less romantic than oak and constant personal attention, they produce wines that only rarely have any technical flaws. Of course, the finest wines also receive much of the "traditional" treatment that involves a careful selection of grapes, fermentation techniques, and aging.

No wine, however, no matter how excellent it may be when it leaves the winery, can stand up to the treatment that it receives in many of the country's liquor and grocery stores. Here we are merely adding our voices to the many others calling for the proper storage of wine in retail stores. California's wineries have certainly been doing their best to see that their product is well handled after it leaves their cellars, but gross mistakes still occur. You might have to search for a store that leaves bottles on their sides, out of the sun, and away from heaters in the back room, but it is the only way you can be assured that the wine you are drinking is similar to the one that left the winery.

Economic predictions about the future of the wine industry range from a continuing expansion of sales to a gradual leveling off in the next few years to a possible wine depression resulting from overproduction. The answer will affect not only winery owners and investors, but also consumers, for wine prices reflect costs and profits that have increased only in response to a situation where the demand for wine has far exceeded the supply. Many thousands of acres of vineyards have been planted in California in the past few years, and no one can predict whether the increased quantities of grapes that will become available in the coming years will in fact result in a glut of wine grapes or whether sales will continue to rise and prolong the seller's market that currently exists.

Certainly some leveling off of prices must come soon, as it is not uncommon now for a winery to raise its prices two or three times within a single year. Hopefully the consumer will become sophisticated enough to realize that just because a wine has a Cabernet Sauvignon label and a high price tag does not necessarily mean that it is better than a well-made Zinfandel or Petite Sirah, any more than knowledgeable sherry drinkers think that Harvey's Bristol Cream is the best just because it is expensive and widely advertised.

If prices continue to soar, many people may find themselves financially driven away from the opportunity to enjoy the better California wines. Already large quantities of less expensive Spanish and Italian imports are making inroads in the American market, and wine merchants are turning their attention to previously untapped wine sources in South America, Australia, and Europe. As the consumer's tastes broaden, the end result could be less than beneficial to many California vintners.

Of additional concern is the fact that the investment possibilities in the wine industry have received so much publicity lately that many people are jumping on the bandwagon by purchasing land and planting vineyards. While theoretically this will increase the grape supply and contribute to keeping the price of wine down, in actuality many acres of prime varietals are being planted in soils and climates where they may not belong. The result a few years from now may well be a lot of "ordinary" premium grapes that will not contribute to the overall quality of California wine.

While there is certainly room in California for an unlimited number of vintners who produce good wines, the current situation, where any small winery can sell a White Zinfandel for $6 because of its rarity and a large company can sell a watery Chardonnay for $3 because of its name, must come to an end.

Again, the choice is ours. If we, as consumers, insist on good value for our money, then wine will take its proper place as the most interesting and diverse beverage in the world and not be left to become the province of only the rich.

Most of the changes that we have noted over the past several years in the California wine industry have been those that one could expect in a rapidly expanding and, at the moment, very profitable business. As far as quality is concerned, there are at least a few bright spots in the overall picture that were not there when the first edition of this book was written. Perhaps the most encouraging sign has been the generally higher quality of California Chardonnays, which on the whole have more varietal character and interest than those of a few years ago. A few of the larger wineries still make only average wine from Chardonnay (and other) grapes, but many of the smaller wineries in particular have been quite successful with what many consider to be the king of the white grapes. California's other whites are still sometimes plagued by rather low acidity and somewhat weak flavors, although some Chenin Blancs and dry Sauvignon Blancs are very promising.

In the reds, the Cabernet Sauvignon remains the variety capable of producing the finest wine, and the best California Cabernets may hold their heads high in any competition, domestic or foreign. Unfortunately, most California Cabernets still reach the public and are drunk much too young.

Some excellent results have been obtained with Zinfandel recently, though selectivity must be exercised. Many in the full-bodied, tannic style have fancy price tags, although in some cases it is pure speculation as to whether they will live up to their apparent potential.

As far as the average consumer is concerned, California's real potential may lie with the simpler premium varieties. These wines—including the lighter Zinfandels, Gamay, Petite Sirah, Chenin Blanc, and Gewürztraminer—may never attain the greatness of Cabernet or Chardonnay, but they are capable of producing consistent, very pleasant wines that should go a long way toward turning the United States into a wine-drinking nation.

As in the first edition, we have been critical where we have thought it justified. The two faults we found most often were either a lack of varietal character or, where the wine might be a fairly good one, a price that was way out of line with the quality. We were pleased that in this second round of tastings we probably discovered fewer technical flaws—sulfur, oxidation, excessive woodiness, etc.—than in previous years. Now the challenge to the California vintner is not just to make sound wine, but to make good wine.

Even if there have been times when we have been disappointed with the overall quality of a certain vintner, almost every California premium winery seems to come up with at least a few varieties that are pleasant and demonstrate an ability to make good wine. Potential is almost everywhere you look; the big question is whether California wineries will respond to it or let the unprecedented consumer demand for wine tempt them into shaving corners and sacrificing quality for quantity and dollars.

In any case, we hope that we have shed a bit of light on the ins and outs of California wine, and that at the same time we have intrigued you enough so that you will go out and start your own "book" of wine experiments. Wine can be a most interesting and enjoyable creature; treat it with care and respect and it will be sure to reward you. And, while the getting-acquainted period may have its ups and downs, a long and fruitful friendship is in sight. A *votre santé!*

How to Interpret a California Wine Label

There is a wealth of information to be gathered from any wine label. All it takes is an understanding of a few terms and a little experience in interpreting the shades of difference between what may at first glance appear to be two very similar labels.

Name of the Winery   One of the most prominent, and perhaps most important, items to be found on every front label is the name of the winery marketing the product.

Wine Type   Of equal prominence on every bottle is the name of the type or variety of wine contained therein. A generic or proprietary wine may be legally made from virtually any grape variety, while a varietal wine must contain a minimum of 51 percent of the named grape.

In smaller print may also appear the legal classification of the wine. "Table wine" has an alcoholic content of less than 14 percent; "dessert wine" contains 17 to 24 percent alcohol. "Sparkling wine" must result from the fermentation of the wine within a closed container. If the secondary fermentation occurred within a glass container of not greater than one gallon capacity, the wine may be labeled "Champagne"; if secondary fermentation took place in a container greater than one gallon, the word "Champagne" may not be used except in conjunction with qualifying terms such as "Champagne style," "Champagne type," or "Champagne—bulk process." Sparkling wines not labeled "Champagne," such as Sparkling Burgundy, need not state whether they were bottle- or bulk-fermented. Similar restrictions apply to "crackling" or other less effervescent wines. If a wine has obtained its effervescence from artificial carbonation, that fact must be designated. All other wines, whether fermented in bulk or in the bottle, may be labeled "naturally fermented."

Appellation of Origin A "California" wine must be produced from grapes grown exclusively within the state of California. Any label designating a more specific area of origin—for example, Napa, Livermore, or Santa Clara Valley—must have at least 75 percent of its volume derived from grapes grown within that area. The 1972 amendments to the federal labeling regulations require only that the wine be produced within the same state as the area from which the grapes come; thus, wine from grapes grown in Monterey County but fermented at a winery in Santa Clara is entitled to be designated "Monterey County" wine.

Vintage While in the past vintaged California wine had to be produced entirely from grapes harvested and fermented in a given year, recent changes have quite reasonably altered the requirements so that now only 95 percent of the wine must be from grapes gathered in the same calendar year. This allows the vintner to top up barrels or otherwise care for the wine by adding very small quantities of wine from other years and lowers the record-keeping burden a bit as well. In addition, vintaged wines must be from grapes grown within the same viticultural area mentioned on the label, though the wine may still be fermented anywhere in the state.

Alcohol Content By law the alcohol content of California white table wine must be between 10 and 14 percent, while that of a red table wine must fall between 10.5 and 14 percent. The label must state either the actual amount of alcohol in the wine (within a tolerance of 1.5 percent in each direction) or, alternatively, the terms "table wine" or "light wine" may be used.

Net Contents must also be displayed, either on the label or marked in the bottle itself.

Estate-bottled   An estate-bottled wine must have come entirely from grapes "owned or controlled" by the producing winery and "in the vicinity" of the winery. The "control" requirement may be met by long-term leases or contracts with independent growers. It is not precisely clear what "in the vicinity" means; in practice, this generally refers to grapes that are at least within the same county, but a winery near the county line that owned vineyards in both counties might well be entitled to the "estate-bottled" description. Widely separated vineyards are excluded, however; thus wine produced from a blend of grapes from new vineyards in Monterey County as well as vineyards in Napa or Santa Clara could not be eligible to be labeled estate-bottled, even though both vineyards are owned by the same winery.

Those wineries that practice estate bottling advertise that it is an indication of consistency and quality. Their competitors who do not label their wines as estate-bottled claim that the term is an often abused one that favors wineries with large land holdings, regardless of the quality of the grapes. Ownership, they argue, does not ensure quality. Some have told us that several of their varieties are eligible to be labeled as estate-bottled, but to them it's not worth the hassle of getting a new label approved.

While estate bottling is often an interesting indication of which grape varieties a winery obtains from its own vineyards and which ones it must buy on the open market, the individual performance and reputation of a winery are much more important than whether or not the wines carry this particular designation.

Near the bottom of the front label will be found a short phrase that may tell a great deal about how the wine was made.

This will include one of the following statements and the name of the winery.

Produced and Bottled by   This means that at least 75 percent of the wine in the bottle was fermented and finished by the named winery. The 1972 amendments have deleted the former requirement that the grapes also be crushed by the winery; because of the advent of field crushing and improved methods of transportation, the grapes may be crushed elsewhere but the must still has to be fermented by the producing winery.

Made and Bottled by   If between 10 and 75 percent of the wine was produced by the winery and has otherwise been treated similarly to that in the above category, this phrase is the one that will probably appear on the label. This 10 percent minimum is set by the label approval board rather than by federal or state regulations.

Terms like *Cellared and Bottled by, Perfected and Bottled by,* or simply *Bottled by* are used to indicate that the wines have been primarily bought from other producers and then finished and bottled by the winery whose label they carry.

While at first it might seem that the winery that plays a role in its wine from grape to bottle will do a better job than the one that buys wine in bulk and then ages, blends, and bottles it, in practice this is not always the case. Both good and bad wines appear carrying all three of these labels, and some of California's most successful wines may be found in each of these categories.

In addition, the widespread use of fictitious names (which are simply business names that do not reflect the identity of the actual owner) makes it very difficult to know just who that winery mentioned in small type on the label really is. It is fairly common for a winery to buy a wine from another vintner and sell it under its own label. Although you would expect such wines to carry designations like "selected and bottled by," the perfectly legal use of fictitious names permits the statement "produced and bottled by" to be employed. For example, if Sunshine Vineyard in St. Helena purchases a wine from Mountain Winery in Sonoma, an agreement may be reached whereby the producing winery files a fictitious name very similar to that of the winery buying the wine. Thus, while the large print on the label may read Sunshine Vineyard Cabernet Sauvignon, the small print at the bottom will state "produced and bottled by Sunshine Winery, Sonoma." Every letter or word in this section of the label is important, but you must look very closely to detect that the winery selling the wine may not have actually produced it.

The last significant phrase on a front label is the *address of the winery,* which, as noted above, should tell you where a wine has actually been produced; obviously a winery known to be in the Napa Valley cannot really have "produced and bottled" a wine at an address in Sonoma. Unfortunately, this address can refer not only to the place where the wine was actually bottled, but also to the principal place of business of the bottler, as long as it is in the same state. Thus several wines are now "produced and bottled" by wineries located in San Francisco, though the wine itself will actually reach the city only through distributors or retailers.

While all of the above terms have some form of legal requirements governing their use, many other extralegal words also find their way onto California wine labels. As you will see below, some are a little more reliable than others in conveying accurate information.

Private Stock is found on the bottles of a few California vintners. At first glance this term seems to connote a limited amount of wine that has been specially selected from a larger batch to carry a winery's private label. In practice, however, any winery that wishes to may call all of its wines "private stock." It is a meaningless way of getting a few more impressive words on the label.

Vintage Selection or *Private Reserve* wines are also made available by a number of wineries. The reputation of the individual winery is most important in determining if these represent higher-quality wines, though these appear to be two of the more respectable notations to appear on a California wine label and often merit consumer attention. Beaulieu, Charles Krug, and Louis Martini are examples of wineries which offer both regular and special selections of certain varieties, and the latter category does in fact designate a wine that, in the winery's opinion, is of superior quality.

Limited Bottlings are becoming more common, often in connection with some form of *numbered label*. Again, winery reputation must be your primary guide. Sometimes these designations represent a certain segment of a winery's production that is regularly segregated from the rest, rather than being specially or individually selected each year. For example, all of Concannon's Cabernet Sauvignon is bottled as a limited bottling, and all Mirassou wines produced entirely from their new vineyards in Monterey are designated as limited-bottling "Harvest" wines. In other cases this label does indicate a special lot of a particular vintage.

Mere numbering of bottles, however, does not imply any form of quality control; anyone can buy a consecutive number stamper without changing the quality of the wine inside the bottle.

Cask, cuvée, or *bin* numbers are also found on some labels. What they mean varies from winery to winery, though again they generally imply nothing about quality control. They may simply represent the identification of a particular year's blend of wine (Llords & Elwood), wine of the same vintage bottled on different dates (Sebastiani), or wine from a particular year selected to receive special treatment (Inglenook cask Cabernet Sauvignon).

Back Labels

While a careful inspection of front labels can be informative, back labels usually say little that is of true importance to the consumer. Some wineries recognize this and skip back labels entirely, while others use them only to give a short history of the winery. A few use this space for the commendable practice of telling exactly which grape varieties go into the particular wine; you may also search the back label for information about the relative sweetness of a white or rosé. Many wineries, however, use back labels merely as a publicity instrument to heap often undeserved praise upon themselves.

Suggested Reading

For those of you whose appetites have been whetted by this introduction to the world of wine, we would like to recommend the following books for your future investigation.

As a general introduction to the broad scope of wine and wine making both here and in Europe, the best work is undoubtedly *Wine: An Introduction for Americans,* by M. A. Amerine and V. L. Singleton. Published by the University of California Press in 1966, it is available in both hard-cover and paperback editions. For a more technically oriented look at wine production in California, there is the recently revised *Technology of Wine Making* by Professors Amerine, Berg, and Creuss of the University of California at Davis (Avi Publishing Company, 1967). A very comprehensive and recent work on nearly all aspects of wine production is the two-volume *Traité d'Oenologie,* by J. Ribéreau-Gayon and E. Peynaud (in French, published by the Librairie Polytechnique Béranger in 1966). It includes a very interesting chapter on sensory evaluation of wine as well as investigations of many modern vinification methods. Amerine and Joslyn's new edition of *Table Wines* (University of California Press, 1970) is also excellent for those interested in the technology of wine production.

For a fuller view of California's earlier wine history, excellent chapters may be found in *American Wines* by Frank

Schoonmaker and Tom Marvel (Duell, Sloan, & Pearce, 1941) and Philip Wagner's *American Wines and How to Make Them,* published in 1936 by Alfred A. Knopf. Leon Adams' new book, *The Wines of America* (Houghton Mifflin, 1973) gives a more up-to-date view and has some very interesting chapters on California's wine history.

On the touristic side, *Sunset* magazine's *California Wine Country* is invaluable. While a few minor inaccuracies do creep in, it is the most comprehensive book of its type available and is an essential for the traveling wine hobbyist.

Several monthly newsletters and magazines have sprung up recently, and certainly the former are worth investigating as a way of keeping up with the latest vintages and developments. Those we have seen certainly vary in quality and style, so be sure to get a sample copy before subscribing. *Wines and Vines* has been the wine industry's trade magazine for years and, while it is directed primarily to those within the wine-making and -selling realm, it does contain information of interest to the consumer. The more popularly oriented magazines include *Vintage* and *Wine World.* Both have interesting articles, although *Wine World* is perhaps the more California-oriented.

And for those who would like to try their own hand at extracting the nectar of the grape, one of the best guides for the home wine maker is *Progressive Winemaking,* by Peter Duncan and Bryan Acton, published in 1967 by The Amateur Winemaker.

List of Wineries

The following is an alphabetical list of all of the premium wineries discussed in this book. Addresses and phone numbers are included to aid those of you who would like to write or phone with specific questions about wines, distribution networks, or visits to the winery. In some cases a San Francisco address is included; this is the business office, while the other address is that of the winery itself.

We especially encourage those of you who live outside of California and have been unable to find particular wines that interest you to write directly to the winery. Almost all of the large premium wineries have nationwide distribution, and even the wines of many of the smaller ones can be found in a surprising number of cities. An inquiry to the winery will supply you with the name of the nearest distributor and a list of the wines that should be available.

Almadén Vineyards
1 Maritime Plaza
Golden Gateway Center   (415)
San Francisco, California 94111   391-1500

Barengo Cellars
3125 East Orange Street   (209)
Acampo, California 95220   369-2746

Bargetto Winery
3535 North Main Street   (408)
Soquel, California 95073   475-2258

Beaulieu Vineyard   (415)
57 Post Street   392-0157
San Francisco, California 94104 (707)
Rutherford, California 94573   963-3214

Beringer Bros.
650 California Street   (415)
San Francisco, California 94108 788-8194
2000 Main Street   (707)
St. Helena, California 94574   963-2725

Bertero Winery
3920 Hecker Pass Highway   (408)
Gilroy, California 95020   842-3032

Bonesio Winery
11550 Watsonville Road   (408)
Gilroy, California 95020   842-2601

Brookside Vineyard Company
9900 A Street   (714)
Guasti, California 91743   983-2787

Buena Vista Winery
P.O. Box 182   (707)
Sonoma, California 95476   938-8504

Butler Winery
Route 3, P.O. Box 357   (209)
Sonora, California 95370   586-4384

Cadenasso Winery
P.O. Box 22   (707)
Fairfield, California 94534   425-5845

Chalone Vineyard
P.O. Box 855
Soledad, California 93960   No Phone

Chappellet Vineyard
1581 Sage Canyon Road
St. Helena, California 94574

Charles Krug Winery
P.O. Box 191   (707)
St. Helena, California 94574   963-2761

Château Montelena Winery
1429 Tubbs Lane   (707)
Calistoga, California 94515   942-4060

Christian Brothers
P.O. Box 420   (707)
Napa, California 94558   226-5566

Concannon Vineyard
4590 Tesla Road   (415)
Livermore, California 94551   447-3760

Cresta Blanca Winery
One Jackson Place   (415)
San Francisco, California 94111   956-6330

Cuvaison
4560 Silverado Trail   (707)
Calistoga, California 94515   942-6100

D'Agostini Winery
P.O. Box 66   (209)
Plymouth, California 95669   245-6612

David Bruce
21439 Bear Creek Road   (408)
Los Gatos, California 95030   354-4214

Davis Bynum
614 San Pablo Avenue   (415)
Albany, California 94716   526-1366

East-Side Winery
6100 East Highway 12   (209)
Lodi, California 95240   369-4768

Fetzer Vineyards
1150 Bel Arbres Road   (707)
Redwood Valley, California 95470   485-8671

Ficklin Vineyards
32046 Avenue 7½   (209)
Madera, California 93637   674-4598

Foppiano Wine Company
P.O. Box 606   (707)
Healdsburg, California 95448   433-1937

Franzia Brothers Winery
P.O. Box 697   (209)
Ripon, California 95366   599-4251

Freemark Abbey Winery
P.O. Box 410   (707)
St. Helena, California 94574   963-7106

Gallo Vineyards
P.O. Box 1130
600 Yosemite Boulevard   (209)
Modesto, California 95353   526-3111

Gemello Winery
2003 El Camino Real   (415)
Mountain View, California 94040   948-7723

Grand Cru Vineyards
1 Vintage Lane   (707)
Glen Ellen, California 95442   996-8100

Guild Wine Company
500 Sansome Street   (415)
San Francisco, California 94111   391-1100

Hanns Kornell Champagne Cellars
Larkmead Lane, P.O. Box 249   (707)
St. Helena, California 94574   963-2334

Hanzell Vineyards
18596 Lomita Avenue   (707)
Sonoma, California 95476   996-3860

Heitz Wine Cellars
500 Taplin Road   (707)
St. Helena, California 94574   963-3542

Husch Vineyards
P.O. Box 144
Philo, California 95466

Inglenook Vineyards
P.O. Box 269   (707)
Rutherford, California 94573   963-7182
United Vintners, Inc.
601 Fourth Street   (415)
San Francisco, California 94107   421-3213

Italian Swiss Colony
United Vintners, Inc.
601 Fourth Street   (415)
San Francisco, California 94107   421-3213

Kenwood Vineyards
9592 Sonoma Highway   (707)
Kenwood, California 95452   833-5891

Korbel Champagne Cellars   (707)
Guerneville, California 95446   887-2294

Llords & Elwood Winery
1150 South Beverly Drive   (213)
Los Angeles, California 90035   553-2368
1250 Stanford Avenue
Mission San Jose, California 94538

Los Altos Vineyards
P.O. Box 247   (408)
Gilroy, California 95020   842-5649

Louis M. Martini
P.O. Box 112   (707)
St. Helena, California 94574   963-2736

Martin Ray
22000 Mount Eden Road   (408)
Saratoga, California 95071   867-3205

Mayacamas Vineyards
1155 Lokoya Road   (707)
Napa, California 94558   224-4030

Mirassou Vineyards
Route 3, P.O. Box 344, Aborn Road   (408)
San Jose, California 95121   274-3000

Nepenthe Cellars
216 Corte Madera Road
Portola Valley, California 94025

Nervo Winery
19585 Redwood Highway South   (707)
Geyserville, California 95441   857-3621

Nichelini Vineyard
2349 Lower Chiles Road   (707)
St. Helena, California 94574   963-3357

Novitiate of Los Gatos
P.O. Box 128, Prospect Avenue   (408)
Los Gatos, California 95030   354-3737

Oakville Vineyards
P.O. Box 87   (707)
Oakville, California 94562   944-2455

Parducci Wine Cellars
501 Parducci Road   (707)
Ukiah, California 95482   462-3828

Paul Masson Vineyards
330 Jackson Street   (415)
San Francisco, California 94111   362-8082
Champagne Cellars
13150 Saratoga Avenue   (408)
Saratoga, California 95071   257-7800

Pedrizetti Winery
Route 2, P.O. Box 166
1645 San Pedro Avenue   (408)
Morgan Hill, California 95037   779-3710

Pedroncelli Winery
1220 Canyon Road   (707)
Geyserville, California 95441   857-3619

Pesenti Winery
Vineyard Drive   (805)
Templeton, California 93465   434-1030

Ridge Vineyards
17100 Monte Bello Road   (408)
Cupertino, California 94025   867-3233

Robert Mondavi Winery
P.O. Box 106   (707)
Oakville, California 94562   963-7156

Rotta Winery
Route 1, P.O. Box 168   (805)
Templeton, California 93465   434-1389

Russian River Vineyards
5700 Gravenstein Highway North   (707)
Forestville, California 95436   887-2243

San Martin Winery
P.O. Box 53   (408)
San Martin, California 95046   683-2672

Santa Barbara Winery
202 Anacapa Street   (805)
Santa Barbara, California 93108   966-5012

Schramsberg Vineyards   (707)
Calistoga, California 94515   942-4558

Sebastiani Vineyards
389 Fourth Street East   (707)
Sonoma, California 95476   938-5532

Simi Winery
Healdsburg Avenue, P.O. Box 946   (707)
Healdsburg, California 95448   433-4276

Souverain Cellars, Inc.
P.O. Box 348   (707)
St. Helena, California 94574   963-3688

Spring Mountain Vineyards
2867 St. Helena Highway North   (707)
St. Helena, California 94574   963-4341

Sterling Vineyards
1111 Dunaweal Lane   (707)
Calistoga, California 94515   942-4354

Stony Hill Vineyard
P.O. Box 308   (707)
St. Helena, California 94574   963-2636

Sutter Home Winery
277 St. Helena Highway South   (707)
St. Helena, California 94574   963-3104

Thomas Kruse Winery
4390 Hecker Pass Road   (408)
Gilroy, California 95020   842-7016

Tiburon Vintners, Inc.
(see Windsor Vineyards)
1680 Tiburon Boulevard   (415)
Tiburon, California 94920   435-3113

Trentadue Winery
19170 Redwood Highway   (707)
Geyserville, California 95441   433-3104

Viano Winery
150 Morello Avenue   (415)
Martinez, California 94553   228-6465

Villa Armando Winery
553 St. John Street   (415)
Pleasanton, California 94566   846-5488

Weibel Champagne Vineyards
P.O. Box 3095   (415)
Mission San Jose, California 94536   656-2340

Wente Bros.
5565 Tesla Road   (415)
Livermore, California 94550   447-3603

Windsor Vineyards
P.O. Box 57, Old Redwood Highway   (707)
Windsor, California 95492   433-5545

Wooden Valley Winery
Route 1, P.O. Box 124, Suisun Valley Road   (707)
Suisun, California 94585   425-3962

Woodside Vineyards
340 Kings Mountain Road   (415)
Woodside, California 94062   851-7475

York Mountain Winery
Route 1, P.O. Box 191, York Mountain Road   (805)
Templeton, California 93465   238-3925

Yverdon Vineyards
P.O. Box 62   (707)
St. Helena, California 94574   963-4270

Z-D Wines
P.O. Box 900
20735 Burndale Road   (707)
Sonoma, California 95370   539-9137

Appendix

The following section contains our evaluations of some recently released wines from the Golden State, as well as descriptions of new wineries and developments. The California wine scene remains extremely active, and numerous new wineries will continue to sprout in the coming months. You can keep current by watching for articles in wine magazines and for new labels on the shelves of your wine merchant. Or even better, next time you visit the wine country look for new vineyards, buildings, or signs marking the location of a new winery and make the discovery yourself.

Napa Valley

Beaulieu Vineyard

Dry Sauternes (Semillon) 1972   Pale yellow with a pleasant, flowery aroma. Off-dry, with light to medium body and acidity. Varietal flavors are light and somewhat disappointing.   (*)
Château Beaulieu Sauvignon Blanc 1971   Light to medium

yellow in color with a soft, spicy aroma. Medium sweet, with light to medium body and acid. A rather simple wine, but certainly a pleasant one. (**)

Haut Sauternes 1971 Medium sweet, rather undistinguished, with less flavor than the Château Beaulieu of the same vintage. (*)

Johannisberg Riesling 1971 Medium-yellow color with a distinct oily-rubbery California Riesling nose. Off-dry, light to medium body and acidity, with flavors fairly typical of a good Napa Valley Riesling. (**)

Chardonnay The *1971* is another fine Chardonnay. In mid-1973 it appears slightly less complex than the 1970, but another year or two of bottle age will help. Medium in body, with a good blend of fruit and oak in the nose and well-balanced, moderate acidity. A distinctive Chardonnay. (***)

Burgundy The *1970* is a very drinkable wine with good balance, reflecting the quality of the vintage, although it is somewhat softer and will probably have less staying power than the 1964 and the 1968. Medium-red color with a nice oaky-vanilla bouquet, medium body and acidity, and light to medium tannin. (**)

Gamay Beaujolais 1972 Light in color and body, with a tart woody finish. Lacks freshness and fruit. (BA)

Pinot Noir The *1970* is a soft, pleasant wine that is probably at its peak. A touch of early oxidation imparts richness to the nose and flavor but has also contributed to the early maturation. Medium-red color with a hint of orange; light to medium body, acid, and tannin. (**)

Cabernet Sauvignon 1970 Medium-dark purplish red in color with a nose that will develop further but already contains overtones of spice and green olives. Medium in body and acid, with moderate to high tannin, yet surprisingly soft in the finish. A very nice though not overpowering wine, with rich and elegant Cabernet flavors. Should reach its peak in the late 1970s. (****)

Brut Champagne 1969   A nice sparkling wine with pleasant flowery and fruity flavors and a touch of yeastiness to the nose and finish. Slightly sweet, with light to medium body and moderate acidity. Different in style from preceding vintages, being light and fruity rather than rich and mouthfilling.   (**)

Chappellet Vineyard

Cabernet Sauvignon 1970   Medium to dark red in color with a mint-berry aroma. Medium body, acid, and tannin, with good Cabernet flavors. Should develop nicely for several years, although a relatively soft finish suggests the wine will be at its peak by 1975–76.   (***)

Charles Krug

Pouilly Fumé   A new wine from Krug made from Sauvignon Blanc grapes. Dry, with good varietal character and light to medium body and acid. Less fruity than the Mondavi Fumé Blanc but with more grassy-spiciness in the aroma in the style of the Loire wines, after which both were named.   (**)

Chardonnay   The *1971* is similar to both the 1969 and the 1970, though it is perhaps a touch softer and would have benefited from a little more acidity. Medium yellow in color with a rich, oaky nose; medium to full body and good Chardonnay flavors. Should continue to grow through 1974.   (***)

Burgundy 1969   Lighter and less substantial than the 1968, though it does retain a fresh raspberry flavor and clean finish that should make it nice with picnics or light meals. Light to medium body and tannin; moderate acid; drinkable now. (**)

Cabernet Sauvignon 1969   Light to medium red in color with a fruity, slightly woody nose. Light to medium body, acid, and tannin. A pleasant and drinkable wine but one without great Cabernet character. (**)

Cabernet Sauvignon Vintage Selection 1968   A good wine, though less distinguished and complex than the several preceding vintages. Medium-red color tinged with orange; herbal green-olive nose. Medium in body, acid, and tannin. At its peak and should remain so through 1975. (**)

Zinfandel 1970   A soft, drinkable wine with grapey-fruity aroma and berrylike flavors. Light to medium in body, acid, and tannin. (**)

Freemark Abbey

Pinot Chardonnay   The *1971* is the third fine Chardonnay in a row for Freemark. Medium yellow, with a nice oily-oaky nose, medium body and acid, and good, fruity Chardonnay flavors. Slightly less complex and rich than the 1970. (***)

Johannisberg Riesling 1971   Medium yellow in color with a good varietal nose. Fairly full-bodied and dry but with good acidity. The freshest and fruitiest Riesling released by Freemark to date. (***)

Cabernet Sauvignon 1970 (Boshé Vineyard)   The first of what will be special bottlings from a vineyard whose grapes formerly went into Beaulieu Private Reserve Cabernet. Dark color, with a beautiful nose of violets and oak. Rich and almost sweet in the mouth, with light to medium body and medium acidity and tannin. Excellent flavors; should develop well until the end of this decade. Blended with 10 percent Merlot. (****)

Heitz Wine Cellars

Grignolino Rosé   The *1972* has a brilliant rose color and a nice estery aroma. It is dry, with light to medium body and acidity. A good full-flavored rosé. (**)

Cabernet Sauvignon   The *1968* has very good flavor and fruit, a minty Cabernet aroma, and medium-red color tinged with orange. Medium in body, acidity, and tannin, with a future aging potential through the mid-1970s. (****)

The *1968 Martha's Vineyard Cabernet Sauvignon* is a beautiful wine that captures the full flavors and complexity of the grape. Deep color with rich wintergreen-minty aroma; medium body; medium-high acid and tannin. Delicious fruit in the mouth with balance and strength to develop well into the early 1980s. (****)

Inglenook Vineyards

Semillon 1971   A dry wine with a distinctive green-grassy aroma, medium body, and light to medium acidity. Good varietal character but a bit alcoholic and rough in the after-taste. (*)

Grey Riesling 1971   Very undistinguished except for a slight spice in the nose. Dry, with light to medium body and acidity. (*)

Chenin Blanc 1971   A slightly sweet wine of pale color and light to medium body and acid. Not unpleasant but simple, with little varietal character or flavor. (*)

Gamay Beaujolais 1970 A little fuller in style than many Gamay Beaujolais, with pleasant though not outstanding flavors. Light to medium body and tannin, with moderate acidity. (**)

Red Pinot The *1969* (*) has a nice fruity aroma but is less balanced than previous vintages and has a slightly sharp aftertaste. The *1970* (**) will be the last vintage for this varietal at Inglenook, for the old vines have been uprooted and the vineyard replanted in Cabernet. The wine is a nice finale, for it has good color, a pleasant buttery-fruity nose with developing bouquet, and nice flavors that should continue to improve through 1975. Light to medium in body and tannin, with moderate acidity.

Pinot Noir 1970 Medium-red color with slightly deeper and more developed flavors than preceding vintages. Light to medium body and tannin with moderate acid. Fairly soft without need for extended bottle aging. (**)

Cabernet Sauvignon 1968 Medium-red color with an undeveloped, slight berrylike aroma. Fairly well balanced, with medium body, acidity, and tannin, yet at this stage possessing rather simple Cabernet flavors. A few more years of bottle age are needed to see if more substantial character will come forth. (**)

Cabernet Sauvignon 1968 Cask Bottling On the light side for a Cabernet, this wine is relatively simple but pleasant and has promise for some further development through the mid-1970s. Light to medium red in color with a soft fruity aroma, light to medium body and medium acid and tannin. (**)

Zinfandel 1970 A straightforward Zinfandel with medium-red color and a chalky, fruity nose. Light to medium in body and tannin, with medium acidity. Slightly sharp finish but otherwise fairly nice. (**)

Champagne Brut 1968 A dry, austere wine with good sparkle and a pronounced yeasty nose. Light to medium in acid; not overly rich or fruity, yet well made. (**)

Louis M. Martini

Riesling (Sylvaner) 1972   A dry, pale yellow wine with a fresh aroma but rather neutral flavors. Light to medium body and acidity.   (*)

Gewürztraminer   The *1972* is very similar to prior vintages and possesses the nice spicy-flowery aroma that characterizes Martini's Gewürz. Once again, though, the flavors are rather light. Dry, with light body and light to medium acid.   (**)

Dry Chenin Blanc 1972   A dry, rather ordinary wine, with light to medium body and acidity. Slight Chenin Blanc character is present, but the wine would benefit from greater concentration of fruit and flavors.   (*)

Folle Blanche 1972   A dry, light, crisp wine with simple but very pleasant flavors. Light yellow in color, light to medium body, and moderate acidity. A good, drinkable, relatively inexpensive white.   (**)

Gamay Rosé 1972   A very dry, tart rosé with bright-pink color and a pleasant, fruity aroma. Light in body, with medium acidity.   (**)

Zinfandel 1970   Medium red, with some fruit in the nose. Light to medium in body and tannin, with medium acidity. Very young at present, but seemingly less complex than the 1966 and the 1968 were at the same age. Must be tried again in 1974 to determine the effect of additional bottle aging.   (**)

Mayacamas Vineyard

Chardonnay   The *1971* finished its development in wood quite nicely and now has good Chardonnay flavors similar to the 1970. A soft dry wine of medium body and light to medium acidity with the oily-spicy character of oak well balanced in the nose and flavor.   (***)

Oakville Vineyards

Sauvignon Fleur 1972   From Sauvignon Blanc and Muscat grapes. Nice perfumed aroma but rather light in body and flavors. Slightly sweet, with light to medium acidity.   (*)

Sauvignon Blanc 1972 (*van Loben Sels Selection*)   A big, dry wine that has promise of developing nicely with adequate bottle age (mid to late 1974). Medium to full body; medium acidity. At present a mustiness in the nose covers the delicious ripe-fruit smell of Sauvignon Blanc, but hopefully this will dissipate and allow the wine's full flavors to emerge.   (**)

Chenin Blanc 1972   A dry wine with nice Chenin Blanc character, good acid balance, and slight spiciness in the aroma. Should develop in the bottle and retain good flavors through 1974.   (**)

Gewürztraminer 1972   Dry with light to medium body, moderate acidity, and light-yellow color. A clean wine with better acid balance than many California Gewürzes but lacking the intense perfume in the nose and ripeness of flavors of this varietal at its best.   (**)

Robert Mondavi Winery

Johannisberg Riesling 1972   Slightly sweet and pleasant, but with less fruit and flavors than prior vintages. Flowery aroma, with light to medium body and acidity.   (**)

Chenin Blanc 1972   Similar in style to prior vintages, though not as rich as the 1971. Light, fruity, and slightly sweet with light to medium body and acidity.   (**)

Gamay Rosé 1972   A dry, fresh, fruity wine with brilliant pink color. Light to medium body, medium acidity, and slightly *pétillant*. Some berry quality to the aroma and taste.   (***)

Pinot Noir 1970   A soft wine, nearly at its peak, that is pleasant but not complex. Nice cocoa-vanilla bouquet; light to medium body, acid, and tannin.   (**)

Cabernet Sauvignon 1970   A soft, pleasant wine with fine balance, fruity Cabernet flavors, and oaky-vanilla overtones in the bouquet and taste. Medium-red color with medium body, acid, and tannin. Its softness portends early drinkability, yet it should endure the decade.   (***)

Souverain Cellars

The past several years have been busy ones at Souverain. In 1970 owner-founder Lee Stewart sold the winery to a small group of investors, and not long thereafter Pillsbury Mills purchased a majority interest, marking its entry into the fast-growing California wine industry. Mr. Stewart continues to be involved with the winery in a consulting capacity.

An attractive new winery has been built in the hills above the Silverado Trail just north of the Highway 128 intersection. Visitors are welcome for tours and retail sales, but there is no tasting. Grapes will come from contracts with independent growers, some of whose vineyards will be farmed by Souverain's land-management company. Although the new facilities will allow some expansion, Souverain will remain in the medium-size range compared to its neighbors. Pillsbury has grander ideas in terms of production at its new winery in

Sonoma County, Ville Fontaine, described later in this section.

It is too early to make any definite decisions as to what quality trend Souverain will take under its new leadership. Only two vintages have passed, and both of these have been fraught with climatic problems for all Napa Valley vintners. In addition the 1972 wines were crushed and fermented in a brand-new facility. Still it is fair to say that several of the formerly highly successful white varieties have been disappointing, yet the prices are higher than ever before. The fine *1971 Zinfandel* is encouraging, however.

Chardonnay The *1971* has less pronounced Chardonnay flavor than the 1970. Slight oak in the bouquet, but the nose is otherwise undeveloped. Light to medium yellow color with medium body and light to moderate acidity. (*)

Johannisberg Riesling Two different wines were made in *1972*, one from the Napa Valley and the other from the Alexander Valley of Sonoma. The *Napa Valley* (*) is the better of the two, with slight floweriness in the nose, light to medium body, and moderate acidity. The *Alexander Valley* (BA) is unbalanced and has little fruit or flavor of the Riesling. Both are excessively oaky and disappointing compared to the beautiful, flowery Rieslings that Souverain has made.

Pineau Souverain *1971* is a full-flavored Chenin Blanc with some oak in the nose well balanced by soft fruitiness. Dry, with medium body and light to medium acidity. (**)

Green Hungarian 1972 Less interesting than the two preceding vintages. Dry, with light to medium body and acidity, slight oakiness, and not enough fruit. (*)

Cabernet Sauvignon Considerable sulfur is present in the nose of the *1969* and may take several years to dissipate. Underlying Cabernet flavors suggest the wine may improve through the mid-1970s, but there is considerably less complexity than was found in the 1968. Medium in body, acid, and tannin. (*)

Pinot Noir The *1971* is a tart, undistinguished wine with little complexity of aroma or flavor. Simple, fruity nose with slight vanilla; light to medium body and medium acidity. Additional bottle age will probably not be of benefit. (*)

Petite Sirah 1969 A full-bodied wine with medium-high tannin that should probably be bottle aged until the end of this decade to reach its peak. Medium-red color, with an intense woody nose. A little more fruit and peppery Petite Sirah flavor would help, but the wine has character and still should develop well. (**)

Zinfandel 1971 Medium red in color with a nice fruity aroma enriched with oak. Well balanced, with medium body, acid, and tannin. A very fine wine with good varietal character; enjoyable now, it should be even better by 1975–76. (***)

Spring Mountain

Chardonnay 1971 The best Spring Mountain Chardonnay to date. An excellent wine with light to medium yellow color, pronounced overtones of oak in the bouquet, and rich, complex flavors. Medium to full-bodied, with well-balanced, moderate acidity. Should continue to gain complexity in the bottle through 1975. (****)

Sterling Vineyards

The Sterling winery, located on a hilltop some six miles north of St. Helena, opened its doors to the public in the summer of 1973. The brilliant white buildings are of a Mediterranean style reminiscent of a monastery perched on the hillside of a lonely Greek island. The site affords a spectacular view of the Napa Valley and surrounding mountains and is accessible to visitors only by aerial tramway from the parking lot on the valley floor.

Sterling's wine maker is Richard Forman, who received his training at the University of California at Davis. The winery is owned by the same families that control Sterling International, a company with worldwide interests in the paper industry. Land in the immediate vicinity of the winery was first acquired in 1964, and today some 425 acres are planted in prime varietals to supply all the needs of the winery.

Although Sterling is fairly large, with the current annual production being 100,000 gallons and the ultimate goal 240,000 gallons, the enterprise has been carefully and patiently planned, and this has been reflected in the quality of the wines released to date. Current plans are to sell virtually the entire supply of wines directly through the tasting room rather than through retail outlets, although this is sure to be disappointing to wine buffs from other parts of the nation. If quality is maintained as production increases, the Sterling sales room is certain to be a busy place.

Blanc Sauvignon 1970   A complex spicy-smoky bouquet and flavor arise from the oak barrels in which the wine was fermented and aged. Off-dry, with good varietal flavors and medium body and acidity. Should develop nicely through 1974.   (***)

Pinot Chardonnay   The first three vintages of this wine have been complex and interesting. The *1969* (****) is soft and spicy, with good Chardonnay flavors and fruit. The *1970* (***) has overwhelming oak character, nearly 14 percent alcohol, and a strong flavor like that of a young French White Burgundy. Beneath the oak are medium-full body, moderate acidity, and considerable Chardonnay character that will take until 1975–76 to come forth. The *1971*

(****) is considerably softer and has a better-balanced nose of fruit and the sweet-spicy bouquet of oak. Creamy and full-flavored with moderate acidity, it will mature earlier than the 1970, yet should be kept until at least 1974–75 to be best appreciated.

Gewürztraminer 1971 A dry, light to medium-bodied wine with fairly good acidity and some oakiness. Pleasant, but not as perfumed and spicy as this varietal can be. (**)

Chenin Blanc 1971 This wine is unusual in its varietal composition, having been blended with one-third Chardonnay. The result is a dry wine with a ripe, melonlike aroma, light to medium body and acidity, and a slight roughness in the finish. (*)

Gamay Beaujolais The *1972* is, to our knowledge, the first California wine fermented by the carbonic maceration technique widely used in the Beaujolais district of France. With this process grapes are introduced whole into the fermenting container. The production of carbon dioxide by the yeast causes the individual berries to burst, pouring forth juice and color but leaving the tannin behind in the uncrushed skins and seeds. The resultant wines are intended to be drunk very young, usually within a few months of harvest. Sterling's Gamay Beaujolais was deliciously fresh and fruity and met with such acceptance that similar wines will probably be produced in future years.

Cabernet Sauvignon Sterling's vineyards are heavily planted in Cabernet, and eventually some 70 percent of the winery's production will be of this wine. Merlot is also planted and is used for blending.

The *1969* is a good, if not overly assertive, wine with typical Napa Valley Cabernet nose and nice varietal flavor and character. Light to medium in body with moderate acid and tannin. Considerable oak flavors in the aftertaste. (**)

Zinfandel The *1969* (***) has deep flavors and considerable fruit and body. The aroma has overtones of mint and dill, while the moderate tannin and acidity indicate a fine future for the wine by the end of this decade. The *1970* (***) is deeply colored and possesses a fruity aroma and vanilla bouquet. Quite rich, almost sweet in the mouth, with moderate body and acid. Rather strong and alcoholic in flavor now, the wine has excellent potential for continuing to mature very nicely into the early 1980s.

Sonoma

Buena Vista Winery

Chablis   The *1972* is faulted by a cloudy appearance, probably from active yeast. Dry, with a yeasty-apple-like nose and light body.   (BA)

Gewürztraminer   The *1972* is oxidized in the aroma and flavor, has little fruit or varietal character, and continues a very disappointing trend with this varietal at Buena Vista.   (BA)

Cabernet Rosé   The *1972* is dry, with light to medium pink color and a fresh, fruity aroma, but is less flavorful and complex than preceding vintages. Light to medium in body and acid.   (*)

Burgundy   The *1968* is similar to the 1967, possessing rather simple flavors and little aging potential. Light to medium body, tannin, and acid.   (*)

Korbel Winery

Zinfandel 1972   A soft, attractive, fruity wine with a berry-like aroma and pretty purple color. Light to medium in body, acid, and tannin. Meant to be drunk young.   (**)

Sebastiani Vineyards

Chablis   The *1972* is very similar to the 1971, being overwhelmed by a sulfurous nose and flavor.   (BA)

Pinot Chardonnay 1972   A dry wine of simple flavors and little Chardonnay character. Pale-yellow color, fruity aroma, and light to medium body and acidity.   (*)

Johannisberg Riesling 1969   Less rich and distinguished than the 1967. Dry, with light-yellow color and light to medium body and acidity.   (*)

Gewürztraminer 1972   Slightly sweet and simple, but a rather pleasant wine. Light yellow in color, with a flowery aroma and light to medium body and acidity. Less spicy than the best Gewürzes, but its light sweetness and smoothness will probably make it popular among beginning wine drinkers.   (**)

Chenin Blanc 1972   Disappointing for its lack of varietal and fruit flavors. Light in color; sweet, with light body and light to medium acidity. Very undistinguished.   (BA)

Green Hungarian   Though rather light in flavor and body, the *1972* is clean and slightly fruity and possesses more developed flavors than the preceding vintage. Pleasant, light, fruity nose.   (*)

Grenache Rosé   The *1972* has a nice bright-pink color and a fruit-ester aroma. Slightly sweet, with light to medium body and acid and very pleasant flavors.   (**)

Vin Rosé 1972   A not unpleasant, though fairly ordinary, dry rosé with bright-pink color and a slightly musty aroma. Medium-bodied with light to medium acidity.   (*)

Ville Fontaine

Ville Fontaine is destined to be a new, large Sonoma County winery with a production goal of two and one half million gallons annually. It is owned by Souverain Cellars and was financed by the Pillsbury Company. The first vintage was 1972, with crushing and fermenting having taken place at the parent company's Napa Valley facilities. Each winery will have its own wine maker and grape sources, and thus you may expect their styles to be different.

The new winery is located some two miles south of Geyserville, alongside Highway 101, and is scheduled to be completed in the fall of 1973. A tasting room and restaurant will be open for visitors. The varietals to be produced have not definitely been determined, but will probably include, besides the three already released and described below, Chardonnay, Cabernet Sauvignon, Pinot Noir, and Zinfandel. Distribution will be nationwide.

Grey Riesling 1972   A nice light, white wine meant to be drunk young. Fresh, estery aroma, light to medium body, and medium acidity.   (**)

Chenin Blanc 1972   A fairly dry, slightly *pétillant* wine with light to medium body and acid. Light-yellow color, not particularly deep in flavor, but pleasant.   (*)

Gamay Rosé 1972   A bright-pink wine with a lovely fruity-strawberry aroma. The flavors are less distinct than the nose, but the wine is pleasant and well balanced, with 1 percent residual sugar, light to medium body, and medium acidity. (**)

Santa Clara-Monterey

Llords & Elwood

Chardonnay After *Cuvée 5* was first released, the winery noted a slight yeast deposit in the bottles and attempted to recall them to correct the problem. Unfortunately not all were returned, as we have occasionally come across a bottle of the original lot still on a retailer's shelf. The presence of a small amount of yeast is not in itself harmful, but as the wine ages, there is risk of some autolysis, with release of off-flavors. Be sure your bottle of *Cuvée 5* does not have a fine, powdery sediment before you purchase it.

Cuvée 6 has a slightly spicy, leafy nose and medium body. It is dry, with light to medium acidity, and would have benefited from more freshness and fruitiness. (*)

Rosé of Cabernet Cuvée 7 Medium sweet, with a deep-pink, almost light-ruby color. Not as fresh and Cabernetlike as prior *cuvées,* it will probably be enjoyed most by those who like intense sweetness in a rosé. (*)

Mirassou Vineyards

As more of Mirassou's Monterey County red wines have appeared on the market, it has become noticeable that the

Cabernet Sauvignon and Petite Sirah often have a pronounced bell pepper-asparagus character in the nose that many, ourselves included, find overpowering. The exact origin of this aroma, or why it should be found primarily in these two varieties, remains a mystery, but its persistence through several vintages suggests it may be a characteristic imparted by the soil rather than a wine-making fault. Its presence is an intriguing challenge for Mirassou's wine makers, and hopefully they will soon find a way to soften its impact.

Chablis 1972   A dry, light, crisp white wine whose tartness would probably be best balanced by shellfish.   (*)

Monterey Riesling 1972   A pleasant medium-sweet wine whose medium-yellow color is freshened by a hint of green. Slightly spicy aroma and moderate acidity. From Sylvaner and Colombard grapes.   (**)

Johannisberg Riesling 1972   Light-yellow color with a beautiful, flowery Riesling nose. Off-dry, with light to medium body, medium acidity, and a clean, fresh finish.   (***)

Chenin Blanc 1972   Medium sweet, with good acidity and some spicy-melon quality to the aroma. Like the 1971 a good wine, though not as intense and ripe in flavor as the 1970. Considerable sulfur was present in the nose at the time of release, but this should dissipate by early 1974.   (**)

Gewürztraminer 1972   Delicate, pleasant, spicy-flowery aroma. A dry wine, with light to medium yellow color, light to medium body and acidity, and good varietal character.   (**)

Petite Rosé 1972   Medium pink-orange color with a soft, rich aroma. A dry, light, fruity rosé with good acidity and clean, well-developed flavors. The best Petite Rosé since the 1968 vintage.   (***)

Burgundy 1970   Less rich than the 1969, with medium-red color and a green-peppery aroma probably arising from the

Petite Sirah in the blend. Ready to drink, with light to medium body, acid, and tannin.   (*)

Petite Sirah 1970   Medium red with a distinct bell-pepper aroma. Soft and smooth, with light to medium body, acid, and tannin. Should develop until 1974–75 in the bottle, but lacks the richness and depth for longer aging.   (*)

Gamay Beaujolais 1971   A very drinkable, fruity wine with a berrylike aroma and bright medium-red color. Light to medium body and tannin and medium acidity.   (**)

Cabernet Sauvignon 1970   A relatively light Cabernet with medium-red color and a pronounced green-pepper aroma. Light to medium body and tannin and moderate acidity. Will be fairly quick-maturing.   (*)

Zinfandel 1970   A well-balanced, drinkable wine with medium-red color and a fruity aroma. Medium body, acid, and tannin. Slight oak character in the bouquet.   (**)

Harvest Zinfandel 1968   A rich, ripe wine with good Zinfandel character to the aroma and flavor. Medium red with slight orange color, light to medium body and acid, and medium tannin. A very fine wine, enjoyable now.   (***)

Champagne au Naturel 1970   Very dry, with good sparkle and a slight yeast character to the nose. Well balanced, with good flavors similar to the 1969.   (***)

Sparkling Gamay Beaujolais 1970   Dry with bright red-purple color and good fruit. Well balanced, with considerably more character than the typical sparkling red wine. (***)

Paul Masson

Zinfandel   Masson's newest red is a soft, pleasant wine with a minty-cocoa nose. Light to medium in body, acid, and tannin. Enjoyable now, without the need for further aging.   (**)

Livermore

Concannon Vineyards

The Concannon tasting room is now open daily.

Dry Sauterne (Dry Semillon) 1972   Quite dry, with medium body, light to medium acid, and a rough finish that would have benefited from more fruitiness. (*)

Château Concannon 1972   A fairly nice medium-sweet wine, with ripe Semillon flavors. Light-bodied with light to medium acidity. Not overly complex, but pleasant. (**)

Sauvignon Blanc 1972   Medium yellow in color; dry, with a spicy-woody nose. A pronounced woody flavor and inadequate acidity make this wine less successful than the 1971, although some varietal character is discernible. (*)

Moselle 1972   An off-dry wine with pronounced woodiness in the nose and flavor. Light to medium in body and acidity. A fruitier flavor is needed to balance the wood and alcohol. (*)

Johannisberg Riesling   The *1972* is slightly fresher than the 1971, but it is still rather heavy in wood bouquet and flavor. Medium-bodied, quite dry, with light to medium acidity and a touch of spice. (*)

Zinfandel Rosé   In *1972* this wine is once again a very dry rosé, with a touch of tannin and strong flavors. Medium-pink color with light to medium body and acid. For the person who favors a very dry, austere rosé. (**)

Petite Sirah 1970   Medium red in color with a pronounced black-pepper nose. A full-flavored wine with medium body and acid and medium-high tannin. At present it has a rather strong woody aftertaste, but further bottle aging is necessary. Certainly a good wine now, with a chance to offer greater rewards in the late 1970s.   (**)

Wente Brothers

The Wente tasting room is now open daily.

Dry Semillon   The *1972* seems to have less character and flavor than prior vintages. A dry wine with very light nose, pale color, medium body, and light to medium acidity.   (*)

Sauvignon Blanc 1972   Less distinctive and fruity than the 1971. Dry, light to medium in body, rather low in acidity, and with a slightly bitter finish.   (*)

Château Wente 1971   This label has now replaced the Château Semillon. Light yellow in color with some Sauvignon Blanc and Semillon character in the nose. Rather light-bodied, with light to medium acidity. Certainly not unpleasant, but very simple.   (*)

Gamay Beaujolais 1971   A wine of light flavor, body, and acid, and no character.   (BA)

Zinfandel 1969   Light to medium red in color with an attractive briary-fruity nose but rather bland flavors. Light to medium in body and acid, with moderate tannin.   (*)

News from the Smaller Wineries

Napa Valley

Tom Burgess has purchased the old Souverain site off Deer Park Road on Howell Mountain, and in 1972 crushed the first vintage for BURGESS CELLARS. Visitors are welcome here daily from 10 to 4, although because of the limited supply of wine there is no tasting. The drive to the winery through the hills on the east side of the valley provides a beautiful view of the wine country below. The first wines include a *Chenin Blanc,* a *Chablis,* and a *Rhine Wine,* all of which are clean, though rather light in flavor, and a *Grenache Rosé* that has a pretty pink color but could use a little more fruit. A *Cabernet Sauvignon,* a *Petite Sirah,* a *Zinfandel,* and a *Burgundy* will also be offered in the future.

Charles Wagner has been growing grapes for some forty years, and in 1972 he founded his own winery, called CAYMUS VINEYARDS. It is on Conn Creek Road, off Highway 128 near the Silverado Trail. The 1972 vintage wines include a *Johannisberg Riesling* and a *Pinot Noir Rosé* (labeled *Oeil de Perdrix,* or Eye of the Partridge), both of which were a bit expensive for their not-overwhelming character. *Cabernet Sauvignon* and *Pinot Noir* were also produced and are currently aging in oak. Mr. Wagner earned a good reputation as a home wine maker, so hopefully some fine wines will be produced from Caymus in the years ahead. Visitors are requested to make an appointment before stopping by; wines will be available both through selected retail outlets and by case lot at the winery.

The SUTTER HOME WINERY is continuing to produce some fine *Zinfandels* from Amador County vineyards. The *1970 Lot 2* is full and rich and should age nicely for five to ten years. The *1971* is the lightest of the past several vintages and may be drunk now. It has light to medium body and tannin and fresh Zinfandel flavors. In *1972* two wines were produced, one from the familiar *Deaver Vineyard,* the other from the neighboring *Ferraro Vineyard.* In the barrel both taste like substantial wines of good character that should age very well.

Several other small wineries have recently been founded in Napa and will be offering their wines in the future. DIAMOND CREEK VINEYARDS is located on Diamond Mountain, to the west of the valley, and will be producing only *Cabernet Sauvignon*. LYNCREST VINEYARDS, off White Sulfur Springs Road, in the hills also to the west of the valley, is already known as a source of the grapes for Heitz Cellars Pinot Blanc and will soon be offering bottles of its own *Chardonnay, Pinot Noir,* and *Johannisberg Riesling.* CLOS DU VAL is evidently the name that has been selected for a new winery to be located off the Silverado Trail east of Yountville, although during the fall of 1972 it was being called the Napa-Bordeaux Wine Company. The reason for this is that wine maker Bernard Portet received his training in France and is the son of the *régisseur* of Château Lafite Rothschild. Production will be limited to *Cabernet Sauvignon* and *Zinfandel.*

FRANCISCAN VINEYARDS will be a good-sized operation whose first harvest will be 1973. The winery and tasting room are on Highway 29, one mile north of Rutherford. In the Chiles Valley, on the other side of the mountains that form the eastern boundary of the Napa Valley, an old winery has been reopened and named the POPE VALLEY WINERY. Before Prohibition, this was an active wine-growing region, and perhaps this new winery will start a renaissance for the area.

Sonoma

Sonoma County is the home of two new wineries, whose first vintages have produced some very successful wines. DRY CREEK VINEYARDS is located at 3770 Lambert Bridge Road, in the Dry Creek area, west of Healdsburg, and is open to visitors on weekends. Wine maker David Stare first released his *1972 Chenin Blanc* and *Fumé Blanc* in the spring and summer of 1973; both are nice wines, with the latter being especially fruity and having excellent Sauvignon Blanc character. A *Chardonnay* will be offered this winter, and next year a *Cabernet Sauvignon,* a *Zinfandel,* and a *Napa Gamay* will be added to the list.

Farther south, on Laguna Road near Forestville, Joseph Swan has been making wine for home use for many years. In 1969 he took out a winery license and founded the JOSEPH SWAN WINERY. He has replanted an old vineyard on his property with Chardonnay and Pinot Noir, which should come into production in the next few years, and while waiting for his own grapes he has been making *Zinfandel* from a vineyard in the Dry Creek area. The *1969* vintage is one of the most delicious Zinfandels we've tasted and has an especially complex vanilla bouquet from the Nevers-oak barrels in which it was aged. The *1971* is lighter but still has good flavors, and the *1972,* tasted in the barrel, should develop nicely. Mr. Swan's limited supply of wine will be sold both at the winery and in a few select retail outlets.

San Francisco Bay Area

The DAVIS BYNUM WINERY has recently acquired a winery building off West Side Road, in Sonoma's Russian River district. When grapes from vineyards in this area are added to those of the winery's Whitehall Vineyard, in the Napa Valley, production will be increased, and, for the first time, buyers in states other than California may find Bynum table wines on their retailers' shelves. When remodeling of the Sonoma building is complete, visitors will be welcome; the exact address and hours may be obtained from the Albany tasting room. Among Bynum's recent wines are a *1972 Traminer* and a *French Colombard* that are not very exciting, a pleasant and pretty *1972 Petite Rosé,* and a *1972 Nouveau Burgundy* made from Early Burgundy grapes, which is a soft and very drinkable young red wine. A *1971 Charbono* and *Petite Sirah* tasted in the barrel show promise of being very fine, full-flavored, and complex wines.

Contra Costa and Solano Counties

About an hour's drive east of San Francisco are three wineries, by no means new, which we recently visited for the first time. The CONRAD VIANO WINERY, on the outskirts of Martinez, has much of the atmosphere and friendliness of a small country farm. Jugs of two-year-old and bottles of five-year-old *Zinfandel* are offered along with several other varietals. The wines are honest if not overly charming and are fairly priced.

In Solano County the CADENASSO WINERY, near Fairfield, is visible from heavily traveled Interstate 80 near the Highway 12 crossroad. Several very inexpensive varietals are produced, the high point of which is a *Pinot Noir* whose varietal character compares very favorably with many higher-priced wines from larger wineries.

Across the interstate highway on Suisun Valley Road, in an area of charming two-lane country roads dotted with oak and orchard and vineyard, may be found the WOODEN VALLEY WINERY. Jugs of generic wines are abundant there, although the varietal wines they offer are actually made by a large Sonoma winery.

The major business of all three wineries is the production of jugs of country red and white wine. Every weekend their courtyards are filled with people who have traveled from near and far to exchange empty bottles for full ones. Those of you who enjoy a glass of your own house wine as a frequent accompaniment to meals would do well to take a day off to visit this countryside and see if you find a brand to your taste.

Livermore Valley

The VILLA ARMANDO WINERY, in Pleasanton, has opened an attractive new tasting room, and now California residents may stop by and select wines that for years have been sold almost exclusively on the East Coast. The specialties of the house include *Oro Bianco,* a light, sweet Muscat, and red table wines such as *Zinfandel, Barbera,* and *Pinot Noir* that have seen several years of redwood aging. The reds are straightforward and honest, but have more wood flavors than charm. Jugs of generics may also be sampled, and all wines are reasonably priced.

Index

412 *Index*